ROCKING
THE CRADLE
OF SEXUAL
POLITICS

ROCKING THE CRADLE OF SEXUAL POLITICS

*What Happened
When Women Said Incest*

LOUISE ARMSTRONG

ADDISON-WESLEY PUBLISHING COMPANY
READING, MASSACHUSETTS   MENLO PARK, CALIFORNIA   NEW YORK
DON MILLS, ONTARIO   WOKINGHAM, ENGLAND   AMSTERDAM   BONN
SYDNEY   SINGAPORE   TOKYO   MADRID   SAN JUAN
PARIS   SEOUL   MILAN   MEXICO CITY   TAIPEI

Many of the designations used by manufacturers and sellers to distinguish their products are claimed as trademarks. Where those designations appear in this book and Addison-Wesley was aware of a trademark claim, the designations have been printed in initial capital letters.

Library of Congress Cataloging-in-Publication Data
Armstrong, Louise.
    Rocking the cradle of sexual politics : what happened when women said incest / Louise Armstrong.
        p.   cm.
    Includes bibliographical references and index.
    ISBN 0-201-62471-0
    1. Incest.   2. Child sexual abuse.   3. Mass media—Social aspects.
I. Title.
HQ71.A753   1994
306.877—dc20   94-18641
                                                         CIP

Jacket design by Andrew Newman
Text design by Dede Cummings
Set in 11-point Sabon by Pagesetters, Inc.

1 2 3 4 5 6 7 8 9 10-MA-9897969594
First printing, September 1994

To Florence Rush

CONTENTS

INTRODUCTION

THE WOMAN ON THE PHONE is returning my call. I have left a message requesting more information about the FMS Foundation. Not to be confused with PMS (Premenstrual Syndrome), FMS, as most everyone by now knows, stands for False Memory Syndrome.

"I don't know the reason for your interest," the woman from the FMS Foundation is saying, "what your story might be. . . ."

"Well . . ." I say, my reticence ambiguous, implying reluctance—which could be taken for an unwillingness to share a so-personal revelation with a stranger on the phone. This is how she takes it.

"But," she says, "you sound like a very sincere person." She pauses and takes a deep breath. "I can tell you how I got involved. Two years ago, my daughter—a young professional woman—began seeing a psychologist. She had always been a happy child, done well in school and in her career. We had never had conflicts outside the normal young-teenage years. And suddenly, this psychologist was programming her." Teariness creeps into the woman's voice. "And—she—suddenly—comes to us and says I—sexually abused her. When she was just a baby.

"She says—she doesn't remember everything. But she knows— I abused her"—there is snuffling here; agonized humiliation—

"by jabbing sticks up her vagina." A pause for recomposure. "I never—this is horrible—and this is what's happening, to so many parents, so many—I can't tell you. And there is *nothing* you can do. Nothing.

"It didn't happen. This *never* happened. I love my daughter. And then, two years ago—she writes us this letter, saying how this psychologist is helping her uncover these so-called memories, and no such thing happened, and that's what they are doing. They are programming people to believe the most horrible things were done to them. And now my daughter won't see us. She won't talk to us. I have lost—my child."

False Memory Syndrome (along with its siblings, False Accusation Syndrome and Parental Alienation Syndrome) is among the more recent retaliatory missiles to be launched in what has by now become the Great Incest War.

It is a war in which I, in all innocence of what would ensue, dropped one of the first depth charges with the 1978 publication of my book *Kiss Daddy Goodnight*—a speakout on incest. Let me be clear: Other women had tried to speak out in other times. Even in recent times, radical feminists like Florence Rush had begun to speak powerfully about incest/child sexual abuse.

It was only fate and circumstance—and, some would say, naïveté—that made me an instrument of breaking the larger silence (back then, when there *was* a silence to break); made me, as we entered an era of ever increasing media mania, the World's First Walking, Talking Incest Victim. A dubious distinction, but one that leads me to speak here in the form of a memoir, an informal biography of the issue of incest. (Informal by necessity: You cannot write a history of a war very much still in progress.)

I came to this issue as a publishing writer; someone whose main focus since the age of seventeen had been the necessity to be self-supporting. Thus, apart from humor and satire and children's books, much of my experience had been in what, looking back, one could call Company America (not yet Corporate America): copywriting in advertising agencies, some large (but not yet gigantic), some smaller. My politics were the politics of sympathy and empathy—with the civil rights movement, with the nascent feminist movement—but my dailiness had me far more involved with product campaigns than with campaigns for social change. In this world, the coin of the realm was not the socially corrective but the clever. By the early 1970s, I was married and the mother of twins: not exactly the profile, certainly in those days, of your militant feminist politico.

And then I spoke out.

What happened next (and next after that) is not a pretty story, though it had, I must say, its comic moments—providing me, for example, with an opportunity to shake Zsa Zsa Gabor's hand on television, an event as incongruous in the context (incest) as it was unlikely in any imagined script of my life. (What she said was, "Dollink, I vould haff keeled him.") Were this saga a film, it would be an epic; perhaps promoted as "A Story of Sexual Violence! Of Power! Of Venality! Of Greed! Of Retribution!"

As a political story, it is a prime illustration of how it is now possible for the powers-that-be to use *noise* to achieve the same end that was once served by repression. It is a story of how readily the solid feminist concept that "the personal is political" can be alchemistically transformed into "the personal is the—public." It is, alas, the story as well of the power of the promise of "help" and the language of "treatment" to infantilize massive numbers of women, emphasizing their fragility, securing their helplessness, isolating them from the larger universe, so cementing their focus on the purely internal that it looms to fill their entire visual screen. All in the name of "empowerment."

This story, reader, has by now come to include real-life tales of the supernatural; alarm about demonic forces loose in the world, eclipsing not only routine sexual atrocities but all hope for rational dialogue.

September 10, 1991. Geraldo's talk show today is entitled "Investigating Multiple Personalities: Did the Devil Make Them Do It?"

To begin, we are introduced to "Kathleen," who, we are told, has eight hundred personalities (and was forced to commit or participate in about thirty murders).

Geraldo then says to another guest, introduced as "Kayla" but now mysteriously billed as "Ellie," "How are you?"

To which Ellie (formerly Kayla) replies, "I'm six now."

This, today, is what passes for dialogue where the issue is related—by disorder, in this case—to child sexual abuse: "How are you?" "I'm six now. How old are you?" "I'm fine."

Now Geraldo explains: "There are more than twelve hundred guests on my panel today, all embodied in these three women, women with terrifying tales of Multiple Personality Disorder, of human sacrifices and of other unspeakable acts. These ladies say the Devil made them this way." The Devil, we learn, in the form of incest and satanic cult abuse.

———

As I write this, books with titles like *Ritual Abuse*; *The Satanism Scare*; *Out of Darkness: Exploring Satanism and Ritual Abuse*; along with those on Multiple Personality Disorder (which is widely rumored to result from sexual and ritual abuse), such as *Uncovering the Mystery of MPD* fight for space on my floor with books that would tell of *Sex Abuse Hysteria*; *Confabulations: Creating False Memories, Destroying Families*, themselves vying for display space with titles like *Invisible Wounds: Treatment of Adult Survivors*; *Secret Scars*, which in turn nudge up against "I"-story books, those by "survivors": *The Family Secret*; *I Couldn't Cry When Daddy Died* . . .

The man from the heating company who came this morning to do our annual boiler checkup had to walk through my study, stepping over and around the piles, nearly tripping over a mammoth loose-leaf binder, *The National Directory of Child Sexual Abuse Treatment Programs*. I do not know what he thought of it all. It is hard to know what any member of the interested but uninvolved public might think or how they could possibly frame for themselves a context in which actual *thought* (as opposed to Superbowl passions, a yay-boo mind-set) could occur.

Indeed, even those feminists who have been paying attention to this issue from the outset are finding themselves driven (or driveled) to the point of confusion. Florence Rush, author of the seminal 1980 book *The Best Kept Secret: Sexual Abuse of Children*, says, "It's just become so impossible, so *twisted*. You can't sort it out anymore."

Consider: Just yesterday (as of this writing) Oprah Winfrey had as guests several women who claimed they had been brainwashed into believing that they had been sexually abused as children—and were now certain they had not. On the panel also was Ellen Bass, coauthor of the most promoted—and most vilified—book on incest, *The Courage to Heal*; she was supporting the endorsement of survivor veracity. Surely an excellent and necessary thing to do. But here is the catch: No matter how much one implicitly trusts that suppressed memories do emerge in adulthood, the charge used by those challenging the reality of claimed assault is correct: The book does not require real memory, offering instead the assurance that if you think you were abused, if you feel you *might* have been abused, you probably were. Within this loose construction lurks the invitation to turn the dreadful actuality of paternal child rape into an experiential metaphor.

And consider: Turn to any presentation by the mainstream media almost any week of the year and you will find assertions of ever greater pathology in ever greater variety ascribed to victims of childhood rape in the home, alongside men arguing that they have been falsely accused, alongside women who, having believed their children and tried to protect them, have in fact lost custody of the children to the alleged perpetrator. With Oprah herself having spoken of her own childhood sexual abuse, along with Roseanne Barr, Suzanne Somers, a former Miss America, we've now got such a thing as could be called Celebrity Incest.

Simply consider the *size* of it all: Psychiatric hospitals nationwide have found a boom market in inpatient programs specializing in incest survivors and the various "disorders" said to result (disorders from which, it is said by some, you can read backwards and infer the abuse)—eating disorders, depressive disorders, borderline disorders, dissociative disorders, Multiple Personality Disorders (have I left anything out?). Consider the aggregate numbers: From 1975 to 1990, "the number of psychiatrists increased from 26,000 to 36,000, clinical psychologists from 15,000 to 42,000, clinical social workers from 25,000 to 80,000, and marriage and family counselors from 6,000 to 40,000. In aggregate, the increase in 15 years has been from 72 to 198 thousand professionals in just those four professions."[1] This explosion roughly parallels the rise of the issue of incest, and thousands (if not in fact tens of thousands) of these professionals now put themselves forward as a resource specifically for incest-related disorders, indicating a fair certainty of an ongoing client population. (People on the whole do not entrust their careers to a specialty problem they anticipate will abate. And people who seek to truly eliminate a problem, and believe in that possibility, do not seek, in such vast numbers, vocation in managing the damages caused by that problem.)

And consider: In my mail comes a flyer for a(nother) incest newsletter, *Raising Issue*, which, we are told, is "a collaborative effort among mental health professionals, trauma survivors, advocates and community educators to provide a forum for raising issues and finding possible answers to often underexplored and underacknowledged questions." Among their first concerns? "The rising incidence of spirit/demon possession models of MPD [Multiple Personality Disorder], and corresponding use of exorcism as a treatment approach." *Exorcism?* (But—should I act surprised? I actually *saw* one in progress—or was it a dramatization?—on HBO's "America Undercover" the other night.)

Oh, no: This is not a story for the faint of heart.

It is no wonder that Stephen King, the master of supernatural fictions such as *Carrie* and *The Shining*, in 1992 turned to far more realistic work with *Gerald's Game*, the story of a woman whose husband, in pursuit of sadomasochistic delights, handcuffs her to the bed, then suffers a heart attack, leaving her (literally) locked in struggle with her memories of previous humiliation/violation: memories of childhood sexual abuse. (*I* think that's realistic.) On this issue, it was no longer possible to compete in the realm of fantastical fiction with what was being presented everywhere as everyday reality.

It is no wonder that an interested observer, coming fresh into the midst of all this after the mid-1980s, would see no coherence, no internal logic to the ongoing events, but only an apparently randomly generated series of dramatic (or melodramatic) occurrences constantly escalating in pitch.

It is no wonder that, given the fundamentalist spin that's been overlaid on the issue—"I believe!"; "I *don't believe!*"; "Infidel!"; "Heretic!"—great numbers of people throughout the land are simply praying for surcease. And are tempted, in ever greater numbers, to pull the plug on the whole issue; dismiss the whole lot, if that's the easiest way to tune out the relentless crossfire.

It is no wonder that, after folks say to me, "Look what you started," they shake their heads and, reaching for *some* point, say, "Well, at least we're talking about it now."

Yes. We certainly are. But it was not our intention merely to start a long conversation.

———

We did have an intention. There was a point. It is understatement to say this is not what it was, to say that this hullabaloo was not what I had in mind, not something I could ever have imagined, when I first began working on this issue in the mid-1970s.

How, then, did we get here? How, in just fifteen years, did we go from total silence—from what was said to be a "dread taboo"—to mothers gagged by the courts, mothers jailed, child credibility again challenged, even adult survivor credibility impugned? How did we get from enforced secrecy, the suppression of children's experiences, women's experiences, such that they were not ever heard—to a level of cacophony such that children's voices, women's voices, are once more not, in any purposeful sense, being heard?

That is the story of this book.

Turbulence ahead: Fasten seat belts, please.

Chapter 1

INCEST:
THE EARLY YEARS

EVEN A PARTIAL SURVEY of the current landscape reveals: Outward Bound programs for incest survivors. A computer network. There is massage therapy and bodywork. There is color therapy (there are safe and unsafe colors). There is dance therapy for incest survivors, and art therapy for incest survivors. For the less physically ambitious, there is even a board game, *Survivor's Journey*.[1]

Incest has generated massacres of women and children in custody courts, a barrage of fire on child welfare personnel and juvenile courts; it has challenged the rules of criminal courts. Even courts that normally deal with issues of fiscal liability have not been immune.

Incest has even spawned its own informal "Annual Goofy Award." The winner in 1993 was a major figurehead of the assault on professionals he sees as dupes of vengeful mothers bent on falsely accusing ex-husbands of child sexual abuse; women confabulating false memories of childhood abuse; untrustworthy children; and interviewers and clinicians who brainwash people into believing that such abuse occurred.

A former pastor of the Lutheran Church, with luminous credentials in the field of psychology,* his openly declared position was that "there is absolutely no evidence to support the claim that child sexual abuse is widespread."[2] Widely cited in the news media and a frequent guest expert on television talk shows, in the winter of 1993, this prominent advisory board member of the False Memory Syndrome Foundation was moved to grant a lengthy interview in *Paidika, The Journal of Paedophilia,* published in Amsterdam, in which he offered pedophiles this advice: "Take the risk, the consequences of the risk, and make the claim: this is something good. Paedophiles need to become more positive and make the claim that paedophilia is an acceptable expression of God's will for love and unity among human beings."[3]

Today, incest and all that surrounds and embellishes it is everywhere. Child sexual abuse—both the routine and the exotic—has become a plot option for daytime soaps, ongoing dramatic series, even mystery stories.

And—with flak flying about who is mendacious and who mis-remembering; who possessed of true wisdom and who merely possessed; who is venal and who is in fact multiple who's—it has become the subject of one of the great screaming matches of all time.

———

It was, of course, not like that in the good old days.

As recently as 1976, the acid fact of paternal child molestation was still securely vacuum-packed in the memories of hundreds of thousands of women. There were signs, however, that it had already begun to corrode the casing.

* He has served, for example, as director of the Institute for Psychological Therapies and as a member of the National Council for Children's Rights, the American Psychological Association, the Lutheran Academy for Scholarship, and the Society for the Scientific Study of Sex.

In the 1970s, feminist literature boldly addressed the need for social change—as distinct from later emphasis on social and economic access. And it was a vibrant force, both in the market and in the marketplace of ideas. Women were speaking out forcefully on rape as a male crime of violence against women. Wife-battering, too—now widely referred to as "spousal assault"—was analyzed as an issue of male prerogative, male right. A plethora of historical documentation was introduced as evidence.

Women organized around these issues in grassroots efforts, starting rape crisis centers and shelters for battered women. The words *patriarchy* and *patriarchal prerogative*—quaint as they now sound—were spoken without apology.

Consciousness-raising groups were a vigorous tool of discovery. "The personal is political" was the aphorism that described the use of shared stories to extrapolate commonalities that fueled analysis, which in turn would lead to activism for social change. Step one: Remove the secrecy that had long protected these violences. Step two: Raise the issues and raise the kind of outcry that would force measures to reduce their incidence.

It bears remembering here that consciousness-raising was conceptually *antithetical* to therapy. In fact, to view consciousness-raising as therapy was to express "anti-woman sentiment by implying that when women get together to study and analyse their own experience, it means they are sick, but when Chinese peasants or Guatemalan guerillas get together and use the identical method they are revolutionaries."[4]

"The purpose of hearing people's feelings and experience," said radical feminist Kathy Sarachild in 1978, "was not therapy, was not to give someone a chance to get something off her chest. . . . It was to hear what she had to say. The importance of listening to a woman's feelings was collectively to analyse the situation of women, not to analyse *her*. The idea was not to change women, was not to make 'internal changes' except in the sense of knowing more. It was and is conditions women face, it's male supremacy we want to change."[5]

(This would later prove high irony, of course, as therapy and therapists would be taken by the backlash to be the embodiment of seditious feminist radicalism.)

It was in this climate and with this understanding that I began to wonder about the hush that continued to encase the issue of child sexual assault, an issue that touched on my own personal history. I decided to open the can.

Over the years, people have asked me why—and my answers tend to vary with the state of the issue on any particular day.

Noted feminist Phyllis Chesler asked me that question once— she was visiting; we were taking a walk. It was 1987 and the climate for the issue had grown dark.

Caught off guard, I heard myself say, "I don't know. I guess I thought I was invincible."

The real answer probably lay, at the time, in a mix of the personal and the mood of the times. Fifteen years ago, for women, speaking up on many issues was differently driven: exploring inner reality was a pathway to identifying external realities, to- ward advocating for change. "Speakouts" were political actions, and there were women speaking out on rape, on wife-battering. Sharing stories was part of a larger goal.

But I do not mean to sound insufferably high-minded. A *climate* is no one's immediate world. And I could hardly have been de- scribed in those days as a social crusader. I was both troubled by, and deeply curious about, the silence surrounding that which had happened to me.

Surely, I believed, in this world, there must be experiential doppelgängers? (I'd had, in high school, one friend to whom something similar had happened, so it seemed clear to me that I/we were not the only ones.) Where was everybody? Why was everyone silent?

I set out in search of what was known about child sexual abuse/ incest. Remarkably little, as it turned out, and of that little, much that seemed more perverse proclamation than knowledge.

In the library, under "incest," there was virtually nothing that did not lead to a door marked "taboo," with all the attendant baggage of myth and divine retribution. I listened at those doors to somber dialogues about tribal exogamy, the pragmatics of marrying outside the family or clan in order to solidify relations and support with outside peoples. None of which had anything to do with my New York father's political or personal interests or motives.

The rest of what one could find in the literature was mainly secreted in psychiatric and sociological works. On the whole, it was remarkably uncharitable toward children. Much focused on children who had otherwise come to the attention of the courts—prostitutes or what were termed "sex delinquents." Since the greatest number of children thus caught and spotlighted were from socially deprived circumstances, the abiding presumption was that this type of behavior was exclusive to the children of the lower class, who were both morally defective and inherently untrustworthy. Reports cited overcrowded living conditions as causative.[6] But the greatest emphasis was placed on the "fact" that the girls were implicated, that they were active "participants."

One classic paper, widely cited, trumpeted this theme unabashedly: a 1930s paper written by psychiatrists Loretta Bender and Abram Blau:

"The most remarkable feature presented by these children who have experienced sexual relations with adults was that they showed less evidence of fear, anxiety, guilt or psychic trauma than might be expected. . . .

"The probation reports from the court frequently remarked about their brazen poise, which was interpreted as an especially inexcusable and deplorable attitude and one indicating their fundamental incorrigibility. . . .

"The few studies that have been made of this subject have been content to consider it an example of adult sex perversion from which innocent children must be protected by proper legal measures. Although this attitude may be correct in some cases, certain features in our material would indicate that the children may not resist and often play an active or initiating role."[7]

Other works suggested that a father's sexual assault could actually be benign from the kid's viewpoint. The upshot of one sociologist's study was that it was the child's "need for affection" that triggered the assault. "The suggestion is therefore made that sexual assault of children by adults does not have particularly detrimental effects on the child's subsequent personality development. Given greater affection—by parents, following the event, or by others in the child's environment—the need for affection, *which may well have predisposed the child to this form of sexual acting-out*, will be outgrown."[8]

(Indeed, almost everything one could find prior to the mid-1970s would give the lie to all the ensuing hullabaloo of shock and horror and hand-wringing and speechifying about dread taboos and, most especially, to the unquestioned assumption that the sexual abuse by a man of his own child is now or has ever been treated seriously as a crime, much less a heinous one.)

As Florence Rush was even then meticulously documenting, there was a long, dark Age of Permitted Abuse. Fathers wielded absolute power over their children's lives; they could be bartered, sold, mutilated, thrashed, starved (and raped) without recourse. Talmudic law decreed that betrothal and marriage could not take place before three years and one day of age. That was not, however, a magnanimous protection of two-year-olds. It simply meant that the female under three had no sexual validity—and therefore had no virginity to lose. "Copulation with one so young was not illegal but invalid. Maimonides assures us that the rape of one under three was no cause for alarm, for once past three, 'she will recover her virginity and be like other virgins.' "[9]

Even comparing the father-child relationship to that of master-servant would be inadequate, since the child had none of the rights of a servant. Within a total patriarchal structure, sexual use of children was permitted and presumed. Not only had children, like women, historically been chattel—male property—but there had always been a greedy interest in sex with children. This could be discerned from the amount of dithering about it that men had done over the centuries.

Under Christianity, sex with children under *seven* was invalid.[10] Invalid meant it didn't count; it didn't happen.

Sixteenth-century jurists decided that ten was the legal age of consent and twelve was the legal age for marriage. During the ten–twelve window of opportunity, sex with a child was a misdemeanor, but given the strong property presumption, it was unlikely that even this mild sanction was enforced where the matter involved sex with your *own* child.

So the measure in all this was legal virginity: the purity of the product a man could put up for sale (marriage). And it is unlikely in the extreme that all this fussing with technicalities would have been of such compelling interest had there not been a whole lot of this stuff going on. But the dickering over the minutiae said nothing one way or another about a child's right to complain, or the likelihood of her being heard, listened to, believed, or of her even evoking social concern (any more than a cow would). Besides: Social survival for female children depended on their shutting up so they could be passed off as pure.

This was the Age of Permitted Abuse.

With the wash of fastidious public morality in the Victorian era, the actuality of child sexual abuse went underground—only to tease rediscovery in the late 1800s.

Feminists then, concerned with male violence in the home, embarked on intervention attempts in the only arena seen as possible for them: among the poor. Engaged in child saving, they discovered hundreds of stories of children sexually brutalized by fathers. So the existence of widespread male predation against children was spoken of, and social agencies intervened to remove the children. But since the focus was on the indigent—who were perceived as morally inferior in any case—the knowlege created no discomfort among the proper.[11]

It was Sigmund Freud, in the late 1800s, who *almost* became the spokesperson on behalf of women's common childhood victimization. Then, listening to women tell of sexual abuse by their fathers, he at first believed them. However, based on the alarming prevalence of these stories, and after introspection about his own childhood (and in the face of hoots, jeers, catcalls from his peers), Freud decided the stories were actually fantasies. (In the language of today, he *recanted*.) Reality, in his revised opinion, was not actual abuse, but rather the child's *wish for*, the child's *fantasy*, of abuse. Girls, this formulation went, loved their fathers and thus hated their mothers; boys, the reverse: hence, the Oedipus complex, leading to imaginary remembered abuse.

To shore up the whole conjectured edifice, Freud postulated penis envy: the biological inferiority of women. As Florence Rush put it, "[T]he female, forever penisless, must always look to a man to achieve any degree of human status; her fantasy of being seduced therefore represented an actual biological need to make up for her natural deficiency. The seduction fantasy represented her everlasting desire for the coveted penis and was implicit in her biology. Therefore Freud found that the incestuous wish of little girls for their fathers was a 'predisposition into traumas giving rise to excitation and fixation.' "[12] Thus, Freud's disciples intoned, the girl's shame and disgust were due not to the actual violation, but to a girl's deep, unconscious wish for her father, her fantasies.

With the introduction of this ideological equivalent of a Rube Goldberg contraption, Freud's colleagues and compatriots breathed a collective sigh of relief, and went about refining this new understanding.

Rush concludes: "The little girl, then, with her innate passion for a penis, is—as in Christian doctrine—the temptress Eve, and if she is violated, the nature of her sexuality renders her culpable. Any attempt on the part of the child or her family to expose the violator also exposes her own alleged innate sexual motives and shames her more than the offender; concealment is her only recourse. The dilemma of the sexual abuse of children has provided a system of foolproof emotional blackmail: if the victim incriminates the abuser, she also incriminates herself."[13]

So it was that we left the Age of Permitted Abuse and entered the Age of Denied Abuse—without ever having to be troubled by anything as strenuous as social or political thought.

The law remained very much in lockstep with the revised received wisdom, encoding the beady-eyed view of vicious, malicious children and ensuring women's and children's continued silence. Commenting on his research into the incest laws of the 1800s and early 1900s, one law student I set to digging writes, "The ironic twist lies . . . not only in the fact that under the . . . rules prosecutrix/victims were almost invariably found to be accomplices, but also in the fact that the victim witness could be found to be an accomplice to a crime which the courts would not acknowledge had been committed. Further irony appears in the fact that, even in some cases where incestuous copulation was violence-induced, failure of the victim to make an outcry or subsequently to report the act has been considered submission, sufficiently qualifying her as a consenting accomplice."

One of the most venerable documents in law, still a reference source today, is John Henry Wigmore's *Evidence in Trials at Common Law*. Born in 1863, Wigmore was the most famous legal scholar of his day: a law school dean, a professor of law, and author of many textbooks and monographs. His views on the credibility of female witnesses in sex offenses first put forward in the early 1900s continue to be held relevant. Wigmore's blunt position was that young female complainants were not to be believed. His overriding concern was "to protect innocent men from false charges." Without specifying evidence, Wigmore *infers* "that many innocent men have gone to prison because of tales whose falsity could not be exposed."[14]

Wigmore was also the progenitor of the law's reliance on psychiatric and psychological testimony in incest/child sexual abuse cases. Familiar with Freud's work—and thus with Freud's (revised) opinion that "such things" did not really happen but were fantasized about by children—Wigmore employed Freud's hypothesis to presume pathology on the part of the complaining young female, and used Freudian ideology as expounded by allegedly objective psychiatrists to condemn any female who would dare make such an accusation.

Indeed, Wigmore relied on letters from practicing physicians to corroborate his theory that women and children routinely made up allegations of sexual assault. Apparently the mildest of these letters recommended psychiatric examination for "every girl who enters a plausible but unproved story of rape."[15] (But where, short of outright confession by the alleged offender, will anyone find a plausible and *proved* story of rape?)

On examination, the authorities Wigmore used in support of his conjured doctrine seem to corroborate the opposite: "The cases from the Healys' monograph used to support Wigmore's proposition that women and girls frequently offer false reports actually seem to show that real sexual acts with these children took place."[16] Thus, what Wigmore's torturing of the evidence would seem to suggest is nothing more nor less than the codification of male-protective social denial: insurance by law that women and children, raped, would not go unpunished should they go public.

Wigmore's legal position, in reality a concoction of personal passion and Freudulent "science," was then handed down to us through history with the solemn and unimpeachable-sounding nomenclature of the Wigmore doctrine.

Thus, the sort of thing one finds when looking up American case law is:

State v. *Kurtz* (1917): "Where the daughter with whom defendant was accused of having incestuous relations was 16 years of age at the time the act charged was committed, and according to her testimony she and defendant had been having illicit relations for a period of about a year before the date of such act, the court stated that she was an accomplice whose uncorroborated testimony was insufficient to uphold a conviction."

McClure v. *State* (1921): "Where, according to prosecutrix's own testimony, the incestuous intercourse with her father continued from the time she was 11 years of age until she was 22, being repeated once or twice a week during all the aforementioned period. . . . The court said it could not believe it possible that these acts could have occurred as testified to by the prosecutrix without her consent, and that the irresistible conclusion from all the evidence was that she was an accomplice in the performance of the act, *if it occurred*" (italics mine).

People v. *Oliver* (1941 Co Ct): "The court without expressly stating whether the act was with the consent of the daughter, who was 18 years or more of age held that she was an accomplice and her evidence must be corroborated. But it is to be noted, as possibly tending to show some sort of consent on the part of the female that she testified that the father had had sexual intercourse with her during the past 8 years, and the court said that the testimony was absolutely incredible, and that it was of the opinion that the prosecutrix was a wayward girl, and was attempting to 'hang' her father for her own delinquencies."[17]

As recently as 1975, a major paper in the *Stanford Law Review* continued to echo Wigmore's unsupported intuition, and advocated treating incest/child sexual abuse as noncriminal, citing as one reason—beyond that of the questionable harm suffered by the child—the likelihood of a criminal prosecution against the parent. More important, the author states, "I believe that such conduct may not always be harmful and therefore the term 'abuse' may be inappropriate. While it will be used in this section, no condemnation of the behavior is intended."[18] Thus, once again, in the absence of any probable cause to believe it—and in the presence of history that proved the opposite—the assertion was made that "criminal prosecution will often result in the father's imprisonment."

What could underlie this passing down, father to son as it were, of a mystical belief couched in the language of a profession that prided itself so on adherence to evidence, to fact? How could the bogus certainty endure that accused offenders would be dragged off to prison in leg irons, when everywhere one found the language of "wayward girls" and false accusations?

Where a girl might complain, for instance, of the *threat* of violence? The court might then point out, with tortuous reasoning, that "there was not one word of testimony that she declined to engage in the alleged act of incestuous intercourse or that she resisted or protested, and since there was no protest or resistance to overcome, a resort to means calculated to overcome it was unnecessary."[19]

Hand in hand with this was the fact that notable personages openly stated that they did not see what the problem was. Sex researcher Alfred Kinsey was simply bewildered by the fuss. In the 1950s he wrote, "It is difficult to understand why a child, except for its cultural conditioning, should be disturbed by having its genitalia touched or disturbed by seeing the genitalia of another person. . . . Some of the more experienced students of juvenile problems have come to believe that the emotional reactions of the parents, police and other adults . . . may disturb the child more seriously than the contacts themselves. The current hysteria over sex offenders may well have serious effects on the ability of many children to work out sexual adjustment some years later."[20] (Setting the precedent for what would later come to seem déjà vu all over again.)

And echoing Bender and Blau et al., Leroy G. Schultz wrote in the late 1950s that "so great can the role of the victim be in sex offenses that many should be considered offenders themselves."[21] Since most of the expert opinion then was that such misbehavior was calculated to be one in a million, it is worth wondering why such a great amount of professional attention was directed to forestalling disclosure.

But there it was, plain as could be, in black and white—what pundits thought when they thought about child sexual abuse/incest. Either the kid was the real offender, or else it was no big deal.

Well. We could fix that, couldn't we?

Wasn't that a reasonable thing to think? After all, it would be hard to argue (wouldn't it?) with the fact that the repeated rape of a minor in your care and trust, whose obedience you are legally empowered to command, constitutes far more egregious wrong-doing than one-shot violation of a neighbor's child.

As for the whole "taboo" business: It was difficult to understand how such sentiments could be found compatible with anything so fraught with cosmic significance as a "taboo," much less a "dread" one. I mean, what kind of a self-respecting taboo could adhere to behavior that so many respected authorities found so inconsequential? And so it could fairly be said (as we would say) that incest was not the taboo, women and children—victims—*talking* about it, raging against it, was the taboo. And that was because their doing so might deliver a healthy whack to the two very convenient masks that screened and protected gross mis-behavior: (1) stuff that's "taboo" doesn't happen, and (2) if the kid says it does, it's either the kid's imagining or the kid's fault.

With the discovery in the 1960s of the "Battered Child Syndrome" and the 1974 codification in civil law of social disapproval, overt avowals of the harmlessness of a man's deliberate sexual aggressions against his own child, and the willingness to see children as the architects of their abuse at the hands of adults, both began to fall out of fashion. But—and here was the dilemma—as it began to be strongly suspected that rape of one's own child was not entirely rare, how could you suddenly start making open charges against thousands of upstanding male citizens; charges of something that overnight and by fiat was being labeled "abuse"? So those early professionals who addressed the issue of incest were increasingly driven to find an alternative focus—one that would continue to avoid spotlighting respectable male citizens. They visited the Oracle (who'd been around for a while and knew what worked), and the Oracle said, "Mom."

And so was developed a list of mothers' multiple and pervasive failures, inadequacies, and sexual shortcomings, which were seen as driving their husbands into the beds of their five-year-olds. It is interesting to note that, in doing so, these professionals came up with a more male-demeaning analysis than anything ever devised by allegedly male-hating radical feminists. The underlying assumption here was that men as a class suffered from what can only be called moral insanity.

After describing a study of "incest families," a pamphlet published by the American Humane Association offered examples of fathers' behavior described by thirteen mothers, behavior corroborated by the child-victim. Included were such things as breaking a radio over the mother's head, burning the child with hot irons, chasing the mother out of the house with a gun, locking mom in the closet while he sexually abused the child. . . .

It would seem difficult, in these instances, to avoid observing who was doing what to whom, to avoid assigning culpability. It would seem difficult, that is, were the assumption that the man was the equal of the woman—a fully developed, responsible adult. That is not, however, the author's assumption. Rather guilelessly (that is, without apparent sense of the magnitude of the insult involved), the author writes:

"After examining the character of the incest family . . . the unavoidable conclusion seems to be that the failure of the mother to protect the child against the contingency of incestuous victimization is a crucial and fruitful area of study. . . . Considering the father offender as a possible source of control of incest behavior seems . . . like considering the fox . . . as guard in the henhouse. . . . The mother is the only possible agent of incest control within the family group."[22]

In fact, it is astounding that this understanding of the male as hopelessly and irredeemably afflicted with diminished capacity was published not by radical man-haters but by an agency affiliated with the mainstream powers-that-be. By contrast, we were operating out of a far greater sense of optimism (sigh) and respect for the male potential to reason (sigh), to listen, to choose.

Perhaps we should have read, in history, the future's blueprint.

But we did not. Perhaps we should have anticipated that much of what we would subsequently witness—including advocacy for decriminalization (even overt legalization), vigorous (relentless) mother-blame—might be foretold by these works. But we did not.

After all, that was *then*, right? That was the "before" in the picture; we'd make the "after." (Right?) Given the sense of *possibility* that derived from the heady energy for truth and change in those days, I didn't even entertain doubt that we could bring change about. Nor did I reflect, then, on the possibility that the change you seek may not be the change that, in the end, you make.

I look back in wonder. Even as I noticed, in 1976 and 1977, bits and pieces of stereotypes and unsupported conjecture that would prove to have the sticking power of Crazy Glue, I was unperturbed.

"Typically, the father and daughter become incestuously involved after the mother has rejected the sexual role with her husband and the maternal role with her daughter. The mother is infantile and dependent, reverses the mother-daughter role, and assumes with her daughter the relationship she wishes she had had with her own rejecting mother."[23]

Or, "In a typical traumatic case, an authoritarian father, unhappily married in a sexually repressed household and probably unemployed, drunkenly imposes himself on his young daughter. . . . Since the father otherwise extends very little attention to his daughter, his sexual advances may be one of the few pleasant experiences she has with him. If she is unaware of society's taboo and if the mother does not intervene, she has no reason to suspect the enormity of the aberration. But when she grows up and learns of the taboo, she feels cheapened."[24]

Or, "The father is a basically inadequate man who drinks a lot. The mother is a very powerful, controlling person, but because of illness, has not been able to function as well as she should and the father has often had to take over the mother's role. As in most of these cases, the mother gave her tacit consent by ignoring what was going on. It gave her a hold on keeping her husband that she could always overlook it on the grounds that he was drinking and didn't know what he was doing."[25]

And, "The mother's role in facilitating the incestuous relationship involved both strong unconscious hostility toward the daughter and considerable dependency on her as a substitute wife-mother. . . . These women had a history of sexually rejecting and deprecating their husbands while simultaneously maintaining satisfactory public facades of female role competence. . . . While rejecting their husbands sexually and generating in them considerable sexual frustration and tension, they played conspicuous roles in directing the husbands' sexual energies toward the daughters."[26]

Over and over and over and over. "A sexual relationship between father and daughter usually arises when the mother, who has become physically estranged from her husband pushes the daughter forward as a substitute to preserve the family."[27]

Given that virtually every professional I asked during the mid-1970s testified that incest was, in fact, *extremely* rare ("perhaps one in a million"), and given that Freud's revised view—that it was all kids' imaginings—still held sway, it was difficult to know from whence these absolute certainties derived, other than some Ministry of Manufactured Information. How could they be so *sure* about that which they everywhere claimed was rarely seen?

But I was (I repeat, incredulously) unperturbed.

After all, these folks just had the wrong take on things. When, in that climate of passion and optimism, we pointed it out, we would prevail.

———

The first thing to do was to clear out the cobwebs of mystification, to organize my own print version of a speakout. (Speakouts were often employed within the feminist movement as a political tool for giving voice to women's real experiences of rape, battering, etc.) What really happened? To whom, and when, and why? With what commonalities and with what effects?

I placed ads in various publications saying I was a woman author doing a first-person documentary book on incest and was looking for others to share in my forum. The summer and fall of 1976, my life centered on the mail. My mail centered on incest.

I was living then in the top two floors of a Greenwich Village townhouse, with my husband and nine-year-old twin sons. Around eleven o'clock every morning, I'd listen for the clank and the splish that signaled the mail being dropped through the street-level slot onto the wide pine-board hall floor. I'd tear down after it.

Occasionally (the book idea was still unsold), there would be a curiously mixed rejection from a publisher. ("The women editors are intrigued. The male editors are not.") Incest, some said, was certainly a *sensational* subject. But since it was so rare, who would the readers be?

(You see what I mean when I use the word *silence?*)

Always, though, there would be letters from women, from all over the country. Sometimes there would be letters from men as well. Most often, those would offer to instruct me at length about the benefits they had derived from fucking their sisters. Occasionally, a man would write in real pain over what his father or stepfather had done to him. Over the months, the number of letters from women reached the hundreds. Included in virtually every one was the fact that they had never told anyone before. How incredible that seemed at the time. An entire aspect of childhood realities totally suppressed, entirely denied, as though by a kind of emotional totalitarianism.

They came, these women, they called, they corresponded, all bearing in trust the story of what had been done to them as children. In part, certainly, they were acting on their own behalf. But there was an added urgency: Perhaps this could help someone else? And, with even greater and more important urgency: Perhaps we could actually make change for children now?

What we were doing not only *felt* radical, it *was* radical—in the sense of unearthing a fundamental truth of women's experience, with a hope for basic change. We were seeking to expose and condemn the permission for male sexual abuse of the children in their care and trust; talking and plotting the overthrow of a centuries-old secret. (As we would learn, it would later come to seem radical beyond consideration—to seek to actually *repeal* this historical male right.)

Seam by seam, we unstitched the vestment of myth from a common but well-concealed truth: Children were regularly molested within the home as a matter of everyday living. And the offenders had done it not in spite of the fact that they knew it was wrong, but because they believed it was their right, or at least *justifiable.* ("My father said it was natural"; "He said he read in a magazine it was natural in nature"; "He said he wanted to teach me about sex so I wouldn't get hurt.") This was authentic testimony delivered to children from, as it were, the offending horse's mouth—before the horse had learned there was instant absolution in simply blaming his wife or, later, his own lousy childhood.

How strange. The most shocking thing to me then about child sexual abuse in the home was how utterly, boringly, banal it was (in its motive, not in its effects). Part of the horror, in fact, lay in the sheer gratuitousness of the behavior. One young woman told of being outside, playing "show me" with a neighbor child. Her father called her into the house and said, "Don't do that. I'll show you mine."

Did he *have* to do that? Of course not. There is no indication that he was half-mad with savage lust or rage, or in the grip of any emotion that overwhelmed a strong sense of prohibition. He simply wanted to, and nothing in the world told him he should not, could not, or must not.

The stories were bizarre in their matter-of-factness, their everydayness, their routineness. Often they were most grotesque in their absurdity. The business of enlisting your child in an activity that violates and frightens her, to satisfy your own—what?

needs?—requires either an outrageous use of father-power muscle (orders, threats) or a truly embarrassing dialogue. ("Come
here and play with my mousie," said one father. "I don't want to,
Daddy," his three-year-old replied. "I'm playing with my dolly."
"You can bring your dolly. She can watch you play with my
mousie.")

To be sure, there were women whose stories were of violent
fathers and stepfathers; there were stories of offending brothers,
whose style was more often than not barbaric; and of uncles,
grandfathers, the lot. But the violence was household-contained,
part and parcel of that same sense of male right to dominance. For
the most part, the women described the ordinary dailinesses of
childhood—three meals, snacks, school, riding bikes—of which
regular sexual violation was a degrading, offending, and bewildering part.

As the particulars were brought into the open, the absurdity of
the adults' behavior, contrasted with the emotional mayhem that
was left in its wake, there were moments of outright hilarity. One
woman suggested a suitable punishment for these offenders: Just
put them on television and make them *describe* these scenes. Not
explain them. Just describe them, in every single, stupid, baby-
talk detail. (The astonishing thing then was how young most of
my new friends had been when the abuse began—three, four,
five. . . .)

Much has been made of the words *shame* and *guilt*; of the kids'
sense that what they were doing was *wrong*. But from what I
heard then, these words distort. The women described rage and
fear of the violation. What "guilt" was described adhered to the
kids' sense of justice: this stuff felt like severe punishment, it *was*
severe punishment—physically and emotionally—and punishment, kids are meant to learn, follows from something you must
have done. *Shame* and *guilt*, as they are used, imply focus on this
as illicit sex, but that was miles away from anything women
described of their subjective experience.

Guilt came, as well, from the endlessly repeated paternal

admonishments that all carried the content: This would kill your mother if she found out. So these women, as children, had been cut off from their mothers, were forcibly engaged in a betrayal of their mothers, and without the protection of their fathers (in fact, needing protection *from* their fathers): in a very important way, the women had been orphaned. (It is a very curious thing to be, an orphan with two parents.)

As for *shame*, that seems to me a poor word to describe what results from total powerlessness and what seems to be a nightly mockery of that powerlessness; a nightly degradation ceremony, overlaid with the outrageous demand that the intervening hours be lived as though nothing were happening. What we were talking about here was sexual slavery: slavery being "a power relation of domination, degradation, and subservience, in which human beings are treated as chattel, not persons."[28] Involuntary sexual servitude which, it has been persuasively argued, should be covered by the Thirteenth Amendment.

(Indeed, that the argument is *very* persuasive can be seen from the moment of the amendment's drafting. In 1865, "Democratic Congressman James Brown of Wisconsin proposed an alternative Thirteenth Amendment, which, among other things, would have created a sweeping exception to the ban on involuntary servitude for all 'relations of parent and child, master and apprentice, guardian and ward.' "[29] That alternative was not accepted by the Reconstruction Congress, but the fact of its proposal explicitly articulates an apprehension about the relevance.)

So much propaganda has since washed by about the villainy of mothers, plotting and scheming to feed their daughters to their housemates, or knowing of the abuse and doing nothing. I must say that, in overwhelming numbers, the women in the mid-1970s—pre-propaganda—stated unequivocally that their mothers had simply not known. This is reasonable: Society had contrived not to know either, and the mothers were neither more nor less than members of that society. As children, visited by threats of what would ensue if they told, the women had not told.

As we talked, as we thought about it, as we listened and discovered, however tangled the personal individual emotions, the target of the greatest expression of anger was clear: It was anger at the grotesque abuse of power and at the *permission* that gendered and engendered that power.

As feminist therapist Sandra Butler would soon write, "I suggest that incestuous assault is not an unnatural acting out of a particular configuration of family interaction or personality types but is simply further along on the continuum of societally condoned male behaviors. We must recognize incestuous assault as culturally and politically sanctioned violence against women and children."[30]

As I listened to women, another thought nudged; more an impression, then, than something clearly formulated. Many, many women described the intense rage their fathers expressed toward their mothers ("that old cow," in one dad's words). The fathers dwelt on the way mom would suffer were she to find out, as though that thought was *almost* delicious enough to invite them to tease discovery. Could it be that in some measure that indeed was the point? That the children had simply been convenient and safe objects for the expression of that rage? Much was subsequently to be made of the "fact" that survivors were often angrier at their mothers than at the perpetrators. It was, even then, part of such literature as existed. I did not hear that from women themselves in the early days of listening. (But to the extent that it was or is true, and is not merely something that is socially and therapeutically encouraged, could that rage derive from the child's intuitive understanding that the abuse does not, in fact, have anything to do with her; she is merely a stand-in?)

Thoughts like these seem, now, in a time sternly devoted to gender neutrality, somewhere between the arcane and the heretical. But the congruence of the evidence then was startling, seemed unavoidable. Since no one had ever acknowledged the prevalence of routine household child rape, no one had ever said out loud that it was seriously wrong nor made provision for accountability. Since no one had ever openly said no to fathers, those fathers who felt like it, did what they felt like. Since the silence was ensured by clear threat of disaster to girls and women as penalty for complaining, everyone could go about assuming that such things didn't happen, and mothers did not have reason to expect they were meant to police their own homes. Since no one talked at all about these assaults, Susie just shut up and, one way or another, endured.

There was a lucidity here that made political understanding of the issue inescapable (we thought). How could it be that breaking the silence would not lead to change?

(How indeed.)

————

Because we were speaking where speech had not been issued before, we had to grapple with language problems. Clearly, an adult coercing sex from a child exclusively for his own gratification is victimization. But many of the women I spoke with were adamant that they not be seen as "victims." They saw themselves, and they wanted to be seen, as *survivors*. That word, which has by now been thoroughly degraded and bankrupted, seemed fresh at the time. It allowed for the notion of serious injury without classifying the injury as necessarily permanently deforming.

If the word *survivor* has since been quite sensibly denounced as a "U.S. psychotherapy term,"[31] that is indeed what it has become, hijacked and debased along with words like *courage* and *power* into the vampirish mental health maw, which drains meaning from the words it puts mouth to before sending them forth to do its work.

But "victim" or "survivor," the issue of permanent injury was nettlesome from the outset. We were, after all, advocating serious censure of men's behavior (after giving fair warning, of course). Serious censure must by definition involve penalty, accountability. How much harm did we have to prove? Women who don't see themselves foremost as victims, who want to be seen as survivors no matter how very badly they have been hurt, are not inclined to embrace the claim that they are "scarred forever." (Some of the women did not want to give the bastards that satisfaction.) But in the absence of that, as historical law told us and as rape prosecution experience showed, women are open to charges of complicity. Still, but, and yet . . . Most especially, we did not want to send the message to kids, to young women, that their fate was, in fact, to be forever damaged. (Was this naïveté? Arrogance? This notion that what we said or did would in the end make any difference?)

Another decision I made, this on my own, was to focus on the stories of white women. Black and hispanic women had written to me as well, but I was uncomfortable with the degree to which using their stories within my framework would play to existing bias that such things only happened among some socially disfranchised "them." In that, at least, perhaps I was correct. Only recently, Melba Wilson, writing of incest in the black community, says, "The fear that I have about saying this publicly is considerable. I worry that this book will be misconstrued and misinterpreted by many in our black communities. Some may feel that I have breached an even greater taboo, crossed a bigger boundary (in their eyes) than incest. By airing publicly some of the uncool stuff that goes on in our communities, I and the other women whose stories are included are exposing the dirty linen that we all know and keep quiet about."[32]

There was no question incest/child sexual abuse was a major problem for minority women. Billye Y. Avery, founder of the National Black Women's Health Project, writes:

"The number one issue for most of our sisters is violence— battering, sexual abuse. Same thing for their daughters, whether they are twelve or four. . . .

"When you talk to young people about being pregnant, you find out a lot of things. Number one is that most of these girls did not get pregnant by teenage boys; most of them got pregnant by their mother's boyfriends or their brothers or their daddies. We've been sitting on that. . . ."[33]

And then there was the matter of the little word *incest* itself. Literally defined as consanguinity or marriage within the bounds within which marriage is proscribed, it carried the baggage of inbreeding and every quip in the Appalachian jokebook. It was also tethered to the quasi-voodoo word *taboo*. But are you really going to say *paternal child rape* every time? (And what about grandfathers, older cousins, funny uncles?) Incest stayed. The word and, in the event, the event itself.

———

Otherwise? The mood was exuberance. It was as though we'd been warned that the stench emerging from the breadbox was emitted by demons who would swallow you alive if you disturbed them. We'd taken the risk, opening the box, only to find decomposing rye, molded and decaying cookies. . . . Nasty, but (we thought) how marvelous. *Those* were things we could get rid of. Look, there is nothing mysterious at work here. Nothing that cannot be cleaned up by a human agency.

All systems seemed go.

My idea was sold. The book was written. What would happen?

We did not expect the world would simply say, "Oh, good. Glad you told us. We'll just cut that out." We had no idea what was going to happen. But (watch out, world) we were going to give it our finest try.

True, there was trepidation as the World's First Walking, Talking Incest Victim was sent out to meet the media. (There was far less media to meet in 1978, nowhere near the current TV babble of cross-talk.) The atmosphere was tense. The sentiment among those who had "shared my forum" was uniform. To be precise, it was, "Better you than me, pal."

Nor did fate allow for out-of-town tryouts. It dumped me abruptly on "The Today Show." A friend, who'd accompanied me, reported that there seemed to be general attention in the

Green Room during the short time I spoke. Except for the two gentlemen journalists, standing behind her.

"Oh, come on," said one. "What nonsense."

"Yeah, she's got it backwards," replied the other. "The trouble is little kids don't get fucked enough."

Oh.

And, true, the book itself was less often treated as a written work than as a human-interest or style-page event. Reviewers, indeed, tended toward barely controlled apoplexy.

In the *New York Times Book Review*, Raymond A. Sokolov (then, I believe, best known for his food writing in magazines) allowed that "Louise Armstrong, a self-described victim of such an assault, must be right to urge a general discussion of father-daughter incest so that victims will gather courage, see that their plight is not unique and be able to do something about it." This much conceded, he adds, "Her research was informal at best (I assume that she did not make it up entirely)." And he suggests that this work, clearly labeled a *speakout*, was "pornography masquerading as science." Science?

"Miss Armstrong," he said, "covers herself with quotations from experts and a kind of feminist rhetoric, but then out comes the rough stuff. And it is very rough and squalid. If you are even remotely sensitive, it will put you off any kind of sex for a while." To which he hastily amends, "I don't mean that incest should not be discussed. I just don't think it should be wallowed in for the sake of titillation."[34]

This same sense of borderline panic was evident, as well, in more than one electronic journalist's reference to the book as being titled Kiss Daddy *Goodbye*.

Overall, though, a tremendous sense of energy and kinship was evoked as more and more women spoke up. On call-in shows around the country, the stories poured in with the intensity and breathtaking rawness of a first-time-revealed secret. "Hi, I'm forty-two years old. When I was five, my father started acting strange when he would come in to kiss me goodnight. . . ." Then the story of what had happened, how she'd pretended to be asleep. Then, "I've been married twenty years and I've never told anyone before. Not even my husband."

These were war stories, told by veterans, about their childhood years as sexual hostages in battles we had never acknowledged— within the American family.

Over and over I was asked the "scarred forever" question. ("Tell me, Louise, are you scarred forever?") Over and over, I passed through (dodged, if you prefer) that question and back to the power abuse. ("Obviously, rape by someone you are meant to trust is acutely painful, but what the women I listened to were more hurt by is the social permission, the license . . .")

Over and over I was asked, "What should happen? What should be done?"

Over and over I answered, "Let's get this stuff stopped. Let's get a consensus that sexually molesting your own child is seriously wrong. Let's dignify the victims' experience. And let's say that from now on, this will be seen as seriously wrong. From now on, there must be accountability."

Corroboration continued to accrue. Most of the fathers, caught and spotlighted, simply did not see what the problem was. One father, on the "Phil Donahue Show" in 1979, said, "I actually in my own mind back then, I thought I was doing her a favor." (What the transcript of the show says is "AUDIENCE: [sounds of remonstrance] [disbelief]."[35] Funny. My recollection is that the audience laughed.) Another man said, "I'm a decent man. I provide for my family. I don't run around on my wife, and I've never slept with anyone except my wife and my daughters."[36]

I believed, then, that the issue could be self-liquidating.

Silly me.

(But still. I still think of those as the good old days.)

Chapter 2

"IT'S A MENTAL HEALTH PROBLEM, STUPID"

THE YOUNG WOMAN on the phone is telling me about a planned gathering in New York, which bears the title "To Tell the Truth." She explains that the first such gathering took place in Santa Fe and drew five hundred people, but she is expecting two thousand to show for this one. She's wondering if I would be interested in keynoting, because they've decided to have a speaker who has written a book on child sexual abuse. (Mygod. By now, she could have just gone out on the street and hailed one.) She repeatedly refers to this planned gathering as an "event" (and into my mind pops, "Incest! A P. T. Barnum Production!"). She tells me that it is meant to be very upbeat, very positive. She is explaining that after the speakers, they are planning to have breakout groups.

Breakout groups?

She explains. "People would choose which breakout group they wanted to go to. And the groups would be facilitated. There would be several rooms; for example, for women survivors, men survivors, clergy—the clergy-abused. It's to give the audience an opportunity to be able to speak, because by that time there will be a lot of things that are coming up for people. There'll be a room for people who have been involved in ritual abuse, um, a breakout group for partners, for gays and lesbians, for families, and for educators and therapists. The one for educators and therapists will be very informational. The other groups will be for people to really have a chance to share."

Caution grips me vise-like as I flash on the last sea of survivor faces I saw from a podium—maybe a fifth of them (well, maybe not *that* many) showing interest in or recognition of what I was saying; the rest uncomprehending, resistant. The way of being they had by then been trained into was being challenged. I wondered then. (I wonder now.) Why had I been invited?

"I see," I say. "And this is supposed to be positive because of . . . what?"

"It's supposed to have a positive note to it because it's focusing on the . . . on, on—recovery. And some of the hopeful aspects of recovery. We're also including someone who would be a speaker who can give an overview of what is going on—with child abuse."

Thinking of my recent two-year tour of the child welfare/foster care system (and the number of children who, perhaps having blown the whistle on their abusive fathers—or perhaps having just acted defiantly as a result of the abuse—have been pulled into that system), I say, "What *is*?"

"What is what?"

"What do you think is going on with child abuse?"

"Well—"

I am confusing her. I am sorry. (But best she finds out before she can only watch helplessly as I single-handedly de-positive her "event.")

She laughs. "I don't understand. I mean, what I'm talking about is someone who can give us some information as to maybe what kinds of programs are being done. How they're different than they were years ago. We're trying to find somebody who has spoken and has information either from a governmental stand-point or a legal standpoint, or what's happening in the community to help people.

"Another aspect would be someone who is an author who has written a book." The person who sponsored the Santa Fe "To Tell the Truth," she tells me, was a person who was an author. "So we were looking for a person who is an author and who wrote a book and would be interested to speak at our function. That's why I was told to call you, because your book is—apparently—very well known and you have spoken before and we thought that if you were interested you could be a perfect person to speak at this event."

"Well," I say. For a moment, I'm at a loss; it's as though this is an interspecies phone call. All that seems to matter is that I have written a book. It does not seem to matter what the book says. (To redo an old line: I am like a dog walking on two legs. The main feature is that I have done it at all.) "The reason I'm hesitating," I say, "is I'm not sure I'm the perfect person at all. You have not read my stuff?"

She hasn't.

"I just think you should be very careful, because I am not a therapy-solves-everything, let's-all-enjoy-being-in-recovery kind of person."

She says that other people in the last planning meeting *had* read the book and said, mmm, yeah, when my name came up. But I have tripped her alarm; there is a note of caution. "When you say you're not a therapy person—what do you mean?"

How does one explain without sounding like one is against help, against befriending, against consolation? "I just have a more political focus. We've lost focus on this as a power abuse, and in my opinion that's the only way to think about this whole thing that's coherent. So I say things that are different from what the survivor movement—or the recovery movement, let me put it; the addiction/recovery moment—have been focusing on."

"Can you give me an example?"

How has this happened? How has this issue been so successfully hijacked by healers and empowerers that silence once again triumphs—this time, despite the noise? "I can give you the example that when I first went out there, the World's First Walking, Talking Incest Victim . . ." I am heading for a point here, about to try to explain what it was we had in mind, what it was we understood (felt sure we did). She interrupts, however.

"You were brave, I'll tell you."

I am floored. The personal is—the personal. We have become a population of stories that carry no larger meaning, that imply no social issue, but are the wampum, the currency, that is the trade of the incest survivor identity.

It was not (I repeat) like this in the good old days.

As writer and theater artist Terry Wolverton, writing about her attendance at the first meeting of the Incest Awareness project, said in 1979, "It was a large public gathering designed to generate interest and participants in the project. A Panel consisting of a psychologist, a social worker, and a counselor discussed the issue from a clinical and objectified perspective, speaking of 'patients' and 'victims,' referring to 'them.' " Wolverton said, "This is my major criticism of non-feminist therapeutic treatment of incest, that it . . . distances those who are seeking help. This dialogue continued with the audience taking up the discussion from the same point of view. An unbearable tension began to fill the room, tension of many women's suppressed pain and rage, until Annette rose to say that she herself had experienced incest, and she needed to discuss it from her own perspective. Other women rose then, identifying themselves, claiming their experience, saying 'I' and 'we.' We saw clearly that we, and not the professionals, are the experts on incest."[1]

How did it happen that women, once strong and clear about the politics of the issue, certain in their desire to follow their own emotional and rational compass toward change, not only for themselves but for children now; to assert their ownership of their experience, the primacy of their analysis, succumbed to a language exclusively focused on personal pathology and recovery: language that is not *theirs* but that of self-annointed experts? This is a question I will explore later.

Now, on the phone, I continue to talk (but really it is babbling). "The women who came forward early on, the women I heard from, did not identify themselves by their symptoms. They were indeed survivors. They had pain, they cried. But they were invigorated by the political analysis of this as a licensed abuse of power; they drew courage from analogies to the issues of rape and battered women. . . ." But I know: I am talking in order to feel my voice. I am reassuring my own need for reason. I am, as far as my phone companion is concerned, yelling into the wind.

As we hang up (with her saying she wants to field what I've said off other people), part of me wants to try one more time to reach out. Common sense, however, prevails. I sigh and think to make myself a sign: IT'S A MENTAL HEALTH ISSUE, STUPID.

When did I first hear the knob click, advancing us from "dread taboo" to "decriminalization" (of that which had never been treated as a crime, the very existence of which had, five minutes earlier, been denied), to "medicalization"—in fact to industrialization?

At my first convention, probably.

I am not much at home in large groups anyway. But it is a disorienting thing, indeed, to walk into a hotel lobby where many suited-up, serious-looking people have pinned to their lapels a three-by-four-inch white plastic-wrapped badge that announces INCEST. One's initial impression is of spoof. A Monty Python sketch on the convention business? An episode of "Fawlty Towers"?

The conference, held at the Bismarck Hotel in Chicago in October 1978, was titled "Incest: In Search of Understanding." Tellingly, it was billed as a conference on "intrafamilial" childhood sexual abuse. Thirty-five people were listed as panelists or speakers. Thirty-five. (It is interesting to note that there were almost twenty more folks listed as members of the *editorial review board alone* at the 1992 inception of the *Journal of Child Sexual*

Abuse, and—let me get up and check. Here it is: The 1990 National Symposium on Child Victimization, titled "Keepers of the Children," lists 856 presenters or panelists. What can one say? "My, how you've grown!"?)

In the bar, the first evening, wearing our little badges, we were the objects of some attention, you betcha. (I wonder where they are now, those other hotel guests whose preview of the issue about to explode came in that clownish scene.)

In sessions, though the surface was genial, the underlying sense was of vigorous competition. You could hear the gears of specialization grinding, the carving up of victim-populations, the negotiations for turf, the vying for funding, for prestige, for place. Never having heard it before, I did not then identify the hum and buzz as the sound of persons professionalizing. (Nor did I know then that professionalizing carries the demand that you transform an issue into one that only *you* can truly understand, using language over which you have exclusive domain.)

Since both Kee McFarlane—then program director of the National Center on Child Abuse and Neglect (NCCAN)—and the center's then-director Doug Besharov were present, and since NCCAN was the main agency authorized to issue monetary grants to demonstration programs, tantalizing dollars, in the form of funding, were present as well.

And so it was here that I first got a glimmer of a previously unconsidered reality, one that would work to isolate this issue from adult rape or wife-battering.

Because of the 1974 Child Abuse Prevention and Treatment Act, child sexual abuse already had a home in existing social policy. That policy dictated civil/social work intervention by protective services and placed the matter of child abuse and neglect under courts that were claimed to be "nonadversarial"—family courts, juvenile courts; courts whose only power over those it found to be offenders (neglectful or abusive parents) was to remove the children to state protective custody (hardly a minor matter, of course; in fact, it can be argued that it is a lesser punishment to be deprived of your liberty for a specified period of time than to lose your children, quite possibly forever). These were courts that claimed disinterest in matters of guilt or innocence, whose stated focus was the "best interests" of children; whose decisions were based on "possible harm to the child."

Thus, at the conference, a protective services official explained why protective services should manage the problem:

"The idea that there is something special about sexual involvement between parents or caretakers and their children, something special enough to require an essentially nonpunitive approach," the presenter said, "can be sensed in the recent extension of the Child Abuse Act to specifically include sexual abuse. . . . It is, of course, the close relation between the perpetrator and the victim that both requires and justifies a nonpunitive approach in these cases."[2]

The nonpunitive approach, as he went on to describe it, focuses mainly on the mother. By pointing out to her the usual pattern— of a passive, dependent wife (who may often be absent because she works or is sick), who in any case is not sexually attractive or cooperative, who invites the child to take over her household responsibilities, and a dominant, controlling husband, who favors the child in any case, which makes him jealous of the child's outside friends—social workers can get the mother to own up to the fact that she has failed in her father-taming role, and to challenge the father's denial and to "get an admission from him." (So not only must mom be taught she has failed in her role as household police person, but she must now stand in for the cops in wresting a confession from the bastard?)

A family therapist then told why family therapy is the way to deal with this "family dysfunction."

A Swedish social expert explained that, while there is rape in Sweden, there is no child sexual abuse. However, he is here (he explained) because most social problems in the United States tend to turn up later in Sweden. (And I raised my hand to express awe at the idea that incest is an American export item.)

One speaker particularly caught my interest, presenting what were, in fact, quite traditional views of incest. Yet, in the new context of language of shock-dread-outrage-horror, these sounded somewhat radical. "It is not uncommon," she said, "for the child to initiate or actively participate in incest. In most cases, we discover that both the parent and the child find erotic gratification in the liaison." Her thesis was that incest is less damaging when the child is young. It is the adolescent, who has internalized society's values, who views incest as a traitorous act. Echoing the centuries of age-dickering, she suggested setting nine years of age as the cutoff point. A child younger than that "does not feel guilty because 'that's just the way things are.' "[3]

There it was again, I mused, this obsession with the child's feeling of "guilt" as the critical matter. Is the reason to proscribe rape concern that the victim has absorbed and will suffer from society's puritanical impulses? And should we, as in earlier days, return to the legal fiction that rape under a certain age does not count, thereby exempting eighteen-month-old babies? Certainly, wherever the shock and horror and dread taboo might be found, it was not to be found in this room.

Of special interest, as well, was evidence that the accomplice-witness assumption was alive and doing quite well—at least in Texas.

Law professor Carla Dowben told us that Texas has had a statute prohibiting sexual abuse of children since January 1849. "However, over the years there has been increasing difficulty in successfully prosecuting for incest following Texas decisions that held the victim of incest to be a consenting partner or an accomplice witness whose uncorroborated testimony was insufficient to convict."

By way of example, she described a 1974 case where the father's conviction was overturned on appeal on the grounds that the thirteen-year-old was an accomplice. The father had offered the child money—for such luxuries as groceries, for example—and the girl was never threatened even though she told him over and over that sex hurt her and she didn't want to do it.

"The Appeals Court concluded that a female who consents or voluntarily enters into an incestuous intercourse is an accomplice witness, and as such there must be evidence linking the accused with the offense other than the victim's testimony. The Court stated that only if the act was accomplished as a result of force, threats, fraud or undue influence is the victim not an accomplice witness."[4]

Again, where was society's much-ballyhooed shock and horror to be found if it could not be found in contemporary or historical reality?

(But never mind. We would point this out: the fact of societal *permission* . . . And *then* . . .)

As icing, there was even a professional philosopher present. To listen to him try to help us evaluate whether paternal child rape is morally wrong, employing the tools of his discipline, was to know what it feels like to be a spoke on a moving bicycle wheel. If you close your eyes all you hear is the hum of the road. If you don't close your eyes, you get seriously dizzy.

In the face of all this, my own presentation, suggesting as it did that incest was, in fact, *the cradle of sexual politics* and that what was needed was a real change of attitude, a revocation of license, seemed sort of spoilsport.

"The real answer," I said, chin out, bucking the tide, "lies less in looking on sexual abuse as a psychological event than as a political one. Men have had the power to enforce our silence; women, our mothers, once small girls themselves, have where necessary been frightened into acting as executors of that power. There has been nothing to stop men from using us as objects to gratify their passing needs. No one has ever said, out loud, that diddling your kid was necessarily a bad thing.

"Indeed," I went on (discovering in this, the first speech I had ever made, the gift of passion in overcoming terror), "the appalling part is that many of our fathers would surely claim they meant us no real harm. It was just a little clean mischief. Just playing doctor. Just a little natural eroticizing of natural affection. Just a little 'tickle,' as Pamela's father put it. Or a weekly 'shampoo,' as Eleanor's father required. Sometimes, as with Sandy's father, it was out and out rape. 'But I know it didn't hurt you, Sandy,' her father said later. 'Because if it had hurt you, Sandy, you'd have hated all men.' [Another interesting supposed benchmark proof of negative effect that would appear again and again.] Pamela's father said, more recently, 'You tell your friend'—meaning me— 'you tell her I still don't see anything wrong with it.' " I said it should be a crime and that a crime comes complete with a criminal and what we do with criminal behavior is assign culpability.

It was like talking about peace at an arms manufacturers' conference. What can I say? They didn't stone me. They were polite—as polite as they would have been if, having wandered by mistake into the wrong conference, I had delivered a peroration on sod farming.

The experience remained unformulated, mystifying, until I got home. The telephone rang. It was one of the conference's sponsors, a pediatrician. He wished to tell me that his cosponsor, the psychiatrist, was a devilish person. He had a scheme—to sell the videotapes he had made of us as we spoke.

This was followed the next day by a call from the psychiatrist. He wished to tell me that the pediatrician, poor fellow, was crazy. That said pediatrician had, the night before, under cover of darkness, broken into the psychiatrist's office, purloined the tapes, and erased portions of them.

Such goings-on suggested to me that the molestation of two-year-olds, and the stopping of same, might not have the new experts' full attention.

———

There were other, early premonitions that things were not going to develop in any way I might have—however hazily—imagined.

A woman called, a social worker, to tell me how much the book had meant to her. (Smile.) To tell me that, based on the book, she was now doing training of other social workers on the issue for the sum of some hundreds of dollars a day. (Frown.)

And yet another social worker called and came to visit. We spoke of one thing and another having to do, as I recall, with the program she was starting in her agency to do counseling for survivors. She also spoke about the book.

Looking at me with that mixture of the intent and the all-knowing peculiar to her trade, she said in a voice full of intimate concern, "You will never, you understand, be taken seriously as a writer. You will always be known as an incest survivor."

Well, now. *That* was a wrinkle (more like a permanent pleat). What did she mean? How did she know? (What made me think she *knew*?) What made her so certain? (Why did I mind her?) Why *not*, why *so*? . . .

She left me with this unassimilable piece of information, the turd she had presumably come by to drop. And she left me also with a piece of (then unassimilated) information about our vulnerability when faced with the arrogant certainty of those who declare themselves seers and *knowers*, and put themselves forward as caring, as meaning us well. (As one feminist therapist has pointed out to me more recently, this is the same con job our fathers did: I'm doing this because I care about you. Trust me, I *know*.)

I set the soothsayer's sooth aside then (well, more or less). The woman was not, after all (though she seemed to be), a bearer of portent. This had not been a visit from a higher power. She was a *social worker*, for crying out loud. With an *opinion*, and what difference did it make, and who told her. . . .

As I say, I set it aside.

———

Crazy, bats, daffy. So much about this issue seemed, early on, just plain nuts. (That it continues to seem so today is still *more* bizarre, given the obsessive conviction that this is a *mental health* issue.)

In 1979 we began to see journalists' reports heralding "Dread Taboo" and "Last Taboo." By the early 1980s, there was a deluge. More books appeared—with pictures of broken dolls or limp, discarded Raggedy Anns on their covers. Everywhere was being spread alarm about the widespread, if unquantified, incidence of incest, using the word *epidemic*.

These reports were the early warning signs that contemporary America's way of dealing with this issue was going to be the creation of social delusion: the recasting of incest as a "disease." The attempt to change not the reality, but the public's *perception* of what that reality was. Clichés like "tip of the iceberg," "pillar of the community," "crosses all socioeconomic lines," were everywhere. Always, the language was the "crime of incest." Even while, at the same time—at the *very same time*—more and more newfound experts and shamans were riding over the horizon advocating "decriminalization."

I was, of course, suitably perplexed. What was an "expert" on incest? Weren't the women to whom it had happened the real experts?

The same old themes were being played—of children's complicity (for favors, or because they didn't know it was "wrong"), of children's secret enjoyment of the event because it was, after all, "sex," of male helplessness, of female malice. . . . "Decriminalization," of course, made eminent sense for two reasons. One was that federal and state funding was not apt to go to those seeking to "break up families" by putting fathers either out of the home or into prison.

A second, equally pedestrian, explanation lay in the fact that the newfound experts—springing forth as from the head of Zeus—had not themselves had the time or the inclination to set out on a listening journey among victims and survivors. When the issue first broke, most of them raced to turn up "what was known," thereby cementing the propagation of the biases of the past, only presenting them now as brand new. (There were exceptions—sociologists like David Finkelhor and Diana Russell, whose work took clear account of the sociocultural, gender-power issues.)

Every now and then a voice of real experience with real children and real mothers and real offenders hove briefly into view. In June of 1981, a Philadelphia judge, Lois G. Forer, wrote to the *New York Times* decrying an article that had appeared citing Dr. Alexander G. Zaphiris, who allowed as to how victims of incest suffer permanent psychological damage and that a high percent of female criminals and prostitutes had been incest victims.

Having made those requisite obeisances to reality, Zaphiris went on to say that the child victim "really loves her father and enjoys the sex."[5]

As Judge Forer wrote with refreshing indignation, "This is a typical statement by male psychiatrists and family therapists who claim that the mother is 'cold' to the father, the child enjoys sex and, accordingly, the mother is at fault."

Citing her experience with rape/incest as an attorney representing child victims and as a judge, Forer said, "Contrary to Dr. Zaphiris's findings, my experience has been that it is often the mother who reports the crime."

In grand but pithy style, she said, "The stereotypes of the father loving and sexually stimulating the child, the child enjoying sex and the mother being an 'accomplice' are, I believe, as false as the stereotypes of the happy 'darkies' who sang in the cotton fields and loved 'old massa,' and the contented coolies toiling in imperial China. The responses of women and girls to outrageous abuse and brutality by the man of the house should no longer be camouflaged by other men, cloaked as scientists and therapists."

And, further warming my heart, she said: "Incest is a serious problem. It is also a serious crime. It should be dealt with seriously. No rapist should be permitted to return to the home where the child victim is. No woman should be coerced into having sex with her daughter's rapist under the rubric of therapy."[6]

But passion informed by evidence and reason would prove weightless against a time-honored and fail-safe way of deflecting blame from errant men caught merely indulging in dalliance within the privacy of the family. Given preexisting social bias and ongoing powerlessness, mothers were simply too easy a fall guy to pass up. Now marching under the euphemism of "family systems theory," women were ever more implicated: If there *was* something wrong with this stuff, for heavensakes why didn't she stop him?

While sentiments toward children might no longer allow laying weight on their wickedness as causative, it remained a credible sell to attribute their susceptibility to their innate sexuality. And even while a new 1970s-born social correctness marginally protected women as *women* from wholesale slurs, nothing had changed in public attitudes toward women as *mothers*. Nothing stood in the way of hauling them out as the real culprits in their husbands' sexual predations, and thus proposing offender *frailty*, rather than offender accountability, as the driving argument dictating a "treatment" response.

As Judge Forer wrote in the *New York Times*, "Prosecutors who demand long prison sentences for thieves frequently recommend psychiatric probation of the incest/rapist, arguing that (1) he is not really a criminal because it was only his daughter, (2) the father is supporting the family and (3) the child has been examined by a doctor, who reports that she was not injured."

Now described in the literature, rather begrudgingly, as the "nonoffending parent," mothers were nonetheless profiled as deeply offensive: They were "so passive and submissive to their husbands that they were unable to protect their daughters from them." They were "the cornerstone in the pathological family system." They had poor sexual relationships, had been married more than once, were dependent on other women and hostile to them all at the same time. Shockingly, they seemed to have "been deprived of self-fulfillment even within the family." They found "secondary gains from their endless suffering." They were "frigid," pushed their daughters in as replacements. They were the "silent partner"; suffered from "passivity, dependency, and masochism." They were "colluding." There was even *proof*. Subjected to such suggestions of what they were *really* like over and over in therapy, a mother would most often "admit eventually that she was party to the incestuous situation and contributed to the underlying causes."[7] Just, I would hazard, to get out of the room: humoring a maniac; backing toward the door . . .

And so the newly risen experts—invisible just one year earlier—could place their full weight on this theoretical high wire, and now posture total certainty. (What choice did they have? A *reporter* was on the phone.) Perhaps somewhat in response to journalistic excitement (this was a *story*, an *epidemic*)—or perhaps, one would prefer to think, because even they had an inkling that this construction was somewhat implausible—the tone they adopted was one of an almost frantic call to calm, replete with assurances that they knew the true way, *they* had the true fix. Not to worry: the workforce would be undiminished. The bastion of the traditional family remained secure.

It was strange. In my travels and in my listening I never sensed, in the public, any inclination to panic. So I could only surmise that the distress existed among the experts, those who intuited, underlying this issue, the potential for a call for serious change, the potential for a severe dressing-down of some of the country's most prominent male citizens; and sensed as well the possibility that mental health expertise just might not gain dominion over this now visibly sizable and potentially prominent and profitable issue. What seemed clear to them (as it seems clear to me now) was that in order for mental health ideology to win, feminist analysis had to lose. (Never mind that mental health ideology could be made more palatable by calling it feminist.)

If the mental health proponents had been worried, they needn't have been. Sensible or not, their formulation was congruent with the overriding imperative to avoid awareness of a grotesquely distorted power-dynamic long permitted within the sanctified family. Despite the headline orgy of outrage and horror, more and more furniture was now being piled against the door marked PROSECUTION (sometimes it seemed like all the furniture in the house): Susie didn't want daddy to go to jail; mommy would go on welfare; daddy would just get out again; you'd be breaking up families; kids couldn't testify in court; and, bottom line, you couldn't get convictions anyway—this last often placed plumb alongside the specter of massive numbers of men carted off to prison in a paddy wagon.

The titillation of the issue was secured: While incest/child sexual abuse had pitifully little to do with "sex," it had everything to do with an abuse of power so gratuitous that it bordered on the absurd. The images created were the stuff of black humor. Turning the aggressions of adult male sexuality against a child who has barely learned to walk and talk, whose objects of ecstasy are crayons, pretzels, and mud, is colossally pathetic. Exposing this as common closet behavior came powerfully close to exposing male predation as the witless exploitations of a bully class.

Even without giving prominence to feminist voices articulating these things, professionals and the media, raising the issue, had led society right up to the brink of discovery; right up to the very edge of true upheaval. And then they pulled back.

Even with only the descriptions of the behaviors—and even without political analysis—the issue was sexy not because it was about sex. But because, even without analysis, the issue in and of itself played peekaboo with a devastating understanding of what underpinned male social dominance, and the role the family, as traditionally structured, had played in assuring its continuance. By dangling, then withdrawing, a serious social revelation, the presentation of the issue would prove to be a breathtaking social *tease*. And it is plausible that that is one reason the media, to this day, does not just get bored and stop playing with it.

In order to keep such full understanding at bay, the powers-that-be had to dance fast. And before any time-lapse for thought or for public consideration, we were presented with a full-scale social policy effort to decriminalize a behavior that had never been acknowledged, never been spoken of, never been majorly prosecuted, never been specifically prohibited in law (what *we* were talking about, that is; intermarrying adult first cousins I don't know about). Somehow, the idea that there already were statutory rape laws, and that, if nothing else, this was statutory rape, never seemed to arise. This was different. It was *family*.

A great deal of attention was directed toward discovering that many of the offenders were in fact *stepfathers*, as though that fact had some cosmic significance; as though it spoke reassuringly of some biological adherence to the old taboo, the avoidance of inbreeding. Listening to this, you would have thought the main concern here was that five-year-olds would wind up pregnant with a defective fetus; you'd have thought that the issue of authority, the issue of trust, were somehow not identical when applied to biological fathers as against stepfathers.

Numerous pilot projects were funded by the National Center on Child Abuse and Neglect, mainly those that strove to keep families intact. Henry Giaretto, director of the most widely publicized treatment center for what were now being called "incest families," advocated use of the criminal justice system as a strongarm to get the guy to confess and the family to go into treatment, known as "diversion to counseling." He said that "the problem becomes even more serious when [the families] are exposed to the criminal justice system. The youngsters see the police cars descending on the home, the father manacled and taken away. . . ."[8]

What police cars? Where? Not a single one of the women I spoke with early on, and only one of the hundreds I would hear from thereafter, reported any police or criminal justice intervention. How could it be that the professionals were the only ones who had heard the sirens?

A 1977 *New York Times* article on the Philadelphia Center for Rape Control told us that "family disruption is often more traumatic to the child than the actual sexual experience"[9]—echoing, uncannily, the old rubric that the real problem the child has with the rape lies in society's attitude. We were told (again) that the child will feel guilty if daddy goes to jail and the family loses its breadwinner.

What made it possible for the powers-that-be to successfully perpetrate the hoax that making no substantive change in the legal approach to incest constituted progress?

For one thing, the members of the press as well as the public assumed that anything so recently touted as a universal taboo must, at the least, have been treated as seriously against the law.

For another thing, we were entering the Decade of Disorders, about to be flooded by the mass social inversion that would come to be known as the addiction/recovery *movement*. After two decades' combative attempts at social change, the American public was disheartened, ready to give up looking outward; susceptible to the message that *real* change was an individual affair. Because of its affiliation with medical matters, the language of treatment and counseling had a ring of the authoritative, of the objectively *prescriptive*, that advocacies for social action never could. Help and counseling implied the benign; had the sound of something far more liberal and enlightened than punishment.

Even more important, underlying all the hoopla of horror, I thought I discerned profound recognition—a recognition compatible, after all, with the prevalence of the event. (And why not? Women may have been silenced, but they were not brain-dead; they knew what had happened to them, even if they had been forced to tuck it away in some locked mind-box.) If, as was by 1979 becoming common currency, one out of ten of these men was in fact molesting his kid,* and if this were to be made seriously against the law, the specter was of one-tenth of the

---

* During these years statistics shot wildly all over the place: from 1 in 100 to 1 in 10 and soon to 1 in 4. While studies like those by David Finkelhor and Diana Russell were meticulous in outlining the behaviors included along with the victim's relationship to the perpetrator, media reports tended to blend under "incest" all degrees of abuse and all stripe of family member. Diana Russell's finding was that 16% of women had been sexually abused by a relative before 18. 4.5% had been sexually abused by their fathers before that age—which nonetheless translates to 45,000 women per million (Diana E. Russell, *The Secret Trauma: Incest in the Lives of Girls and Women* [New York: Basic Books, 1986], 10).

otherwise productive male citizens of the country diverted to making license plates.

A need for a sense of personal safety drove a public will to collude with the definitions of "incest families" and "incest mothers" as "other."

Had women-at-large put it together—the statistics on wife-battering, the incidence of child-rape, the fact that the offenders were "normal" men indistinguishable from all other men—the idea that men were as likely as not dangerous to have in the house (and that you could not tell, in advance, which men would prove to be so), there might be a significant disincentive to family life, even a substantial apprehensiveness toward it.

It was these things, I believe, that in part drove both the demand for therapeutic interventions that targeted the pathology of the entire family, and the concomitant decriminalization passion; that dictated the framing of the issue as a psychological or psycho-relational glitch, with full public relations force placed behind securing household child sexual abuse under a civil, as opposed to a criminal, jurisdiction.

Perhaps key, however: This was simply following precedent. The battering of children when first uncovered had been described as "parental abuse," before quickly being reformulated into the less threatening "Battered Child Syndrome." Medicalization—framing the issue as a *syndrome*, a matter of individual disease or pathology—took the heat off an otherwise volatile issue, one that might uncomfortably challenge paternal autonomy.[10] The child abuse precedent worked to focus attention on incest as a children's welfare issue, with adult survivors sought out largely to provide a kind of Greek Chorus, chanting about the devastating psychological effects (and further validating medicalized intervention). Without survivors actively resisting this role or aggressively using it to turn a political point, there would be a magnetic pull on incest away from other issues of violence against women and toward the far murkier and considerably more sentiment-ridden world of child health.

That turning the issue of child sexual abuse over to a civil intervention system seemed to those in power at the time a prudent course designed to defuse the issue would, later, prove something of a joke. Because the most important thing to know about the civil child welfare intervention system is this: It has always and forever targeted exclusively the poor, mainly poor single mothers—women with no clout and little credibility and no presumed right to take the moral high ground by speaking of privacy rights. The courts designed for such matters—courts cloaked in the language of avuncular concern—had actually been designed as courts of moral opprobrium; to intervene in matters of waywardness, delinquency, general dereliction, and the failure of the disadvantaged to conform to a social ideal. It was the need for public assistance that triggered the state's right to a trade-off of private surveillance and intervention. Though it would not become clear until the organized outcry of 1984, child sexual abuse—so often declared prevalent in the middle class and so very much a male offense—was destined to detonate once it hit the child welfare system.

But it would be a grave error to fail to identify perhaps the most critical reason underlying the urgency for a "medical" response to "incest families." A punitive stance demands consensus. And a substantial (if largely discreet) portion of the population remained uncertain as to just how wrong sexually violating your own child was, and significant voice was being given to those advocating for children's rights—to sex with adults. No one, of course, was *for* child sexual abuse, but a substantial number of substantial people did not necessarily think, in their hearts, that such behavior was abuse. Despite the generalized mime of outrage and hand-wringing, even now—as in the past—candor peeked through—briefly. And an open call was posted by various men's groups for incest as a *children's* right.

A group of men, all with M.D. or Ph.D. after their names, were speaking about "positive incest." They were labeled the "pro-incest lobby." Their claim was that "the rate of incidence is so high as to make prohibition absurd."[11]

John Money, of Johns Hopkins University, was quoted in 1980 as saying, "A childhood sexual experience, such as being the partner of a relative or of an older person, need not necessarily affect the child adversely."[12] Wardell Pomeroy, coauthor of the original Kinsey reports, was quoted as saying, "It is time to admit that incest need not be a perversion or a symptom of mental illness." Adding, "Incest between [sic] . . . children and adults . . . can sometimes be beneficial."[13] As Larry Constantine, an assistant clinical professor in psychiatry at Tufts, explained, "Children have the right to express themselves sexually, even with members of their own family."[14] One researcher asked, "Who knows how much psychic damage we cause our children with such well-meant yet inhuman attitudes? Who knows whether one result [of bending over backwards to avoid any possibility of incestuous involvement] may not be the present rash of feverish adolescent sexual activity with its undeniable results?" And winding up with a rhetorical flourish, "How many adolescent girls have not said, 'It's the only time I feel someone really loves me?' "[15]

An anthropologist wrote that "the concept of abuse may be inappropriate when applied to incest. 'Many psychotherapists,' claims psychologist James McCarey in *Human Sexuality*, 'believe that a child is less affected by actual incest than by seductive behavior on the part of a parent that never culminates in any manifest sexual activity.' "[16]

James W. Ramey, Ed.D, visiting professor, Department of Psychiatry at Bowman Gray School of Medicine, writing in the May 1979 SIECUS Report of the Sex Information and Education Council of the U.S., equated the incest "taboo" with the earlier "taboo" against masturbation, as something that deserved to be relegated to antiquity. Once again diving into the muddy waters surrounding the word *incest* and tying it to the word *taboo*, he writes, "It is in fact one of the most recent crimes to enter the

English criminal law calendar, an event which took place in 1908. To this day incest between *bastard* relations is not criminal in Scotland, nor is intercourse between uncle and niece incestuous in England, or, for that matter, in Rhode Island."[17]

In one particularly confusing passage, Ramey tells us that "many professionals who discover incest in the course of their work with families are careful not to make an issue of it. If they feel that one party to the incest is being grossly taken advantage of, then they find some other reason to remove that person from the situation." So far, it *sounds* as though he's speaking of consanguinity, consenting adults, but then: "for they know that to make an issue of the incest is primarily to punish the victim, since our court system will either remove the child from its home or incarcerate the adult. In either case the victim not only bears the guilt of having broken up the family, but may also be 'sent away' to a foster home or to an institution."[18] If I am correct here, the two choices for the abused child are either being removed from the home or being *sent away* from the home, and thus it is best if everyone just keeps quiet.

My personal adventure with the permissivists began in 1977 when I met with a reporter who was pursuing a story on "positive" incest with a bouncy enthusiasm that conveyed his conviction he was hot on the trail of something *new*. The journalist, Philip Nobile, seemed to find my perspective, if not fuddy-duddy then nonetheless disappointing. He was far more enthused about the findings of a researcher named Warren Farrell, a former board member of the National Organization for Women and author of *The Liberated Man.*

All I really knew about Farrell's foray into incest was that he had run a classified ad in the same issue (June 1977) of *Psychology Today* as I had. His ad read, "INCEST. Research and personal data needed, especially positive experiences including women. Confidential." Peculiarly, he signed this ad "Dr. Sarrel." I can only conjecture that this feeble disguise (other ads he ran elsewhere had a similar signature) was in keeping with his sense that he was doing something deliciously wicked.

The tone of Nobile's story when it appeared in the December 1977 issue of *Penthouse* was, similarly, one of gleeful mischief. Incest, he wrote, "would be just another media trend, faddishly seduced and abandoned after repeated use, were it not for two forthcoming studies that promise to turn the prohibition on its head. Both introduce and uphold the notion of *positive incest*, an especially dissonant oxymoron that will madden therapists and confuse the masses more than the Kinsey reports did twenty-five years ago."[19] Nobile quotes former Kinsey collaborator Dr. Paul Gebhard, director of the Institute for Sex Research in Bloomington, Indiana: "In fact, in the ones that were not reported [to police or psychologists], I'm having a hard time recalling any traumatic effects at all." The Gebhard-Kinsey material was, Nobile reported, to be included in Warren Farrell's work in progress, *The Last Taboo: The Three Faces of Incest*—a work Nobile tells us (apparently as evidence of just how revolutionary this take on things was) that had been rejected by twenty-two houses before being accepted for publication by Bantam for sixty thousand dollars.*

Nobile goes on to report on sociologist Dr. James Ramey, who'd kept his own positive incest manuscript hidden for the past four years, fearing massive misunderstanding.

Nobile does recount Farrell's musing on the fact that his ads calling for experiences of positive incest revealed that 85 percent of the daughters "admitted to" having negative attitudes toward "their" incest. Farrell seems perplexed by this in light of the fact that, "On the other hand, statistics from the vantage of the fathers involved were almost the reverse—60 percent positive, 20 percent mixed, and 20 percent negative."[20]

Recited as discovery, here, is that which had in fact been handed down through recent history: That it is only public *moralizing* about incest that causes damage; that if we would all just lighten up, there would be no problem. ("The average incest

* To the best of my knowledge, this book was never published, at least in the U.S.

participant can't evaluate his or her experience for what it was. As soon as society gets into the picture, they have to tell themselves it was bad."[21])

Incest, Farrell observes to Nobile (based on what, we're not sure), is more likely to be negative in the lower classes, where the alleged offender simply has not had the requisite training in the refinements of rape. (Perhaps, then, the solution to eliminating "negative incest" would be education to inculcate would-be offenders with more elegant incest manners?)

Meanwhile, much continued to be promulgated by fringe groups about children's right to sex with adults. The Rene Guyon Society, with its slogan "Sex by eight or it's too late," gained some media attention, as did the North American Man Boy Love Association (NAMBLA). One 1978 Guyon Society flyer opined that "utter rage in our children's minds over their sexual repression leads to: attacks on the weak and elderly, unreliable service personnel, drug abuse, running away, VD, alcoholism, divorce, suicide, obesity, smoking, theft, and [oddly] unwanted pregnancy." A bit overheated, perhaps, but really not that far from the researcher who suggested that avoiding incest might be what was causing feverish adolescent sexual activity (with its unwanted results).

With the escalating rhetoric of crime-dread-horror, however, professional researchers pursuing "positive" incest could be conveniently pigeonholed with fringe-group eccentrics as kooky proponents of some brand-new sexual libertinism masquerading as a children's rights movement. There was no need to note or consider the significance of this time-honored view, or explore its (closet) popularity within weighty circles.

Thus was the opportunity for retrieving a piece of information crucial to serious consideration of paternal child rape lost to the twentieth century.

To wit: These guys were saying pretty much what our fathers had said.

Chapter 3

THE DOCTRINE OF
EQUAL CULPABILITY

I AM REMEMBERING A PANEL I was on several years ago. Suddenly, a young woman was on her feet yelling, loudly, furiously, fist-wavingly.

"You keep saying men!" she hollered. "You are wrong! Everything you are saying is wrong! I was sexually abused by my mother!"

It was perplexing, that. Not, certainly, the young woman's passion to make heard her own testimony. No one had ever denied the existence of female offenders, although no statistics I am aware of had ever put the incidence of women offenders much over 5 percent. But let us say it is 10 percent of all offenders. Be even more generous: allow 20 percent.

Nor did what I said, I believe, in any way make light of her pain or her struggle or her reality. If both your legs are broken and you suffer internal bleeding, it is equally horrid whether you were knocked down by a Volkswagen or an eighteen-wheeler; your anguish and justifiable sense of hurt will be equally serious.

But if, say, truckers have a tacit license to drive recklessly and command, by legal authority and by the size of their vehicles, the rule of the road—and the drivers of private Volkswagens do not—then an external and overriding issue, challenging that presumption of right, demands attention.

Dark hints pervaded the literature that female offenders were far more prevalent than we knew; and that the fact that we did not know meant that their offense was so much worse, so much more damaging.

Lucy Berliner has been with the Sexual Assault Center at Harborview Medical Center in Seattle, Washington, since its inception in the late 1970s. Now Director of Research, she describes herself as a feminist, although she is clear that working in a university hospital setting makes her part of the establishment; that the goal of Harborview's program and others like it was to gain respect and acknowledgment for child sexual assault as a legitimate specialty area with a clinical focus, within the traditional medical model. She said to me recently, "They're still doing that. At every conference you go to, there will be somebody there saying female offenders are a *far greater problem* than we know, and that we just don't hear about it because it's so much *more* devastating."

The young woman's attack on what I was saying was the first I was witness to. It would not be the last. Whether deliberately or not, such attacks of course served to shore up the carefully neutralized language of "intrafamilial sexual assault" and "parental" abuse and pronounless "survivor-hood" promoted by the language of experts and by the media. Now, it appeared, not only were women causative of what they did *not* do, but they were doubly damned: where they didn't cause it, they did it. Such emphasis would not only further deflect attention from historical male right, but solidify existing bias.

Challenges like these carried an implied warning to those speaking gender politics: To continue this tack of spotlighting male offenders would only make *you* seem like an insensitive bigot, and prove you unfit to converse with serious, open-minded, gender-neutral professionals.

It was beginning to seem like we had gone, very quickly, from being silent to being *silenced.*

The oddest thing about the success with which this was being done was that corroborating data simply could not be found. The open-mindedness was no more than the "experts' " emphasis on a conjecture of convenience. Not seeing a high incidence of abuse on the part of mothers meant it was there, but so much *worse* that no one could speak out. And if that were so—even though it could not yet be seen—then there was no need to challenge *male* privilege; we could simply focus on human pathology.

For all its posture of scientific professionalism, the early decision to mask the gender-specific deliberateness of incest was profoundly political.

Lucy Berliner says, "I believe gender is one of the, if not the, basic organizing principles. It is mostly men doing it to mostly little girls. And what is interesting is how much those who follow the more professional/clinical model have tried to minimize that.

"There's always this business of going in and saying, 'Boys are underreported. It's probably just as common.'

"Well, show me the evidence that boys are underreported. I think that is driven by this desire to eliminate the gender issue, more than by evidence. . . . And in addition to all this stuff about boys being underreported is how they're affected differently. The implication is, '*It's even worse* for boys.'

"There's not a shred of evidence to support that. Again, which I find very interesting. But what is more interesting to me is not whether it does actually affect people differently, but the fact that they need to say that. And the same thing goes for women offenders. Anecdotally, at least, there's universal agreement that people are weirder about women offenders. Either it's, 'I can't believe she did it,' or, once you believe she did it, she's like the weirdest person in the world. It's a very different way of thinking about it."

What this kind of anti-empiricism did was what so much of the ensuing ruckus about child sexual abuse would do: It would play to *feelings*—overriding, outshouting the challenging facts.

The deemphasis of reality would whitewash, even seem to justify, the neutralizing (neuterizing?) ideology being promoted by the powers-that-be—an ideology that was essential in order to deny the feminist understanding.

British feminist Liz Kelly has written, "A slightly different, and in some ways more subtle, dismissal of feminist analysis of the 'male monopoly' is to begin by accepting that *currently* it appears that it is men who sexually abuse children. The implications of this are then neatly sidestepped by an insistence that abuse by women is underestimated, it is just more hidden, and hence not visible in reported cases or survivors' accounts. This dubious claim is justified by asserting that women have more legitimate access to children's bodies: therefore, women are more able to hide abuse of children.

"I do not want to dismiss the fact that a few women do sexually abuse children. What concerns me is the way evidence we *do* have is ignored and evidence we *do not* have is invoked to support an ideological position. By asserting that lots of women abuse too, they just haven't found the survivors yet, the 'new experts' justify refusing to engage with feminist analysis, refusing to recognise men's power in the world and in the family."[1]

That the passion of the young woman challenging me was real, I readily conceded; that her testimony denied my overall point, I did not.

Nonetheless, I was brought up short, almost wanting to apologize, blackmailed by her emotion, which cast me as unfeeling; as though I had said something raucously gauche on an intensive care ward.

But what, I kept wondering, had informed the intensity of her outrage? (Her tone had been several decibels beyond that of ardent disagreement.) Had what I said seemed to lessen the importance of her personal victimization? Did what I said appear to deny her pain? (or indeed have anything to do with *pain*)? And had the issue of incest now evolved into that: a pain competition, a victimization sweepstakes, a demand that the political, which had emerged from overwhelming commonalities, be denied in deference to the perfectly genuine pain of the personal?

Clearly, the claim being staked here was that individuals' wounded identities were paramount. Understanding the issue and attacking the cause on a political level was seen as a competing worldview, one perceived somehow as out to deny individual anguish. The perception denied the distinction between the private and the public and made of the two views, instead, arch rivals in a war for dominance—a war for dominance, alas, among the powerless.

Feminist Celia Kitzinger writes, "Our decision *not* to define ourselves in these terms is not a denial of our wounds, but a shift of focus. We are saying that we are more than the sum of our wounds. And we are asking whose purposes are served by making our wounds central to our identities. When our suffering is the focus, the root cause of that suffering is obscured. When the onus is on us to become well-adjusted, in spite of oppression, oppression can continue unabated. We are turned into nothing more than a new consumer group for the latest psychological developments. Whether they call us 'victims' or 'survivors,' the emphasis is on our suffering, our endurance, our pain, our psychic struggles. As 'victims/survivors' we are defined by that which hurts us."[2]

How had it happened that the personal, of which the political had been born, now sought to suffuse and even suffocate that to which it had given birth?

Saddened, as I left that meeting I realized that now we would be censored not only in the larger world, but would face pressure to censor ourselves—if we were to be at all welcome within the increasingly feeling- and symptom-dominated survivor world as well.

Clearly, that early concern about proving permanent injury was to stay with us. Was it not possible to validate private pain without making it the public focus? Does the absence of lingering life-deforming damage suggest (as the sexual permissivists would argue) that the abuse was not, therefore, abuse?

What of the women who are left out of this picture?

Does the fact that some women escape—for whatever combination of reasons and in whatever way—huge emotional penalty argue against this being an offense, a severe assault? Isn't attempted murder attempted murder despite the fact that the intended victim didn't end up dead?

Why is the assertion that it is men who have long had permission for this behavior presumed either to render all men culpable, or to deny that there are some women who sexually violate children as well? What drives the *need* to wield these either-or's like a giant Crayola, scribbling over the larger picture? (That there was a need to do so would grow increasingly clear.)

British anthropologist Jean La Fontaine writes, "There are some indications that sexual abuse by women may be under-reported, but the evidence so far is rather weak. . . . Much of the evidence, when examined closely, can be seen to refer to the practice in some states of recording mothers as guilty of sexual abuse when they failed to prevent it happening. . . . The insistence that there is much sexual abuse perpetrated by women which is never revealed may be the product of discomfort with the idea that this sexual problem is solely a masculine one. The effort to find indications of female abuse of children may, like the denial that the problem exists, be a reaction to the overwhelming evidence that sexual abuse is perpetrated by men, who are the figures of authority in Western, as in most, societies."[3]

And why did women so heartily collude in this deception? Perhaps there is something in this: that victims/survivors of paternal child rape know more surely than any the dangers in challenging paternal authority. And know that if safety is what you are seeking, it does not lie there.

———

If, as is true, the issue of incest was not born in a vacuum, neither did it develop in one. The social context of the 1980s was vigorous backlash. Increasingly common was the usage of the word *femi-*

nist as an epithet. As though to reassure itself, the media seemed to do an annual obituary of the women's movement, alerting us that we had now entered the era of "postfeminism." Indeed, stories abounded of the gains women had made in the workplace; profiles of female corporate and professional success were prominent. Anger at violences fell out of fashion; celebrations of access came in.

In the light of all this good news happy-talk, the ongoing, relentless presence of violences against women—rape, battering—were sidelined as wallflower issues; rather plain and considerably past their prime; conversation-killers, not on the media's A-list.

The charge intensified that identifying offenders in rape, wife-battering, incest, as male, was not a fact but a radical man-hating ploy, and those who did so were leftovers from another era.

Perhaps inevitably, all this was put forward in the name of equality. On the issue of wife-battering, for example, those feminist writers Ann Jones identified as the "standard-bearers of equality" contended "not only that women and men are evenly matched in physical combat, but that men might in fact be getting the worst of it."[4] As Jones notes, the media jumped on the battered-husband bandwagon, and other researchers hopped on as well.

Indeed, 1980 brought forth the epiphanous introduction of the Battered Husband Syndrome—a syndrome said first to afflict 25,000 husbands, then 20 percent of all husbands, and finally 12 million men—before it vaporized, leaving behind no evidence that this was, or ever had been, a galactic problem.*[5]

---

* Disappeared *for the eighties*. It has recently been reintroduced as a significant problem in David Thomas's book, *Not Guilty: The Case in Defense of Men*, wherein the author reports findings that show, among other things, that "the more highly educated a man is, the less likely he is to be violent toward his partner. Female violence, on the other hand, increases with education. In fact, college-educated women were nearly twice as likely to assault their partners as college-educated men." It is hard to know what to make of this ominous bit of data, and unfortunately the author does not help us out. (New York: William Morrow and Co., 1993), 181.

The result was the inception of what I would call the Doctrine of Equal Culpability. Briefly, this can perhaps best be illustrated in the playground, where the squabbling little girl and little boy are both screaming. LITTLE GIRL [to the intervening adult]: He hit me! LITTLE BOY: I did not, but so what, she hits me!

The Doctrine of Equal Culpability achieved prominence alongside the coronation of the Conservative Right in 1980 and the procession celebrating the Religious Right. Those of this persuasion spoke in code—of the "traditional" family—but it seemed quite evident that their passion was, in fact, only partly a response to issues like women in the workplace, and far more vigorously a response to the sense that within the traditional family, fathers were losing traditional control.

Paul Weyrich, father of the New Right, wrote in the *Conservative Digest*: "There are people who want a different political order, who are not necessarily Marxists. Symbolized by the women's liberation movement, they believe that the future for their political power lies in the restructuring of the traditional family, and particularly in the downgrading of the male or father role in the traditional family."[6]

But it took conservative economist George Gilder, the intellectual darling of the Reagan administration, to make the conservative male's fears quite graphic.

It was Gilder's take on things that, were women not to humor men's private little violences, men as a whole would run amok. The marketplace would disintegrate. Civilization would collapse.

Gilder's thesis is that it is women's job to socialize men: "The crucial process of civilization is the subordination of male sexual impulses and psychology to long-term horizons of female biology. . . . It is male behavior that must be changed to create a civilized order. . . . Women domesticate and civilize male nature. They can destroy civilized male identity merely by giving up the role."[7]

He said: "Deprived of his role as provider and protector, the man, like males all over the world throughout human history, will leave. As a general rule of anthropology, the likelihood of his presence in the home decreases in direct proportion to the aggressiveness of the woman."[8]

Turning away from the family, Gilder tells us that the man frequents all-male bars, behaves loudly and abusively, watches televised football for hours and bombards himself with the music of male sexuality. "Otherwise he is obsessed with women. He tries as much as possible to reduce them to their sexual parts and to reduce their sexuality to his own limited terms—to meaningless but incessant copulation."[9]

His thesis was one that, in fact, had a female proposed it, would have provoked the male riot that so concerned him: Following in what was beginning to appear to be a wearyingly long tradition, Gilder seemed to believe that men as a class were moral idiots.

Men, Gilder told us, commit 100 percent of the rapes, 95 percent of the burglaries, represent 94 percent of the drunk drivers, 70 percent of the suicides. And, he told us, they represent 91 percent of the offenders against family and children. These family offenders, his view suggests, were the men whom mothers and wives had failed to properly socialize. Given that failure, the implication was, women's ongoing captivity was no more than a necessary trade-off in defense of the larger serenity.

Were these women and children (as well as women and children in general) given a means of egress, then men's natural savagery would be directed toward society. Women thus had to sacrifice their bodies and those of their children in order that this insane order of (his view suggests) inferior and out-of-control power freaks remain in social and political power. A noble national sacrifice was thus implicitly called for. One so noble, in fact, that it is hard to believe the only social reward offered for this act of heroism was the label "masochist."

If that was the *theory*, then crying "women do it too" was the technique.

The Family Protection Act, introduced into Congress by Senator Jesse Helms in 1981, was designed to repeal nearly every legal achievement of the women's movement. It proposed, among other things, repealing all federal laws protecting battered wives; banning federal funding for legal aid for women seeking divorce; and providing tax incentives for men whose wives stayed home and had babies. It proposed, in other words, locking all the doors that had so recently been marked Exit. Neither the Family Protection Act nor the New Right made reference to paternal child rape/incest—at that point.

As though they were not reading the news of male violence against women in the pages of their own papers during a decade when the number of rapes doubled and the number of women seeking shelter from homicidal husbands shot up 100 percent[10]—the press chose instead to discover the drawbacks of access feminism in the absence of social change: We were now told that women had made their gains, they were trying to "have it all": they'd been given time to play in daddy's office. Now they wanted to get married and have babies.

At the same time, in response to increased pressure to enforce child support, men's rights groups emerged, demanding (absolutely deadpan) *equality*, including what they saw as a corrective to rank discrimination: They wanted the equal right to redefine fatherhood and father's rights to custody of their children. The September/October 1982 official newsletter of the Men's Equality Now International Coalition offers evidence of how far some fathers are driven to go in sheer desperation at being deprived of their children's companionship. It is instructive:

"In August truck driver John T. Parish of Grand Prairie, Texas, joined the ranks of mass murderers who appeared in that state this summer. He gunned down ten (10) people of whom six (6) died, then drove his eighteen (18) wheeler through a police barricade, a police car, and over a policeman (who survived) before he overturned the truck and was shot to death."

Parish, we are told, was an easygoing, friendly man with no police record. His roommate told police that his real problem was he kept getting routes to California instead of to Indiana where he wanted to go so he could see his six-year-old son. "How many such cases," we are asked to wonder, "can be traced to the simple fact that some man has lost his family and cannot take the pressures society places on him as an absentee provider?"[11]

We also learn of William McKenney, serving fifteen months for breaking and entering, who "sawed through the bars of his jail cell, along with three other men, and escaped." All because he wanted to see his newborn daughter and the officials wouldn't give him furlough because the last time they had, he hadn't come back.

Far from being confined to avowedly activist men's groups, this degree of empathy with fathers' plights and sympathy for fathers' rights would be reiterated a number of years later by one of the leading psychiatric experts hired by fathers in child sexual abuse/custody cases.

Dr. Richard Gardner testified on behalf of Marc Friedlander that he should get temporary custody of his two sons because his wife, Zitta, was thwarting Mr. Friedlander's visitation rights.

During the custody hearing, in July 1988, Zitta Friedlander was walking to her car after work when Mr. Friedlander shot her thirteen times.

At the murder trial, Dr. Gardner (again testifying on Mr. Friedlander's behalf) said, "I believe that after 27 months of progressively mounting frustration and suppressed fury . . . one day, after another failed attempt at visitation . . . [Mr. Friedlander] became acutely psychotic and murdered his wife." In other words, the man was simply driven insane by his custodial frustration.[12]

The net effect of this testimony seems to be, once more, a man presenting a male as dangerously wired and morally out of control. This is not a fundamental belief I have found expressed in any of the serious feminist literature (were it so, change would not even be worth trying).

As with the pro-incest lobby, there would seem to be a felicitous concordance of opinion and feeling between what some might view as chest-thumping misogynists and those schooled in institutions of learning and science.

The Men's Equality Now newsletter tells where materials are available to help win cases for (1) successful damage suits for alienation of children's affections; (2) the reduction or elimination of child support for alienation of affection and/or denial of visitation; (3) successful changes in custody (same reasons); and (4) paternity cases—"How to Fight—How to Win." And the newsletter makes known a lawyer who "has manuals and other material on winning child custody."[13]

Couched in all manner of feeling-speak, much of this passion for gaining their children's custody was clearly dictated by economics, in the face of increased pressures to enforce child support. And so it had always been.

Smack up until the dawn of the twentieth century, children had economic utility and fathers rarely relinquished custody. When, in the late nineteenth century, they began to do so, it was the result of the industrial revolution and compulsory public education rendering children an economic disadvantage.

Then, suddenly, not only did mothers gain custody rights, but the father had no further duties of child support.[14]

Nor have fathers'-rights advocates ever been at all reticent about declaring their economic motives. As attorney Maurice Franks wrote in his 1983 book *Winning Custody: A No Holds Barred Guide for Fathers,* "You're at war; and the sooner you recognize this fact and act accordingly, the healthier your future.

"Has it occurred to you that in a divorce action children can be a valuable commodity? That a child in the home is like money drawing interest in the bank, or rather like money invested in solid municipal bonds, paying tax-free dividends?

"Well, think about it. There's a good chance that your children's mother has thought about it." That is because she is "calculating": she has figured out that she can get x number of dollars a month from you to support your children while they are living with her, and zilch if they are living with you. "She will have decided that having the children with her will maintain her image as The Respectable Mother, whereas, if you have the children, she will view that as detracting from her appearance as a responsible citizen. For, you see, that kind of woman does not view things in terms of love, or what is best for the children. She never sees anything from the aspect of what it means to someone else; only from the angle of what such-and-such action means to her."[15]

But if one significant motive informing the men's rights/fathers' rights movement was economics, another—for some men— would seem to be rage: a rage against the apparent strengthening of women's rights, most particularly in the family; and a change in both mores and means that made it possible for women to leave, as well as the setting of limits on the male right to domesticized violence. It was a rage tied to the abortion battle, the battle over who owns women's bodies and who owns the end product (the children). (It would not be long before fathers' rightists would begin arguing that not only fetuses but frozen embryos were "half theirs," and suing to prevent girlfriends from having abortions, or ex-wives from donating the embryos.) Fathers' rights groups drove a movement to increase "joint custody"—even in cases of wife-battering. ("The guy may beat the living daylights out of his wife but could be the greatest father in the world to his children. A man who beats his wife has a problem with adult women, not necessarily with children," said a spokesperson for the Canadian Council for Family Rights.[16]) The "friendly parent" standard was born: the recommendation that custody be given to the parent most likely to encourage visitation. There was a push to insist on "mediation" in cases of divorce—even (perhaps especially) in cases of wife-battering and incest.

Indeed, I recall a New York City meeting to address the perils of mediation for women, sponsored by the National Center on Women and Family Law. The mood was somewhat grim. This was clearly a major threat to women victimized by domestic violences of all sorts. I was not meant to be a presenter. However, I was asked to address the issue.

Mediation and child sexual abuse?

Mediation is, by definition, a negotiated settlement involving *compromise*. People mediate about *wages*, not about attempted homicide and rape.

"It is not," I said, "negotiable." Period.

———

The direction things were taking was beginning to become entirely clear. We had brought the issue of incest out from under wraps only to find that—exposed to the toxic climate that prevailed—it had begun to hemorrhage uncontrollably. News of family treatment programs was ever more celebrated. Profiles of the "incest family" proliferated. The new mythology of paternal child molestation was being drummed into our heads the same way the story of the discovery of America had been in grade school, creating an emotional belief in a "truth" that worked to stonewall reality. (Who do you really *believe* discovered America?)

All but unnoticed except by those paying close attention, the Doctrine of Equal Culpability crept into law: Statutes now faulted the mothers who "knew or *should have known*," the mother who "failed to protect" the child from paternal sexual assault.

As I traveled, as I spoke, it was unavoidable: Things were getting worse, if anything, for children now and for the women, their mothers, who sought to protect them. (I did not know, then, that this "worse" would prove to be far from "worst.") Social workers, protective service workers would report on cases:

• Two girls, aged seven and nine, sodomized by dad over the years while mom was out, finally told mom—who reported it to protective services, who reported it to the Sex Crimes Unit. An officer arrested dad at his job. Case went to court. At the preliminary hearing the assistant district attorney would not take the case because the children were too young and their testimony would not hold up in court.

The D.A. said, "We don't take cases we can't win."
Outcome: The family went home to live together.

• Dad raped sixteen-year-old daughter who told mom. Mom took her to a physician because dad argued there was something wrong with the child for fantasizing about sleeping with dad. Doctor agreed she was disturbed. Parents had her placed in a psychiatric institution.

Eight months later dad got drunk and said, "I fucked my daughter and it was the best fuck I ever had."
Outcome: Mom divorced dad.

• Mom found out dad was molesting daughter. She didn't have enough money to leave home. Daughter was placed in foster care, where she was raped by foster father.

Outcome: Mom dropped the allegations against dad and daughter came home. She felt it was better to be molested by dad than raped by foster father.

The issue of incest, so recently raised, had had no chance to achieve prominence as a political issue, historically derived from male right, before it was gobbled up whole by our society's sanitation engineers: the psychiatric/mental health establishment. But that is retrospect.

We continued to try. We continued to believe. Because we were speaking in greater and greater numbers, our voices seemed, to us, loud. And because what we said seemed so congruent with experience and with reality, what we were saying seemed overwhelmingly clear. And because we were able to address the personal within the framework of the political, harmony seemed possible. Action seemed reasonable. Change continued to seem inevitable.

In 1983, feminist Andrea Dworkin said in a speech: "Incest is the first assault." She said, "Incest is terrifically important in understanding the condition of women."

Of the sexually abused child, she said, "Her whole system of reality, her whole capacity to form attachments, her whole capacity to understand the meaning of self-respect are now destroyed by someone whom she loves."

Then she said, "Incest victims are now organizing in this country, and they are organizing politically. One of the reasons that they are organizing politically and not psychiatrically is because they understand that it is the power of the father in the family that creates the environment that licenses the abuse. They understand that probably better than anyone who hasn't had the experience understands it. They have seen the mother's fear of the father; they know their own fear of the father; they have seen the community support for the father; they have seen the psychiatric community's support for the father; they have seen the legal system's refusal to treat the father like a criminal; they have seen the religious leaders' refusal to take incest as seriously as the grave crime of homosexuality. They understand the world in which women live. . . . Incest victims are truly at the center of our political situation. They have been, in my opinion, the bravest among us for speaking out about what happened to them when they were children. And they are organizing to get children some protection, some rights; and the women's movement has to be more serious in understanding that the connection between women and children really is political. The power of the father is what makes women and children a political underclass."[17]

In 1983, as well, there was a conference called "Pulling Together II: Surviving and Stopping Incest." Organized by the Pennsylvania Coalition Against Domestic Violence, it brought together incest survivors and activists from rape crisis centers and battered women's shelters. Speakers at the conference emphatically condemned recent American Bar Association guidelines that proposed provisions for prosecuting mothers under child sexual abuse laws, or subjecting women who should have known of the abuse to civil liability.

Emphasis was placed on devising strategies to stop incest, rather than simply engage in problem management. Even *therapy's* value was questioned, as some survivors "described years of searching for a helpful therapist and years of therapy after that. . . . All survivors who spoke stated that a political consciousness about violence against women and children helped remove the terrible isolation and guilt caused by their own experience of incest."[18]

Feminist activist Valerie Heller said, "What I hear from many abused people is that they feel guilty and then I share my understanding of guilt. I suggest that maybe what they are feeling is anger and rage, pain and sadness, and betrayal and confusion and hate from being used and not guilt as men and society have defined it."

The conference was viewed as a "big first step in incorporating incest survivors into the women's movement and the anti-violence against women movement."

Ah, well.

Key here is to notice that a distinction is made between the women's movement and the antiviolence against women movement. Joan Pennington, formerly an attorney with the National Center on Women and Family Law and currently director of the National Center for Protective Parents, cautions me against assuming that the battered women's movement was ever a part of the mainstream feminist movement. It was, she says, a grassroots movement of women activists, aligned with feminist principles but distinct from organized feminism.

Radical feminists, early on, grasped the point of including "private" violences against women as a significant part of their analysis, including sexual assault on children.

Florence Rush, speaking in 1971 at a rape crisis conference, said to great acclaim and comprehension:

" That the sexual abuse of children, who are overwhelmingly female, by sexual offenders who are overwhelmingly male, is part and parcel of the male dominated society which overtly and covertly subjugates women.

" That the sexual molestation and abuse of female children is not regarded seriously by society, is winked at, rationalized and allowed to continue through a complex of customs and mores which applauds the male's sexual aggression and denies the female's pain, humiliation and outrage.

" That sexual abuse of children is permitted because it is an unspoken but prominent factor in socializing and preparing the female to accept a subordinate role; to feel guilty, ashamed, and to tolerate, through fear, the power exercised over her by men. That the female's early sexual experiences prepare her to submit in later life to the adult forms of sexual abuse heaped on her by her boy friend, her lover, and her husband. In short, the sexual abuse of female children is a process of education which prepares them to become the wives and mothers of America."[19]

But not very gradually, the decade of the 1980s brought an ever greater denial of feminist voices. A new veil of silence began to descend, woven of a magical new hi-tech fabric. This fabric was permeable by the personal, but it acted as a filter, blocking out the political. All that began to get through were *stories*: battered women's *stories*, rape victims' *stories*, incest victims' *stories*.

This would prove to be a silence more powerful than suppression precisely because it could be posed to us that the telling of stories was change. It offers the picture of change, of a new freedom to speak, a new willingness on the part of society to hear (so long as all they are hearing is stories). And nothing then has to happen. And seeing this picture of progress, people feel good, and even the victims, telling their stories, feel they are in the picture and they feel good.

And the point to all these stories is rendered invisible, and social discomfort is rendered unnecessary, and those trying to remind everyone that there was a point are rendered irrelevant.

And no one need stop to wonder why, if all of this is progress and all of this is change, little kids keep getting raped and molested by male adults in a position of trust.

Feminist antiviolence activists continued their activism and continued to speak, but outside of public hearing and public view.

That this was so made the hijacking of the newcomer incest issue at all levels, child and adult, all the more smooth and all the more total. Treatment, counseling toward keeping families intact (as the expression goes), won greatest support, all based on the fulcrum of the "incest mother": she who colluded, or had the nerve to work or get ill, who denied and rejected her child. The pain adult survivors expressed was handily translated into pathology by mental health clinicians and more and more shingles began to appear on door frames, advertising those specializing in the treatment of incest survivors.

It was not only incest that was all but suffocated by a move toward medicalization—but all parts of the antiviolence movement. (It was simply that incest had not had a chance to establish itself within that framework.) The search for funding by those starting or running shelters for battered women led increasingly to state and federal governments and to private foundations and agencies. These power groups, after all, were willing to fund "help" which was defined as psychosocial treatment, often counseling for battered and batterer à deux. As a trade for monies, they increasingly demanded to define the issue their way—as one of victim-pathology: They were there to fund private, harmonious, household resolutions, not social revolutions. The medical lexicon began to revise the understanding of battering—from the problem the woman *has*, to the problem the woman *is*.[20] Thus, very much as would happen with adult incest survivors and with the maternal protectors of assaulted children, victim labeling occurred as a matter of policy instituted at the federal and state level—and in the name of benign assistance.

By 1984 I had begun referring to the fact that we seemed to be witnessing the birth of an incest *industry*—a staggering array of clinicians and counselors and therapists and researchers and authorities and experts, all with their careers sighted on one aspect or another of incest and its aftermaths. (But "incest industry" was a phrase the backlash would soon find euphonious and useful and of service to their different agenda, and co-opt.) In truth, by now, this issue—once so peacefully encapsulated in quiet—had begun more and more to resemble an ant colony on speed. Clinicians rushed hither, researchers rushed thither, trainers rushed yon. . . .

Little remark was made of the fact that you now had a "heinous crime" and a "dread taboo"—with no particular censure of the offender. Indeed, one hardly heard speak of the offender (without the hyphenation of -treatment). Few seemed to notice, much less mind, the inherent absurdity. As law professional Michael J. Rosenthal noted, arguing against a policy of decriminalizing child abuse (presumably including child sexual abuse): "Imagine the sense of injustice and the contempt for law awakened by the following hypothetical courtroom scene:

"JUDGE (*to the defendant*): You are charged with killing (or seriously assaulting) your two-year-old son. How do you plead?

DEFENDANT: Your honor, I admit that I killed (or seriously assaulted) my son, but I have a defense.

JUDGE: What is your defense?

DEFENDANT: Your honor, my defense is that it was child abuse."[21]

Incest, medicalized, was neutralized; stripped of its character as a deliberate act of aggression, a violence based on the belief in male right. As a female-censuring "illness," it much better suited the politics of the Right. Billed as help and treatment, it equally suited the sentiments of the Left. And it far better suited a media which was expressing ennui with feminist politics (*Enough* already. We *talked* about that.) and beginning to focus—ever more tearfully—on children's need for their fathers, and the rise of the New Age, sensitive Dad.[22] The feminist political understanding of the inherent power abuse, and the permission, dimmed from all public view.

Survivors continued to speak out, some of them politically. But, finding little support from an increasingly embattled feminism, they went where solace was everywhere promised: to therapists. The stated goal of most survivor therapy and counseling in the early to mid-1980s was forgiveness of the offender.

Welcome to the Age of No-Fault Abuse.

Chapter 4

RINGLING BROTHERS AND BARNUM & BAILEY PRESENT . . . INCEST!

IT WAS BEGINNING TO BE CLEAR: However little the social response to the issue of incest improved anything for children and women, it held astonishing promise as spectacle. Not only was avoiding the obvious going to require Olympian expenditures of both energy and cash, but the ensuing multiple tangles, pratfalls, and high-wire acts had the potential to turn into the Greatest Show on Earth. What you saw going on would depend on which ring you were watching.

The ring with some of the funniest acts was the one devoted to offender treatment.

"Diversion to counseling" was the cry of the decriminalizers. The ostensible goal, in keeping with the family preservation so dear to conservatives' hearts, was to reunite the families. Perhaps I was alone in finding this idea peculiar: that, even for those of conservative bent, there was sound fiscal rationale to keeping our

most abusive families intact, while letting more reasonably constituted families founder for such trivial reasons as, say, a man's
whim that it might be more amusing to try something else.

Perhaps more peculiar was the blanket assumption that this
was inarguably in the best interests of child victims who, we were
repeatedly told, did not want their daddies to go to jail. Child
victims, of course, had not been asked their opinion, nor had
adult survivors. In fact, I know of only one such effort that has
ever been made. Based on responses from 273 young people who
had experienced some form of sexual victimization, 95 percent
felt that abusers should be prosecuted, and 87 percent of them felt
that this should be so if the offender were a family member.[1]
Clearly, however, this sort of thing was not what policymakers
wanted to hear.

And so were begun many offender treatment programs, most
derived from work with rapists of adult women. By 1990 the
number of specialists treating sex offenders would explode from
twenty-nine to more than eleven hundred.[2] A great number of the
therapies focused on the male sex organ, as though it, as an
independent actor, were the real offender. They measured "its"
arousal pattern, providing minute calibrations with a device early
on referred to as a "penile transducer."

Hours would be spent, for example, with a rapist who expressed his fondness for stories about rape and torture of women,
and who had actually raped thirty-three women and gone to
prison on three different occasions.

The researchers presented this rapist with three audio descriptions: of a nonsexual assault on a woman, of the rape of a woman,
and of mutually-consented-to heterosexual sex.

The audio portion for the nonsexual assault was colorful: "She
starts to scream out. You just put your hands, put your hand over
her mouth . . . She's trying to get away now. She's screaming,
going toward the other room. You grab ahold of her and you pull
her to the ground."

The out-and-out rape was not a whole lot different: "You put your hands around her mouth. You stop her from screaming. You just struggle with her. Pulling her to the ground. You've pulled her to the ground. You're going to rape her. You feel her body right underneath, right underneath you there . . . You're going to screw her . . . She's trying to get away. It's no use. You've overpowered her. You've pinned her down, and now you're shoving your dick right into her."

And then comes the nonviolent one (in which the girl is really begging for it).

The upshot of this for our known and convicted rapist was that on the physical assault he achieved 13 percent full erection. His score was 37 percent on the no-holds-barred rape. And only 7 percent on the shucks-she-wants-it version. The researchers report that "by dividing the percent full erection to the rape stimulus by the percent full erection to the mutually consenting intercourse scene, we calculate the subject's proclivity to rape."[3]

Thus proving that it can be proved that a confessed and convicted rapist is turned on by rape.

Continuing along the lines of this "modality," incest offender treatment programs would show the alleged perpetrators pictures of naked kids and, if they got an erection, deliver to them a penile electric shock or, in some cases, a shot of ammonia up the nose— known as "aversion therapy." (It never ceases to amaze me the things you can do in the name of treatment that you could never get away with in a circumstance called punishment.)

In 1981, I received this letter:

Dear Colleague:

The Sexual Behavior Clinic has recently received funding from the National Institute of Mental Health to provide evaluation and treatment to incest offenders and child molesters. Patients are seen on an outpatient basis, and there is no charge for any of the services provided.

There are several requirements for participation. First the patient/client must be 18 years of age or older and nonpsychotic. Second, he must have involved himself sexually with a female child, either related or unrelated to him. Thirdly, he must want to do something to stop that behavior. Finally, he must not be under legal coercion to participate in this treatment program. Treatment can only be given to those men voluntarily seeking treatment for their sexual behavior. *Likewise, if the patient/client is dissatisfied with the treatment at any time, he can simply stop the treatment without further consequences.* (italics mine)[4]

This last certainly seemed a more than generous way to treat self-confessed rapists and child molesters.

The "diversion to counseling" buzzphrase was used by those trying to keep up the appearance of serious sanction while eliminating the practical need to pursue such. It attracted its own host of newfound experts and entrepreneurs, its own blizzard of papers and gabble of conferences. The absence of any evidence that the treatment actually worked did nothing to dampen enthusiasm (since the goal of eliding the crime issue was served, and more funding seemed always to be there to support that goal).

Comically enough, twelve years after getting this letter I received a report of a study conducted by the Minneapolis *Star Tribune* that concluded that rapists and child sexual abusers were *more likely* to be arrested for new sex crimes if they completed psychological treatment than if they were never treated. Most of these sex offenders had never been to prison. The study tracked 392 rapists, 375 child molesters, and 165 incest offenders. "Treatment in Minnesota's much praised treatment programs did not work, except to keep many sex offenders out of prison. Many judges released any offender willing to submit to treatment." The good news was that "in contrast to rapists and child molesters whose victims were not children in their families, male incest perpetrators were less likely to be caught re-offending . . . *usually because their victims grew up and became less accessible*" (italics mine).[5]

Facts such as these, however, have not seemed to present any impediment to continuity. Recently, I received promotional material from Farrall Instruments about its Portable CAT-600—a penile erection-detector—with these bulleted features:

- Assess both males and females*
- Built-in intercom and audio mixer
- Three-year limited warranty
- Proven software & assessment technology
- Controls stimulus times

And, they add (the mind boggles here):

- Legal cabin baggage on commercial airlines

"The Portable CAT-600," the information reads, "is used in conjunction with your laptop computer to provide state-of-the-art assessment technology at practically any location." Even, obviously, on a commercial flight between, say, Boston and Denver—no doubt to widespread passenger appreciation.

Here's how this compact technology works. You sit the offender down in a comfortable chair (on commercial airlines, this supposes business class). You attach something called a strain gauge to the guy's penis. "The client is then exposed to a number of audio and visual stimuli which have been carefully selected to simulate the real-life cues that initiate deviant action." The plethysmograph records changes in arousal and prints out a graph for you.

Here, under the category "children," are some of the visual stimuli provided for your client's delectation:

"BB-31 BARB—Girl, 14, 5', 86 lbs. 29-23-30, long, light brown hair. Clothed in blue jean cut-offs and tube top. All scenes in bedroom. Model is clothed to partially clothed. Noticeable bust development and pubic hair."

---

* I do not know what the practical applications are for females. I am not sure I want to know, either.

In the next-listed sequence, Barb removes her panties, then puts on a short nighty. The scenes are in the bedroom, on the bed and couch. "This set shows very seductive facial expressions and explicit body exposures."

(It also, of course, provides very explicit corroboration to the molester's imagining that the kids *want it*. But never mind . . .)

Next you get to see Barb sunbathing nude on the patio, in bathroom and bedroom, etc. Very seductive, we are told, and explicit.

Your client digs boys? Try JEFF, age eight, four feet eight inches, sixty-five pounds. ("Completely explicit.")

Your subject prefers little girls? How about MISTY? Age five, two feet six, forty pounds. Measurements: 14-13-14. Long, light brown hair, brown eyes. Wearing blouse, jeans, undressing to nude. "Good facial expression. Child friendly and seductive."

Next: MISTY nude in bedroom and bathroom. "Good body exposure. Showing off to observer."

And, it says in this literature, "All scenes as staged by Farrall Instruments are as realistic as possible. All recognizable models in staged scenes have signed Model Release which are on file with Farrall Instruments." Presumably, even five-year-old Misty.

Most interesting about this pornography-for-professionals is that Farrall Instruments claims they will develop *your* slides. "Most film processors will not develop films which have a sexual content. In many cases films of this nature are destroyed or 'lost.' As a further service to our customers we have made arrangements with a processor to develop and mount Ektachrome film for our customers. You can send your film to us for safe processing." All you need is a personally signed statement from the "therapists" who will be using them.

An article challenging the claims for penile plethysmography appeared in the July 1991 issue of *Medical Aspects of Human Sexuality*.[6] Nonetheless, in its promotional material, Farrall Instruments tells us that "a 1990 survey in the United States by Fay Honey Knopp and William Stevenson indicated that 21% of the juvenile and 32% of the adult programs surveyed used the plethys-mograph." And that Farrall Instruments, Inc., has, to date, placed 275 chart recorders and 130 computer-type plethysmographs.

Further, we learn from the brochure (titled "The Portable CAT-600, the Portable Sex Offender Assessment System, NEW from Farrell Instruments") that Dr. James Breiling of the Antisocial and Violent Behavior Branch of the National Institute of Mental Health "has said that any restrictions on a specially trained clini-cian's ability to use the plethysmograph in assessing and treating sex offenders 'would be analogous to depriving a physician of the right to obtain x-rays in cases of broken bones.' "7

Yet another ring grabbed the spotlight early on: prevention pro-grams. The idea here was to go into the schools and teach the children about "good touch, bad touch"; to instruct the kids to tell if anyone touched them "inappropriately."

Predictably enough, this produced controversy: These pro-grams were scaring children, making them suspicious and afraid, teaching them about sexual matters not appropriate to their age. The obvious challenge, however, failed to be posed: If you were talking about the most insidious form of child sexual abuse—incest, sexual exploitation by fathers—why were you going into schools and telling *kids* to say no? Why weren't you going into corporations and boardrooms and telling potential or actual *of-fenders* to say no?

British feminists Mary MacLeod and Esther Saraga write, "The most alarming implication of the orthodox explanations [those involving "family" dysfunction] is in the current view of preven-tion. *There is virtually no discussion about decreasing the likeli-hood that men will abuse.* . . . Instead, prevention is envisaged in terms of programmes like 'Kidscape' which teach children to say 'no.'. . . But children do say 'no'—and it makes no difference, except possibly to increase the threats against them. 'I said "no," said one 17 year old in a recent TV programme, 'but he said he did it because he loved me, and that all fathers do it in their families. . . . I would have had to kill him to stop him.' "

This approach, MacLeod and Saraga said, "carries risks, particularly for the very children it seeks to help. It makes children responsible for adults, and may also make abused children feel even more guilty."

They suggest that real prevention would involve *"changing the way that boys learn to be men, and changing our expectations of men."* A step forward, they say, would be changing the law to enable suspected abusers to be removed from a family during investigation (rather than removing the child), which would send a clear signal that "men's power and freedom of action within families is unacceptable if they abuse it."[8]

But directing programs toward boys and men would direct attention to men as potential abusers, to men as current and potential offenders—the very thing that decriminalization and medicalization were designed to *prevent*. Directing programs toward boys and men would cast light on the notion of offender *responsibility*—and, therefore, on accountability. Under the medical model, incest is a "family problem," with everyone playing a "role." No matter how often it is reiterated that "incest is never the child's fault," directing prevention programs toward children in fact defines the role ascribed to them even while claiming there is no such thing. Kids are not dumb. They hear that.

In terms of cost/benefit—a popular measure of social programs—it could readily be argued that the benefit of these programs is to the status quo. And the cost is absorbed by the child.

As British feminist Jenny Kitzinger has suggested, teaching children to say no means telling a five-year-old that power is something for her to take or to give away. Since men are clearly free to see the child's body as their property, and since children know this power exists, this sweet message simply acts as a bewildering lie. Further, at least one study showed that prevention programs actually make abused children feel that the abuse is indeed their own fault. You have given them to believe that they are *supposed* to have power to prevent abuse, after all.[9]

By necessity, prevention programs always elided the uncomfortable daddy-connection: They simply would not have been tolerated otherwise. Even while stating that most offenders were "someone the child knows," these programs traded on acceptable fears of those outside the family. Even while mumbling somewhere about abusers sometimes being trusted family members, they posed the solution for the child as being to "tell someone you trust."

Prevention, of course, is a feel-good kind of word—it sounds medical/clinical and implies a robustness and optimistic right-mindedness, along the lines of proper nutrition and daily workouts. Programs that give the appearance of *doing something,* without doing anything substantially threatening to the status quo, sound safe to everyone concerned. As promoted by the purveyors, such programs have at once the patina of the most excellent child-caring intentions. And they carry little risk: It is difficult to challenge what or how much you have actually *prevented.*

But—look here (this is uncanny): On the very day I write this, the *New York Times* carries a story on its "Health" page headed, "Abuse-Prevention Efforts Aid Children," which would seem to belie what I have just said. Reporting on a study by sociologist and longtime sexual abuse researcher Dr. David Finkelhor, the story indicates that what the prevention programs in fact help children to do is fend off sexual assaults *by strangers.* (Since, according to Finkelhor, the most effective programs were those that "involved parents and got them to talk to their children about preventing sexual abuse," it would seem reasonable to assume the "parents" cooperating were not themselves presumed likely to be suspect.)

It is a problem with studies of all sorts in this area that they do not separate out incestuous assault from other forms of child sexual abuse, so you are often left with an apparition of evidence, which gains credibility as it is cited in later literature.

But here is where a real question arises: From the story, we learn there are about two hundred thousand substantiated cases of sexual abuse each year, *a number that grows by 10 percent annually*. If the number grows by 10 percent annually, how can it be said that prevention works? Well, because: " 'The rise in cases may attest to the *effectiveness* of the abuse-prevention programs,' said Dr. Finkelhor, since by far the largest number of cases go unreported."[10] Well, but how do we know that the largest number of cases in fact *still* go unreported—if the prevention programs are "working"?

And here is another question: If two hundred thousand cases of sexual abuse are substantiated, then haven't those assaults already taken place? And is that prevention? Or is it case-finding? (And if it is case-finding, why call it prevention? Why list—as one promotional piece does—a pamphlet called *He Told Me Not to Tell*, which discusses "understanding the problem, talking to the child, and what to do when a child has been assaulted" as a *child abuse prevention handout?*)

And if *prevention* is indeed a code word for *case-finding*, and if the good news is that the children, because of prevention programs, have been more willing to tell, then wouldn't it be worthwhile to look at what happens after the children have told before we declare this good news?

Such a look would most definitely be enlightening.

It would take you, as it has taken me,* into the world of foster care/child welfare. The kids in that world who spoke with me did not have a whole lot of praise for what had happened to them. They spoke not only of coercive removal from their mothers as well as from their fathers but of coercive counseling, which chronically reiterated that it was not their fault, what had happened, but ceaselessly probed, at the same time, their individual shortcomings, their emotional temperatures.

---

* A journey documented in my book, *Solomon Says, A Speakout on Foster Care* (New York: Pocket Books, 1989).

Many of them thus developed a paper trail focused on their pathologies, and a great many then wound up in psychiatric facilities of one sort or another. Not—as you might think—because they were "sick," but because they were under a kind of psychiatric surveillance. And because the system, when it had nowhere else to put them down (as not infrequently happens) could handily label them and place them there.

Caseworkers' testimony corroborated what the kids said.

One young woman told me she'd gone into protective services work two years earlier thinking she could protect children. She said, "I'd tell them, 'Trust me. You can tell me the truth. I'll protect you.' Now," she said, "I still tell them, 'Trust me. You can tell me.' But—now I know—I can't protect them."

Another said, "The hardest part for me—the thing that I always felt was the most ugly—was the way the court system would treat the kids. Basically, one of the things that the court system would do—in the case of an incest kid—would be rather than say, 'This is an incest kid,' they would take the kid into court on a 'dependency' petition, saying, 'This child is being truant. This child is running away. This child cannot be handled by the family. And therefore . . . they cannot keep this child. And therefore we are gonna place this child.' But never saying the words, 'Incest was going on.' It was making a deal with the parents. 'You place your child and we're not gonna say what it is.'

"And it looks like the kid is at fault. It looks like the kid is delinquent."[11]

As part of *prevention* efforts, a Spiderman comic was produced and distributed, perhaps the ultimate expression of the by-then-current incest theme song, "You are not alone." As a child, kids learned, Spiderman also had been sexually abused. (As far as I know, the question was never raised as to how many small girls identified with Spiderman.)

The production and dissemination of prevention/identification materials became a prodigious business. As a professional, you could buy for your class or your clients picture books like *My*

Body Is Private ("Julie knows that her private parts are not to be touched. Julie narrates this non-threatening introduction to the painful subject of child abuse."); *No More Secrets for Me* ("*The man at the arcade tries to buy Nickie stuff so she'll sit with him.* Through a series of realistic vignettes, boys and girls encounter various situations of sexual abuse and learn what they can do to prevent it.") Through a catalogue you can even purchase "the finest anatomically correct dolls available," which are "unconditionally guaranteed." (To what? For what? Against what?) These dolls, we are told, are "not toys. They are currently in use nationwide in the offices of police, courts, investigators, therapists and interviewers." They are also fully washable, extremely durable, and fully clothed, including underwear. A full set—including Grandmother and Grandfather—is $389.[12]

There were even prevention "games" developed. One, for example, *The Talking and Telling About Touching Game*, was a brightly colored poster sheet directed primarily at elementary school children.[13] The only "goal" of this game is to answer twenty-four questions successfully. (Colorful as it is, that does not sound like much of a "game" to my inner child.) "Successful" answers, for the most part, involve telling "a trusted adult"— despite the fact that, as the authors of the parents' and teachers' guide to the game suggest, the molester often *is* a trusted adult. Any suggestion of what will quite likely happen *after* the child tells—the intervention of protective services, the charge against the mother of "failure to protect," the removal of the child to the foster care system—is entirely absent.

The game's authors seem to have no qualms: They are doing good. The tone of the game's questions have that frantic cheeriness children become accustomed to humoring in adults, but which, in this context, seems vaguely lunatic:

Question 20: "Let's pretend that someone did touch your private parts or tricked you into touching his private body parts. What should you do if he tells you that you will be in big trouble if you tell anybody because *you* did the wrong thing? What if he says he will hurt you or your mother or the other kids in your family if you tell? What if he says: 'I could go to jail, so don't tell anybody what we did'?" Yes. And what if that someone's name is daddy? And what if you've already seen him hurt your mother and/or the other kids?

The suggestions for your version of the correct response to this question is, "A child is *never* the guilty party in a case of child-adult sexual contact. Tell your children that there are laws to protect them and your family from abusive adults. Let your children know that you plan to personally protect them from any adult who threatens to harm them." But should you tell them that the laws to protect them from the abusive father or step-father include the prospect of their removal from you? What this really amounts to is playing the Walrus and the Carpenter with real little kids. Remember? "Oh, oysters come and walk with me upon the briny beach. A little walk, a little talk . . ." Remember? (Chomp.)

"The child must be protected from the individual who assaulted him or her," reads the parents' and teachers' guide. "This may involve removing the child temporarily to a safer home—but always remember that the child's safety is more important than any minor inconvenience required to protect the child." *Minor inconvenience?* Do you know how long it takes the average mother to get her kid back from foster care? Two years. Do you know how many foster homes a child can be placed in in two years? "No situation," the guide assures us, "is hopeless. There are programs designed to help the child, family members and even the offenders—but nothing will work until YOU take action to protect the child. . . . Seeking help is the first step to healing the hurt. Seeking help is an act of love for the child."

By the mid-1980s, I would begin to hear from those who had, as children, succumbed to the lure of telling. And been removed. In connection with subsequent events, none of these kids even once used the word *help*. ("Has anyone," Florence Rush asked in 1971, "ever thought of the fantastic notion of getting rid of the father?"[14])

It is surely ironic (in light of this) that *The Talking and Telling About Touching Game* was billed as a "safety game."

The zeal, the urgent ebullience, the declarative certainty about Doing Good and Healing and Help, was almost entirely uninformed by reality. It was reminiscent of child-saving in the early twentieth century, and its lofty goal of nonpunitive intervention was, from the beginning, contradicted by the existing practices of a "service delivery" system that not only held mothers accountable for whatever happened to children, but was in any case a system in chronic chaos.*

However, to paraphrase an old rubric about South America, most people would rather do anything about child welfare than read about it. And so all the public could be counted on to know was that the *system* (to use the word loosely) espoused the best possible intentions, and that for some reason every few years scandal erupted, usually triggered by a child's death, and the media reported the system was broken. It was then reiterated that caseworkers were underpaid, overworked; burnout was high; turnover was rapid-fire; there weren't enough homes to place kids in; and some of the homes kids were put in were themselves abusive.

Nonetheless, since middle- (and certainly upper-) class America held a clear and correct, if unstated, understanding that child welfare intervention—both historically and in the present—targeted only the poor, most frequently poor single mothers, the

* Here, for example, is a far from atypical charge against a child welfare agency: "The American Civil Liberties Union this month sued Wisconsin and Milwaukee County, charging they are denying Milwaukee children their constitutional rights under state and federal law.

"The lawsuit, filed June 1 [1993], asks the federal court to order the state and county to reform the county's child welfare system. . . ." The suit charges that higher-ups in the Milwaukee County Department of Health and Human Services know about the system's failure, but refuse to protect child-victims of family abuse and neglect. Also, when they do remove the kids to foster care, they fail to provide services and even placements. Particularly interesting is that according to Marcia Robinson Lowry, director of the ACLU's Children's Rights Project, this particular system is not even in financial difficulty" ("Child Protection Report," 19, no. 12 [11 June 1993]: 1).

role assumed by the majority of socially respectable persons was that of spectator—there to go 'yay' at the idea that Something was Being Done, and 'boo' when the Something proved disastrous.

This class-targeting has never been a very pretty idea; thus, it is seldom introduced in proper society. Certainly those engaged in such work do not advertise their activity in those terms. Rather, it is glossed over as being a mission of "help," and a "service."

Nonetheless, the fact that it targets the poor and most particularly poor single mothers is *known*. It is not inadvertent, and when mentioned, is not denied.

In an interview with Professor Alfred Kadushin, a prominent authority and coauthor of *Child Welfare Services* (1988), a leading textbook on the subject, I asked whether protective service intervention should, if it is to be truthfully a "service" to children, be class-undifferentiated.

"Okay," he said. "It should be undifferentiated. I'll say it should be undifferentiated. But how are you going to undifferentiate? What goes on in middle-class homes is not subject to referral. It is protected in some measure. Would you then ask that the agency be provided with the prerogative of going into homes, defying the autonomy of the family? Have access to middle-class families?"

"I'm asking you," I said, "are you comfortable with saying that the poor are then necessarily the focus of an intrusive intervention?"

"I'm not comfortable, but I see that this is inevitable. And I'm comfortable with the fact that if we can't deal with all of the situations, we can at least then deal with some of the situations that become accessible to us. I'm ready to opt for half a loaf. With the certainty that I'm not gonna get the whole loaf. With that, I'm comfortable."

"I hear what you're saying—that half a loaf, and at least you're doing something. But are you comfortable that those who need a hand up are getting a boot down? Losing practically all they have left—their kids? There's a reason for some discomfort in targeting people who are already victims."

"It's done all the time. The school does it constantly. If you take a look at your disciplinary problems—at who is removed from school, or who's put in which classes. I'm not comfortable with it, but it's part of the way the social organization is set up. And I'm not gonna change it, and you're not gonna change it. And I'm uncomfortable with it, but I'll live with my discomfort."

But—would middle-class fathers whose kids spoke up live with theirs? Household child sexual abuse "cut across all socio-economic lines." It was abundantly present in prosperous households. Children (and mothers) were being beckoned forward, with assurances that "help" was available.

And, with the rise of the issue of incest, for the first time in history, upstanding white males were being reported as abusers: The addition of sexual abuse to other definitions of abuse and neglect more visible among those living in circumstances of social disadvantage and deprivation implicitly extended the limits commonly taken to be "legitimate state intervention into family life."[15]

For the first time in history, interveners, under the auspices of the state, were faced with the daunting prospect of crossing manicured lawns (bordered by swimming pools and tennis courts) to inform a white male professional or corporate executive that there had been a report that he was raping his child; to inform him that the child had spoken up about it (perhaps following a "prevention" presentation) in school.

Suddenly, a system whose major insulation from constitutional challenge—challenge about abrogation of due process rights, of privacy rights, of parental versus state authority—had been its overriding high moral purpose (rescuing children from the poor and the powerless according to its definition of *abuse* or *neglect*), suddenly that system faced the awkward challenge of opting out of its part of the social class–specific bargain.

Incest hit the child welfare industry like a souped-up explosive device. Although the initial fanfare would be introduced in a different ring—apparently outside the ring marked *traditional family*— it would soon move to its own spotlighted circle, creating spectacle indeed.

Chapter 5

NINETEEN EIGHTY-FOUR

SEPTEMBER, 1993. I have just finished a phone interview with one of the leading experts in the field of child sexual abuse.

He has characterized as "neo-traditional" the view that child sexual abuse is a largely male violation.

Neo-traditional.

I am kind of pleased with the sound of it. I have never been grouped with anything so solid-sounding and respectable before.

Neo-traditional.

———

There was an odd atmosphere—a combination of disappointment and relief—as the year 1984 arrived, as though it were not quite living up to Orwellian billing. In retrospect, this seems a misperception, certainly within the framework of the incest issue.

In Orwell's *1984*, after all, Winston Smith's society was in the midst of the social engineering that would ultimately, by alteration of language, make it impossible for Oceanians to think politically incorrect thoughts: the perfection of Newspeak and Doublethink.

"The B vocabulary consisted of words which had been deliberately constructed for political purposes: words, that is to say, which not only had in every case a political implication, but were intended to impose a desirable mental attitude upon the person using them." The word *oldthink*, for example, "was inextricably mixed up with the idea of wickedness and decadence. . . . But the special function of certain Newspeak words, of which *oldthink* was one, was not so much to express meanings as to destroy them."

By 1984 (the actual year), it can plausibly be argued that some version of this was evident, as "spousal assault" was everywhere used to stand in for "wife-battering," and the commonplace sexual assault of children by males who held power over them had been solidified in the lexicon as "intrafamilial sexual abuse," which, in turn, was a symptom of "dysfunctional families."

By 1984, the noun *incest* had become a commonplace verb: "I was incested when I was five." (Which sounded sort of like, "I was baptized when I was five.")

We were treated to seemingly endless ominous warnings about something called the "cycle of violence." Abused children, it was everywhere intoned, become abusers.

This incantation had not only the ring of scientific predictability, but it implied a kind of hereditary causality, a gene running amok down the centuries.

Implicit in the cycle of violence was the insufficiency of merely saying that paternal child molestation is a gross violation of a child and a grotesque abuse of muscle and power. Rather, it was necessary to find for the issue some tag that would render it a public health problem and further justify medicalized intervention. The implication that, without treatment, victims were social time bombs doomed to explode on their children, lent further urgency to treatment. What the cycle-of-violence shibboleth, repeated endlessly in the media, did, of course, was to convey that message to the children themselves—to desperately awful effect—as they grew up and became parents themselves. Therapists spoke to me of the suicide of certain adult clients whose children approached the age they had been when they were raped.

For all this talk of incest-transmission, there was slim evidence, if any. If it was true that a number of caught and spotlighted offenders now began to allow as how they too had been raped as children, it was also true that offenders had not said that early on. So it was impossible to know to what extent they were using this as a formula to mitigate their accountability.

Most important, it made no sense. Offenders continued to tally at over 90 percent male, and the majority of victims tallied as female, seemingly canceling the validity of a cycle of violence.

Challenged with this apparently contradictory fact, however, experts responded that sexually abused females grew up to *marry* offenders, that's what it was! This suggested that they had some kind of clairvoyance, some parapsychological radar, which enabled them to determine *predictability*—when the experts could not, even after the fact, find any personality anomalies in perpetrators, nor any way to assert that this man's behavior could have been predetermined. But *she* knew, they said (she *must have known*).

What the cycle-of-violence shibboleth did was to exonerate men who committed abuse (because they had themselves been abused as children), and to implicate women who chanced to have married those men (because the women had been abused as children).

What the purported cycle of violence did, in line with everything else, was to shift focus from the deliberate, planned, calculated sexual assault on a child by a male adult into the realm of some quasi-biological-behavioral determinism. It obliterated all need to deal with what our fathers had said, early on (when they were still spouting uncontaminated truth): "I don't see anything wrong with it." It obviated the need to deal with the number of venerable people who continued to question whether "the harmfulness of incest has any existence outside of the incest taboo." Who asked, "Is the harmfulness of incest solely a consequence of the shame and guilt attendant on violating a taboo?"[1] Who, in fact, said out loud and in respectable company that they didn't see anything objectionable about it.

And—for all the expressed concern about children—it invited well-meaning people to appear on television at all hours of the day or night, telling twelve-year-olds who might be being molested in the now that their inevitable fate was to themselves become that which they so fiercely hated in the now—molesters.

It is truly amazing what adults will do when they are let loose to express their good intentions toward children.

Newspeak had rendered the issue of incest safe to present for public consumption.

In 1984 *Life* magazine covered over twenty pages with a special report headed "The Cruelest Crime, Sexual Abuse of Children: The Victims, the Offenders, How to Protect Your Family."[2] *Newsweek* did likewise with a cover story, "Sexual Abuse: The Growing Outcry Over Child Molesting," which was heralded as "A Hidden Epidemic."[3]

Television took the issue to prime time with ABC's "Something About Amelia," about which columnist Nicholas von Hoffman wrote perceptively, "Americans with a new topic 'medicalize' it. In the ABC movie, the police are pushed to the background: the shrinks take over. Incest is demoted from being a crime and a sin to being real, real bad, but a disorder, nevertheless; a candidate for help, for therapy."[4]

Following the airing of "Something About Amelia," we were told that child sexual abuse/incest reporting shot up by as much as 900 percent.

The year 1984 witnessed "Kids Don't Tell," and a five-and-a-half-hour PBS program, "Child Sexual Abuse: What Your Children Should Know," which aired in September. About this last, John Corry wrote in the *New York Times*, "What is missing in the series, admirably conceived as it may be, is a sense of sin. We are enlightened. We are informed. We are almost reassured: child sexual abuse, after all, may be prevented. What we do not get, however, is a feeling for the emotional wreckage that the abuse leaves in its wake. 'Some adverse consequences' doesn't really do it. . . . In a way, a felony is seen as a misdemeanor: wickedness becomes only an ethical lapse."[5]

But those few published voices who took issue with the now-sanitized presentation—male voices, it is to be noted—were in the minority. Overall, the response seemed to be one of near festivity. The silence was being broken. Help was available. Families could have counseling and be kept intact. (Nothing, really, had to change.)

As television, incest was "in." The hurdle had been jumped. It was now available as a plot feature to all future shows.

———

As though to chasten anyone who challenged the new sensitive/therapeutic understanding, two morality plays were even then being staged that would at once make simple, commonplace incest seem minimalist, prove the folly of hard-line prosecution and the hopelessness of attempts to seriously censure offenders against children—and give a national forum to a virulent backlash.

It was a backlash that could have been anticipated—but only within a feminist framework; only had there been any residual awareness in the larger community that what we had challenged when we first spoke out was the cradle of sexual politics. Removing that awareness—that in raising the issue what you were challenging was a profound sense of male entitlement—left both the professionals and the public unprepared for the fact that the portion of the male population who chose to act on this entitlement were on the verge of a declaration of war.

Since public speech on incest was now so carefully tamed, the backlash had an immediate edge. Their speech had vigor. They had the ability to muster a state of dudgeon, seize the moral high ground with their intemperate tone, and recruit a militant army.

When the backlash first showed itself, it was not around the issue of incest as such. Rather, they made their maiden appearance on the scene where the cameras had already been set up—

around the large-scale abuse charges in Jordan, Minnesota, and the McMartin Preschool abuse case in California. While these kinds of allegations of multiple-offender abuse are not my primary focus here, they had several impacts that can't be ignored. For one thing, they brought a bit of Grand Guignol onstage—an introduction of wickedness, murder, torture; the sense of *sin* that had been sanitized out of plain old paternal child rape. Involving criminal prosecutorial proceedings, they had theatrical qualities that call-this-800-number, help-is-available presentations never could. They dwarfed the issue of routine household incest— virtually normalizing it, making it seem, well, *homey.*

I would presume to guess that those are the reasons the backlash first surfaced around these cases. They offered a dramatic entrance onstage. And because of the outsize nature of the allegations that emerged, they offered a forum in which to make credible the suggestion that, hey, this stuff was *incredible.* They were the perfect place in which to propose the notion of child sexual abuse as *preposterous.*

But the fact that those cases were where the backlash first showed its flag does not automatically mean mass-abuse cases were its focal concern. The coincidence between the first time state intervention was ever directed to middle-class white males, and the backlash, which would initially organize as Victims of Child Abuse Laws (VOCAL), is too conspicuous to ignore. Unquestionably, over the previous decade, with an increasing number of imprecations to the public and to professionals to report any suspicion of child abuse, a certain number of innocent people had been pulled into battle with the protective services system, and these people too were drawn to VOCAL.

But it was with sexual abuse allegations that anger cohered and was translated into the organized action that debuted on September 19, 1984.[6] Twenty-four adults in Jordan, Minnesota, had been charged with sexually molesting children, including their own. Many of those charged were respectable citizens within the community; the high drama of the trial that ensued drew much media fanfare, and escalated as some of the children began to talk of more than massive child sexual abuse. They spoke of having witnessed a child murdered; of stabbings, shootings, decapitation, mutilation. . . .

After months of to-do, the prosecution was dropped. Much mud was slung and many accusations flew—most notably directed against the prosecutor, R. Kathleen Morris, who was alleged to have fumbled the case, but also against the professionals who had interviewed the children and who, it was said, had programmed the kids, led them, and contaminated their testimony.

Indeed, Jordan offered the backlash a national forum in which to, at first, hum a few bars of what would become their national anthem: that the children were no more than innocent victims of adult interviewers, interrogators, and therapists who were programming them, leading their minds to untrue beliefs with poisonous questioning techniques; and that the adult defendants were being piteously denied their rights: judged guilty until and unless they could prove themselves innocent.

The press found the refrain catchy, and, encouraged, more verses were added and the ditty was amplified nationwide, leaving an indelible imprint of doubt in the public's mind.

As child sexual abuse expert Dr. Roland Summit writes, "The [negative] legacy of Jordan might be appropriate if it countered a real threat to civil liberties and if the exculpatory argument were substantiated in forums other than adversarial deadlocks. If the massive and unprecedented discovery of sexual abuse during the past ten years has led to overkill, and if specialists self-trained in innovative interviewing techniques are creating fictitious atrocities, then there is reason for the public media and the courts to rally on behalf of a class of falsely accused adults."

But, as Dr. Summit points out, "If the children *were* victimized as they once claimed, and if criminal courts provide exculpation of adult suspects, then there is nothing in the juvenile courts, the clinical establishment or the public media that can validate those claims and protect those children against a simplistic and unsubstantiated exculpatory argument. . . . In the presence of reasonable doubts about adults' criminality, there is no countervailing offer of reasonable belief in the ordeal of the children."[7]

In fact, the reality of the proceedings did not bear out the innocent-being-railroaded hype. Though it received minimal media attention, a commanding opinion rendered on review by the United States Court of Appeals found that due process had indeed prevailed and the civil rights of the accused adults had, in fact, been legally observed. And there was no evidence that a passel of venal therapists and interviewers had conspired to warp young minds and pervert the children's testimony.

The plaintiffs in the appeal (i.e., the accused), the appeals court said, "attack various decisions by the guardians, therapists and attorney, for example, to recommend against visitation, as proof of conspiratorial purpose. In essence, they contend that the performance of their duties by these professionals was directed and tainted by a conspiratorial purpose to frame the plaintiffs." This the appeals court decided amounted to no more than unsupported allegations of malice.

Further, the court rejected the "inference that law enforcement personnel are necessarily less entitled to rely on details of criminal activity described by children than those described by adults."

And the court added that "absent any information concerning improper questioning methods, we are at a loss to understand how a psychological evaluation or therapy can be accomplished for a juvenile suspected victim of sexual abuse if questioning itself is not permitted."[8]

Indeed, the appeals court found reason that the charges should not have been dropped but should have been more forcefully pursued. Floyd R. Gibson, senior circuit judge, wrote, "The detailed accounts of sexual abuse given by the children required the authorities to act, and their action, as the court holds today, is protected. The children's accounts are so startling and egregious, however, that it is difficult to accept the prosecutor's dismissal of the charges against the parents and other parties charged. . . . The children's accusations, if true, demand the prosecution of the guilty parties. The prosecutor's action in dismissing the charges leaves this shocking and abusive affair in limbo."[9]

Nonetheless, if all of this was too little reported, it also was too late. By then, the majority of the public had most likely forgotten the words of one six-year-old boy who had testified as a victim in the case. When asked by the defense attorney if the child were worried that his father would sodomize him, he turned to his father and said, "You won't do that no more, right?"[10]

What did continue to echo in the public's mind was the virulent rap about the *railroading* of *innocent citizens*.

What struck me as I watched the daily reports of the brouhaha was that what was being enacted here—to go with the double-think and doublespeak—was a double bind. Nobody much wanted to say that it was okay to sexually abuse children. On the other hand, to entertain the suspicion that it was rampant in a small community was to envision the possibility that none of the previously held public pieties bore much relation to actual reality. It was one thing to recite, as a mantra, that incest "cut across all socioeconomic lines" and something else entirely to seriously consider that the behavior of a child molester might lie beneath the visage of the fellow who was an esteemed member of your Kiwanis.

The limbo of doubt served the backlash well. Doubt lasts longer in the public mind, causing more indigestive discomfort, than either conviction or exoneration.* And *irresolution* kept sufficient doubt alive to taint less publicized cases across the country.

The doubt cast about therapists' interviewing techniques and about certain experts' credulousness would prove triumphant when extended "downward" to less flamboyant cases involving

---

* Many fewer people have recall of the 1984–1986 Country Walk case in Florida, in which Frank Fuster, owner of the Country Walk Babysitting Service, was convicted of fourteen counts of child sexual abuse and sentenced to 165 years in prison.

"only" a child's accusation against a father, provided it was couched, as it always was, in acceptable doublespeak: Yes, of course, child sexual abuse is rampant and awful to contemplate. But. Such an accusation is never true when it is made in any particular circumstance by any particular child against any particular man. It can only be attributed to the evil machinations of treating and interviewing adults, and most particularly, to the deviousness and pathology of the believing adult who brought the child's accusations forward to begin with.

And so, in the end, what ensued from the Jordan episode was cacophony, and, in the public mind, cognitive paralysis. (These people, after all, were not denying that child sexual abuse/incest were widespread and oh-so-too-bad and to-be-punished-when-found. They were not saying it was okay. They were just saying it wasn't here, in this case, now. . . .)

Above all—since nobody hearing reports of the events in Jordan could find any coherence in them, any context for them, nor, in the end, any resolution—a level of general apprehension was generated that I had not sensed before. Specters of organized evil-doing by adults (or maybe organized malice by professionals?) had been raised and then left walking among us like the undead. The net effect was that the case generated a three o'clock in the morning kind of intense but free-floating anxiety. It furthered public susceptibility to any parent-like reassurance that, non-sense, everything is just fine, what's going on here is nothing but a hysterical witch-hunt.

Witch-hunt was precisely the cry issued by VOCAL. However, in deference to the prevailing "med-speak," what was now billed as an epidemic of false allegations was given the honorific title "False Accusation *Syndrome*."

VOCAL's literature spoke in "preserve the family" terms, de-crying intrusions into the privacy of the home, entirely compatible with Reagan-era sloganeering. ("What VOCAL seeks to resist and change—abuse of government power to foster witchhunts and violence done to innocent people—has been a part of human history for thousands of years."[11]) However, implicitly, the word *family* was code for a unit that included a male. Indeed, it was the absence of same that had long rendered single mothers, particularly poor women, suspect and vulnerable to the very state intervention that was now being challenged by men with such gusto and indignation.

Quite simply, men were astonished and outraged at being treated the way poor mothers had long been treated without any such organizational protest. But then, poor single mothers were not accustomed to getting much in the way of attention by speaking of fairness, justice, due process; their rights. (Indeed, such talk on the part of a targeted poor single mother would most likely be reflected in her case record as "paranoid, uncooperative." *Uncooperative* is the word I most often heard applied to mothers and foster mothers alike, triggered by anything from assertiveness to a worker's failure to communicate a scheduling change. The foster mother argued, the mother didn't show up: uncooperative.)

Within the protective services system, VOCAL was claiming (quite justifiably), the supposition is one of fire at the first whiff of smoke. Many professionals are mandated to report any suspicions of abuse, and the public is asked to. The investigation is made by social workers/caseworkers, and "likelihood" of abuse can lead to an agency decision that it is "founded." The subsequent court-ordered removal of the child to state care occurs heedless of parental protestations of innocence. This is entirely consistent, however, with the basic standard of judgment that underlies the rationale for allowing this kind of extralegal or supralegal power to the state—avoiding the standard of proof beyond a reasonable doubt.

And it had never bothered anyone—so long as it remained as undemocratic in reality as it was in historical rationale; so long as it did not affect anyone in a position to complain.

The doctrine that gives the state the right to intervene against parents on behalf of children, *parens patriae*, can be traced back to fourteenth-century England, where it was asserted as the "sovereign's responsibility toward the property and later the person of the insane." It was then extended to include children of property: "The King as political father and guardian of his kingdom, as the protection of all his subjects, and of their lands and goods; and he is bound, in a most peculiar manner, to take care of those who, by reason of their imbecility and want of understanding, are incapable of taking care of themselves."[12] (Quite probably, the sovereign's concern then was not the children but the property they were "of.")

The doctrine, as proposed by Lord Blackstone, bluntly stated, "The rich indeed were left at their own option, whether they will breed up their children to be ornaments or disgraces to their family."[13] The state's solicitude was directed entirely at the children of the poor.

In colonial America, as well, the first statutes focused entirely on parental poverty, and on children orphaned or illegitimate. With the passage, in 1865, of the constitutional amendment prohibiting involuntary servitude for blacks, the question of indenture being, in effect, involuntary servitude, arose. The solution was to rename it: thus was born the placing-out system.*

The development of societies for the prevention of cruelty to children in the last quarter of the nineteenth century signaled an adherence to the original intent of *parens patriae*: the legalized, coercive removal of children from the suspect poor. However, almost from the beginning there was a tension between the police function allowed the state, implied by *parens patriae*, and a social work approach. Once again, the solution was language: The coercive intent of the state in its police-power guise was formulated in the language of care and concern.

On and on the thing rolled, through the establishment of Family Court, the development of the Children's Bureau—gathering

---

* Charles Loring Brace, the first secretary of the Children's Aid Society, came up with the idea of draining New York City of what was seen as an "infestation" of vagrant children by shipping them out West where there was a need for their labor (i.e., Placing Them Out).

bureaucracy. It was given a major boost as a "system" with the 1962 publication by C. Henry Kempe, a pediatrician, of findings about what Kempe initially called *parental abuse*—then quickly revamped under the less frightening and accusatory heading Battered Child Syndrome.[14] This new discovery generated widespread interest, kicked up public indignation, and brought amplified funding. Again, all predicated on the social distance between those who labeled the problem (middle-class professionals), and those who supported intervention (middle-class citizens), and those targeted as the objects of attention (namely politically powerless, lower-class families).

In 1974, the Child Abuse Prevention and Treatment Act went into effect, and in jig time each state had a protective service, affiliated with juvenile/family court, and the power to petition for removal of children from homes where they faced "possible harm" from abuse or neglect.

And here we all were, content and secure in the knowledge— recurring scandals aside—that poor children were being rescued from bad or impoverished or incompetent "parents," mainly single mothers with the odd socially disadvantaged male thrown in. Until, that is, the discovered infamy of incest/child sexual abuse and the anarchic nature of *this* "illness"—that it "cut across all socioeconomic lines."

From their inception, juvenile/family courts have been cast in an openly declared paternalistic role, far different from the role ascribed to criminal courts. The standards of judgment are different, as are the goals. Where the standard of evidence in criminal court is proof "beyond a reasonable doubt," in these lower courts the standard is "preponderance of evidence." Where criminal courts place a primary value on the accused's due process rights, these courts hold as their highest concern "possible harm to the child." The key value here is not "presumption of innocence." But presumption of innocence is what respectable men deem their due. They were *victims* of these outrageous intrusions long allowed by this (now misapplied and *unconstitutional*) child abuse legislation. All of a sudden, this system, so long applauded for its most excellent intentions, wasn't *fair*.

This, essentially, is what VOCAL's message was.

By contrast with other backlash groups, however, VOCAL's tone seemed positively mellow. A group called Men International quickly put out a flier and began running ads in the VOCAL national newsletter claiming there were over five hundred thousand false reports of (code phrase) "child abuse" every year.

"But," the flier tells us, "there is new hope. We have developed a specialized team, capable of assisting on cases anywhere in the nation. The team is made up of the best experts available in the United States. We call it the 'Annihilation Team' because our aim is to destroy false allegations. You can call it the 'A-Team' for short. We mean business." The flier is signed "The Avenger."

In retrospect, if the case in Jordan presaged what lay ahead, it can also be seen as a kind of warm-up act for the Big Event, the one in which Satan would be introduced to the public—for the first time in a century—as a major player. (Talk about a dramatic comeback.)

You will remember the McMartin Preschool case in Manhattan Beach, California (if you were sentient in 1984 you could not have missed it). It overlapped the Jordan case in time, but it continued way beyond it, and, had they been diabolically designed to do so, together these cases could not have offered a more convincing, if somewhat reiterative, demonstration to the public that you could not get there from here, in terms of criminalizing and prosecuting cases of child sexual abuse (be they incest or otherwise).[15]

You will remember: To begin with, in the fall of 1983, a few mothers with children at the preschool became uncomfortable with the way "Mr. Ray" (Raymond Buckey), who was Virginia McMartin's grandson, behaved—very physically—with the children.

Several weeks later, a two-year-old boy returned from the

preschool with blood on his anus. The Los Angeles Police Department began an investigation, sending a letter to the parents of the hundred or so children enrolled in the school, reporting to them that Ray Buckey was under suspicion, and asking them to report any indications that their own children had been abused.

The parents, naturally, then posed that question to their children. A few said Mr. Ray had indeed done something to them. Kee McFarlane, now a consultant to Children's Institute International in California, was asked to interview the children. Soon the children were implicating not only Ray Buckey but Peggy Buckey (Virginia McMartin's daughter and an employee of the school). As more and more parents brought their children in for interviews that were being videotaped in order to spare the children repeated questioning later, the number soon climbed to the hundreds. The backup was such that appointments were being scheduled for three years later. Indeed, parents were bringing in children who had attended the school in the past as well. And the children now began talking about being drugged and tied up, raped and sodomized, penetrated with pencils and other objects.

They talked of the "movie-star game" and the "doctor game" and the "cowboy game" and the "tickle game" and the "alligator game" and the "horsey game." They talked of gerbils, turtles, rabbits—pets at the school—being killed in front of them, and of being told that's what would happen to their parents if the children ever told.

Then the Devil was ushered onstage, as the audience—all of America—sat spellbound.

Some of the older children, former students at the school, talked of having been forced to drink rabbits' blood in an Episcopal church nearby. They said they had been abused by other people wearing black robes and carrying black candles.

Some kids began to speak of visits to a local cemetery where bodies were exhumed and hacked into pieces. And all this gained some credibility when the state closed a day-care center operated by the Episcopal Church: Children there had been found by doctors to have been sexually abused.

Soon, five other nearby preschools were under investigation. And children there described the same events as the McMartin kids had.

A conspiracy theory gained media attention when Kee McFarlane testified before a televised congressional subcommittee, expressing concern that the children's accounts of abuse at different schools in several different cities were so similar. She said, "I believe that we're dealing with an organized operation of child predators designed to prevent detection. . . . The preschool . . . serves as a ruse for a larger, unthinkable network of crimes against children."

Seven indictments were handed down by a Los Angeles grand jury: against Ray Buckey, his mother, his grandmother and sister, and three other former teachers at McMartin school. There were 115 separate counts. By 1984, 400 children had been interviewed at Children's Institute, with 350 saying they had been abused by somebody at the school. By now, children were talking about having been taken out of the school to be abused—one, in a van while going through a carwash. Others told of having been driven careening in the van to a doctor's home with a half-dead baby bouncing around inside.

To the protest that all this was not only unthinkable but incredible, the reply would be made that fewer than ten years earlier, the very idea of widespread child sexual abuse/incest had been similarly unthinkable and incredible—thus tying the credibility of those children's stories to the credibility of most reports by survivors. But if the higher court's ruling in Jordan had been too little, too late, all of this coming in tandem with Jordan seemed too much, too soon.

The preliminary hearings were to determine whether the prosecutors had sufficient probable cause for the judge to order the defendants to stand trial. The hearings alone lasted twenty months, and cost more than six million dollars, filling forty-three thousand pages of testimony (over five hundred volumes).

The defense mimicked that in Jordan: brainwashing by the social workers/interviewers. This was made even more concrete here because videotapes could be produced of interviews, and the techniques used in talking to the children could be examined repeatedly and in exquisite detail. When, despite the chaos and uncertainty and the turnover in prosecutors and the confusing courtroom testimony of the children, the judge ordered the case to trial, it was already January of 1986. It would be a year and a half before the trial finally began; almost four years after the first charge against Ray Buckey was made.

It is hard to think of another uproar in history where, in the end, nothing much happened, yet where the event had such a far-reaching, indelible effect—on the children and parents, on the professionals who, once again and in ever more grandiose language, were portrayed as the real abusers—brainwashers of youth and defilers of the good names of adult innocents. And on the viewing public.

With McMartin, the backlash refined its techniques of mockery and the sniper tactics that would keep those professionals advocating for no more, really, than a fair hearing for the children, always in the position of *reacting*—to challenges to their methods, innuendoes about the flaws in their methods, and, perhaps most important in the long run, to the rise of figureheads said to be their equals and opposites as experts, who were gifted with less reticence and a far less inhibiting sense of decorum.

I have always had an odd sense about these backlash experts. Although I know they have names and distinct identities, so much of what they have said and so many of their tactics carry the echo of history that they have always seemed to me *insubstantial*. As though their voices, echoing through history, were those of ancestral beings.

While the professionals listening to children had taken pains to build (albeit early-stage) theory and research based on the radically challenging notion that the voices of women and children might be pointing to something society needed to hear, the backlash had built nothing but hi-tech amplification for the booming voice of the status quo. What they *had* taken pains to build were troops. And in a shooting war, it is the guys with the troops who have a decided advantage.

Having tested the mettle of their attack strategies on the national stage, proponents of the backlash were now ready to march forward, decrying as false allegations any allegations that came to light (all the while deploring the actuality of never-here, never-now child sexual abuse/incest).

But by now you may have noticed the true impact of Jordan and McMartin:

By now, incest, the routine, historically permitted, sexual assault of a child by a male in authority in the home, was being rendered diminutive, pedestrian, by contrast—further eradicating any place in the script for the identification of the role of longstanding normative gender politics.

In the large-scale abuse cases, women were hoisted into the spotlight as accused co-offenders, cementing conviction—even absent convictions—about the Doctrine of Equal Culpability.

A residue of generalized unease was created, an unease that would come into play again later on. It was an unarticulated susceptibility to the idea that evil was loose in the world, perhaps in the form of satanic dalliance, involving not ordinary men choosing to nobble around with the kids during naptime, but otherworldly forces (which again diminished the import of regulation-issue incest).

And with the introduction of testimony about black-robed figures and church rituals and bizarre forms of transport, the backlash had been handed the blunt weapon of the apparently ludicrous with which to bludgeon children's credibility and cry even more loudly, "social hysteria!"; "witch-hunt!"—and to engage in ever louder mutterings about vendettas being launched nationwide against upstanding citizens plying their simple routines.

All of which "educational" materials they could carry back with them to their own home turf as supporting evidence when their own or their cohorts' children spoke out about sexual abuse.

Had Jordan and McMartin been manifestations of deliberate strategy—the staging of a spectacular production, to magnificent backlash benefit, at state expense—one would have to applaud it as brilliant. In the event, it was simply events—which men whose delicacy about their rights in such matters had the perspicacity to personalize, and to use as spin.

But if all this was diverting, it was also diversionary. It was not even near where the Great Incest Massacre was taking place.

Chapter 6

THE GREAT INCEST
MASSACRE I

IT IS 1992: I am reading *Defend and Betray: A Victorian Mystery*, by Anne Perry. By page 100, I have intuited what lay behind Alexandra's murder of her husband, the esteemed general. (And to think I once was able to turn to such books for *diversion*.) And so I press on, seeking confirmation, to page 271, where . . .

"I know why Alexandra killed the general! . . . And my God, I think I would have done it too. And gone to the gallows before I would have told anyone why."

"Why? . . . For God's sake why?"

"Because he was having carnal knowledge of his own son!"

"Dear heaven! Are you sure? . . . General Carlyon— was . . . ? Hester . . . ?"

"Yes—and not only he, but probably the old colonel as well—and God knows who else."

"No wonder she killed him . . ."

"What else could she do? . . . There was no one to turn

to—I don't suppose anyone would have believed her. They'd lock her up for slander, or insanity, if she tried to say such a thing about a pillar of the military establishment like the general."[1]

Aha! So it was, in fiction. And so it is, in fact.

———

January 9, 1984: Following the first airing of the made-for-TV special "Something About Amelia," Ted Koppel, on "Nightline," is taking the hour to calm the emotional turmoil he presumes has been created nationwide. He is about to break an important barrier: the focusing by a major network news program on the subject of incest. The point of this hour, he tells us, is not exploitation, but rather an occasion "to chase away some demons."

We will meet some guests, Koppel says, who will appear in shadow—perpetrators and victims—as well as some experts.

And so we do.

Speaking to one silhouetted perpetrator, "Jim," Koppel says, "Do you understand now, as a result of therapy, what it was that first attracted you to a little girl? I mean, why would you want to have sex with a child—a child, period, but least of all, your own child?"

And Jim replies thoughtfully, "There's not any one exact answer as to why I turned to my daughter. There was a lot of contributing factors that led up to it. *One thing with my daughter, a lot of times I would turn to my daughter out of anger with my wife. Like if I would get angry with my wife, I would say to hell with her, I don't need her. I've got my daughter. I can turn to her*" (italics mine).[2]

How, I wondered, watching, could anyone fail to hear this? Jim's motive was rage at his wife. She was the target. The child was the weapon. And yet here we were, in 1984, instead of listening, deploying professionals to strip-search male psyches and dissect erections (if you will forgive the assaultive imagery).

Plain as the nose on your face, it seemed: Incest, in its intent, was often a form of violence against women, coincidental to which children were being raped.

How often? Well *I* didn't know. But surely we could find out? And wouldn't that be a good thing? Because where this rage against women is the intent, doesn't the very mindlessness of the father's motives enhance a thousandfold the abuse—above and beyond what a passing pedophile might have done? Doesn't this aggravate the betrayal of trust and amplify the pathos? The child sees the father (albeit monstrously transformed). And the offender sees mainly a way to (metaphorically speaking) break the thing that would hurt his wife (or ex-wife) the most? That just seems so—*mean* (I am tempted to say it should be against the law).

But there I was, going off again—in the direction no one seemed inclined to take. Looking for *simple* explanations instead of complex pathological forces.

Still, it is tempting to think that, had anyone listened to what the men themselves had to say, perhaps we would have witnessed less carnage later. Perhaps it would have made sense then, to those in authority and to the public, that this male rage at their wives drove not only the abuse, but might well have driven separation and divorce to begin with. And that this same male rage at their now ex-wives made it not only plausible but far from unlikely that abuse of the child would begin following divorce—in the same way that more battered women and their children are murdered after they leave the relentlessly assaultive marriage. And that the question here, as with battered women, was not why would the woman stay (that dreadful incest mother). It was why would the men continue to seek to punish them? Continue to not let them go?

Perhaps, had anyone then listened, we could have avoided the wholesale massacre of those children who told, and those mothers who acted to protect them.

"Mom Sues to Save 'Abused' Son"3
"Court Gives Kids to Abusive Dads"4
"Mother Cited for Keeping Child from Ex-Husband"5

These headlines from the mid-1980s were soon met, matched, and drowned out by others heralding the views of the now-organized backlash, flush from their trial missions in Jordan and McMartin:

"False Accusation of Child Abuse—Could It Happen to You?"6
"Has a Child Been Molested? (A Psychiatrist Argues for Reforms in the Way Child Sexual Abuse Cases Are Investigated)"7
"A Bitter New Issue (Some Accusations of Child Abuse Are False)"8

Adult survivors (I had taken to saying) do not threaten the status quo. It is the children now, and the women—their mothers—who seek to protect them *now*, who threaten the status quo.

This was not, among survivors, who saw themselves as a movement determined to gain "empowerment," a popular thing to say. In my own (and only) defense, I said it because it was what I now witnessed: Everywhere I saw the ravages of a war in which women acting protectively now were being savaged; in which children were being torn from those mothers and delivered into the care and control of those men the children had stated were their sexual violators—where they were not otherwise being wrenched away, into state custody.

Women simply could not win for losing.

Since, by the early 1980s, statutes in virtually every state faulted the mother "who knew or should have known" or who "failed to protect," both women still married, just discovering the abuse, who raced to seek protection for the child and women who had not cottoned to the abuse yet, were at severe risk of losing custody to the state. For example:

In the Matter of Katherine C. and Others, Children Alleged to be Abused.

"A natural mother, who had no actual knowledge of the sexual abuse of her child by her husband, the child's stepfather, in their home, will nonetheless be held to have allowed the abuse . . . if the objective evidence available to her should have prompted adequate protective measures from a responsible parent similarly situated: good faith, good intentions and even best efforts are not, per se, defenses to a child protective petition since to hold otherwise would frustrate legislative efforts to prevent avoidable injury to children."[9]

"In Matter of Alayne E. this court contended that it sympathized with the respondent mother in her efforts to shield her daughter from an abusive father. And yet, the court's sympathy did not prevail because of the simple reality that the mother's efforts were insufficient and inadequate to protect the child."[10]

"In Matter of Shane T. this court, while acknowledging the efforts of the respondent mother to protect her son, nonetheless made a finding of abuse against her."[11]

In sum: "Parents must be zealously and consistently dedicated to their children's welfare. The obligation is fundamental and absolute. It may bring parents into conflict with each other and with their own respective needs and desires. When this occurs, the only appropriate parental response is clear. The welfare of the child must prevail."

A ringing exhortation, yes? *The only appropriate parental response is clear. The welfare of the child must prevail.*

Now look:

"Mother Defies Custody Terms": "A Rockville mother of two is vowing to go to jail rather than comply with a court order that her daughters, ages 2 and 4, be allowed to visit the father, the mother's ex-husband, on Sunday."[12] The children had indicated to the mother that the father was sexually abusing them.

Or, "A Mute Girl's Story: Child Abuse and the System." Filed from Los Angeles, this story begins, "There is a small girl here, now 5 years old, who rarely speaks. She is, according to her psychiatrist's testimony, an 'elective mute' who refuses to talk as a result of sexual abuse by her father that started before she was 2.

"The child's mother . . . says she appealed to the police, doctors and lawyers to help her safeguard the child from abuse, but in the face of the father's denials could not prevail.

" 'Nobody would listen to me,' " the mother said. " 'Everybody told me, "You're going through a divorce, all women say that." ' "

And so the mother sued the doctors and lawyers who did nothing to help. She said that "even when a medical examination found evidence of sexual abuse after a weekend visit with the father in February 1981, her complaints were ignored, and she was subsequently found in contempt of court because she refused to allow the father to visit the child." Either she would allow the father to take the child for a weekend visit or she would go to jail.[13]

Or this: "A trial court on Staten Island recently determined that a battered woman had 'abused' her daughter under the new Family Court Act where her daughter was sexually abused by her stepfather in her home when the natural mother was out of the house, had no knowledge of the abuse and had affirmatively attempted to protect the child from the violence of the step-father in times past."[14] The court found this woman's failure to have the stepfather excluded from the home equivalent to "allowing" him to commit sexual assault on her daughter.

And so what we were looking at was the nonnegotiable demand that women act to protect their children from abuse by the children's fathers—and their utter denigration, vilification, discrediting, and surgical excision from their children's lives when they tried to meet that demand. Nowhere in this imprecation to believe and to act did there appear caveats cautioning skepticism or suggesting they'd best wait and see what developed further, or that they'd best marshal irrefutable proof before believing and acting.

And so women would discover—one by one by one—that, wittingly or not, they had been set up as marks and stooges by a fundamentally fraudulent and duplicitous social response. Unequivocally ordered, in stentorian tones, to believe and to act, they would come to find out that there was, in fact, no way within existing procedure that they could safely do so. And not only were existing procedures against them, but it soon became clear that there were major forces marshaled against them as well. That it was exactly on this terrain that the backlash forces had chosen to stage the major battle of their war.

To make things even more sinister, it soon became clear that this was to be a denied battle in a denied war, despite the visible casualties: Rendered in Newspeak, it was held to be simply a matter of "custody disputes."

It was a battle waged by fathers in the name of justice, due process, a citizen's rights. And it was a war waged in halls said to be ones of justice. Interestingly, it was a battle that could not have been so effectively waged, much less won time after time, without the groundwork that had been laid by all that earlier public education, put out through the media: that is, without the redoubtable "incest mother." (Never has the rotten mother been of such service to her country.)

You remember the incest mother. She who disbelieves the child, tells her to shut up, facilitates the abuse (and then denies it); she who will choose the man over the child every time? You remember. The Incest Mother. The one, who, when her daughter discloses the abuse, in school perhaps, will be instantly slapped with a charge of "failure to protect," her child removed to foster care.

That's as it should be for the real incest mother. The one who refuses to believe this is happening (and doesn't much care even if it is). That's how you can be sure the child is being violated: when mom is the identifiable culprit. "How could you ever think of such a terrible thing?" says the incest mother. "Don't let me ever hear you saying anything like that again!"

Dr. Lee Coleman is a California-based psychiatrist and founder and director of the Center for the Study of Psychiatric Testimony. Along with Dr. Ralph Underwager and Dr. Richard Gardner, he was part of the group of medical men lending their credentialed support to the insurgent forces against those mothers who believed their child's accusations of abuse, and against the psychiatrists, psychologists, and attorneys who believed them as well; against False Accusation Syndrome, if you will (or must). Here, he is addressing a meeting of VOCAL:

About the mother who says, "Don't let me ever hear you saying anything like that again," he says, "Now, in a classic situation where the male figure is the alleged perpetrator, that is the kind of statement you might hear from a mother who is still married to the father, or who is still living with, and wants to continue living with, the live-in boyfriend—yes, indeed, that is the kind of thing that you might hear. That is the classic, intact-family, incest situation. . . . That makes sense when a mother who hears that her husband has molested a daughter may in fact have more loyalty to her husband than to her daughter, for emotional reasons, for financial reasons, and there may be a lot of other reasons. . . .

"Now, we have a situation where the mother and the father have divorced each other. They hate each other. And they are fighting over the custody of the child. Do you think that you are going to hear that mother say to the child, 'How could you ever think such a terrible thing?' 'Don't let me ever hear you say that again.'?"[15]

You see how it is with the real incest mother. There was only one small problem with this incest mother: Now that women had been so strongly alerted that incest was real and widespread, that disbelieving mother didn't very often exist. (If she had existed in the past, where the laws would equally implicate the child should she speak out, her behavior could in itself be interpreted as child-protective.)

But the relative noncorporeal existence of this mythological creature would not prove much of a handicap, since years of propaganda had by now given everyone to believe in her—as surely as they had believed in all the other pathogenic mothers that had been conjured for us as explanatory over the years: schizophrenogenic mothers, refrigerator mothers (said to cause autism), mothers who caused their sons' homosexuality (which always reminds me of a lovely bit of subway wall graffiti: "My mother made me a homosexual." Followed by: "If I get her some wool, will she make me one too?"). . . .

By the mid-to-late-1980s, if there was one thing everyone would verbally have agreed to about incest, it was that it was up to a mother to protect her child from her husband's sexual assault. But—having achieved this universal accord, this coast-to-coast affirmation—along came the increasingly powerful Male Protective Brigade to slam shut all the doors that would have made such protection possible (all while we were beckoning kids forward, all the while trumpeting that "help is available!").

Here, as in the preschool cases, as in the Jordan case, the sheer unbelievability of events worked for the backlash. Case after case washed by—from the most notorious case of Elizabeth Morgan, whose young daughter Hillary told of sexual abuse by her father (and where not only did medical findings corroborate the abuse, but where a child by a former wife had also testified to sexual abuse). Morgan would set a record for the longest jail term served on a civil contempt charge. And on to the case of Virginia LaLonde, April Curtis, Liisa Archambault, Jeannine Athas, Kitty Kruse . . .

Neither the mainstream news media, nor (in consequence) the public, took note of any context in which these cases occurred, other than that of a "custody dispute." Each of these cases appeared as an aberration, absent even a hint that they might be united as signifiers of rampant and vicious gender bias and gender assault. Each of these cases was presented as arbitrary, as though it was not part of a deliberately staged, all-out assault on women.* As it became unavoidable that an awful lot of these cases were remarkably similar, the backlash put out the word that charges of sexual abuse were merely the latest ploy in angry-woman divorce tactics.

Thus, not only was the general public permitted to assume that in each of these cases the mother must have done something wrong (or was making false accusations), but each of the women, first hearing what her child was saying to her, set forth on her protective course oblivious to the sheer power of what she was taking on; certain that she, smart, competent, with an entire biography of abiding the law, would surely prevail.

Each of the women went from shock and horror as comprehension dawned as to what her child was saying, to a quick reaching out to the protective services advertised as being the first place to report. And then to an attorney.

Following advice, each of the women would scrupulously document what the child said, and begin to keep files of medical reports and psychological evaluations of the child. Eventually, as the cases went to hearings and as psychological evaluations were ordered of her, and as further examinations were done on the child, and as further hearings were held and further evaluations accrued and further hearings were held, the documents came to fill boxes, then cartons, then more cartons....

---

* The results of a recent study in Orange County, North Carolina, however, show that over a five-year period between 1983 and 1987, in all contested custody cases, 84 percent of the fathers in the study were granted sole or mandated joint custody. In all cases where sole custody was awarded, fathers were awarded custody in 79 percent of the cases. In 26 percent of the cases, fathers were either proven or alleged to have physically and sexually abused their children. *Contested Custody Cases in Orange County, North Carolina Trial Courts, 1983–1987: Gender Bias, the Family and the Law* (Committee for Justice for Women and the Orange County, North Carolina Women's Coalition, 1991). Summary, at 1. Cited in H. Joan Pennington, Esq., "The Hardest Case: Custody and Incest," National Center for Protective Parents, Inc., February 1993), p 25 at footnote 62. Available from the National Center for Protective Parents, 1908 Riverside Drive, Trenton, NJ 08618.

The more women did as they were instructed to do, the more likely they were to be labeled obsessive.

The more they tried to gain protection for the child, the more likely they were to be labeled hysterical and vindictive.

They could not look calm (calculating). They could not look upset (emotionally disturbed).

Watching these cases as they proceeded through years of domestic litigation was like watching in excruciating detail as sadistic boys gleefully tormented small animals; the tormentors' delight only enhanced by the victims' struggles, as the victims, using every resource at their disposal, fought back. Laughing in the face of both logic and evidence, the accused fathers won and they won and they won. There was nothing the mothers could do to gain parity in a world where other guys controlled all the often-hidden, sometimes improvised, rules.

Unfair, as a word, doesn't cut it. Take the instance of Mikey:

The facts were thus: "For a period of six months commencing February, 1984, Respondent observed her four year old son's change in behavior. Mikey suddenly exhibited an unexplained fear of men. He clung to Respondent's skirts when he saw unknown men in the street. His behavior toward his father changed. He suddenly resisted going out with him alone or being picked up by him. He masturbated excessively, undressed in public and acted out in a sexually aggressive way with other children. He regressed to defecating in his clothing. He suffered from sleep disturbance, awakening from nightmares screaming 'Don't do this to me. Leave me alone.'

"The record is devoid of any proof that Respondent knew that her husband was sexually abusing their son. When she learned the specific details of the abuse from her mother (who elicited them from the child), she took appropriate action. She informed Child Protective Services, took the child to his pediatrician, and removed herself and the child from the marital residence." An earlier finding had determined the child was in fact being sexually abused by his father.

Well, okay. Is that good enough? No.

Suddenly, out of nowhere: "The issue before the court is whether Respondent neglected her child . . . by failing to exercise a minimum degree of care in not providing him with psychiatric or psychological care, and thereby contributed to or caused impairment of his emotional health."[16]

Where did *that* rule come from? How did that become the paramount issue?

And what if Mikey's mom *had* taken him for psychological counseling? Many other women found themselves specifically faulted for doing so: Taking their children for psychological evaluations and counseling was then said to exemplify an "obsession" with sexual abuse.

Any child could have told you that there was something wrong with this picture. Within several years there would be thousands of kids who could tell you in no small detail just what was wrong—from their raw experience of having become, with their mothers, entrapped in that picture's squiggly, contradictory, persecutory, go-nowhere-but-into-captivity lines. Many adults await us in the future to tell us of life in court-licensed sexual slavery.

And so for women there now were two doors marked Exit: report the abuse to protective services; or take the child and leave, seeking divorce. But on the other side of both doors was a sheer drop, a descent through the various floors of purgatory and, for most women and children, the ultimate arrival in hell. Two doors marked Exit—but no means of egress. The punch line for this joke played on thousands of women and children was that this was a "system" having a "response."

Could we have foreseen this? Yes. I suppose we could have. (What we could not have foreseen was the complete excision of any way for the public to understand it, any forum for explaining it.)

Indeed, one of the earliest victims to be sacrificed on the child-protective altar had been brought to my attention well before incest as an issue popped out of the darkness. It had seemed outrageous then (and something we would need to fix, right?).

In deference to the fact that the child involved is now over eighteen (and I do not know her whereabouts and cannot get her consent), and out of profound respect for the fact that alleged perpetrators carry a litigious gene, I will call the child Alice; her mother Mary Lou—and change other names as well.

From the court documents now before me, we learn that Mary Lou had been divorced from "Harry" in 1975. Custody of the infant child had been granted to Mary Lou with visitation to Harry.

In the winter of 1976, Alice, then five years old, had complained to Mary Lou that Harry had sexually molested her. At once bewildered, perplexed, and alarmed, Mary Lou turned to a local but nationally respected child psychiatrist, "Dr. Smith," as well as to a local clinical psychologist, "Dr. Judith Wright." Their separate opinions were that Harry had indeed sexually molested the child. And Dr. Smith advised Mary Lou not to allow Harry further visitation. (Remember, we are dealing with 1976 here, two years before incest would explode on the human interest pages of newspapers nationwide. Dr. Smith was operating on child-protective common sense.)

The following month, Harry filed in the trial court, seeking to have Mary Lou held in contempt for failure to allow visitation, and seeking custody for himself. Mary Lou's attorney filed to overrule that motion, appending the evaluations of Dr. Smith and Dr. Wright, and seeking to curtail visitation or at least forbid it to be unsupervised.

The judge, "Judge Cain," proceeded to trial, commanding Mary Lou to proceed with proof in support of her motion to terminate visitation.

At the trial of the case some four months later, Judge Cain

began by commenting that it was up to Mary Lou to prove reason to terminate visitation, and up to Harry to prove reason for a reversal of custody. No further mention was made at that time of any charge of contempt of court.

The court's findings and judgment, however, included a specific finding of contempt against Mary Lou: "The petitioner has willfully and continuously violated various orders of this Court, without justification and with no showing of mitigating circumstances."

He explained: "It might be suggested that this time the petitioner has an excuse for at least the denial of visitation, that being a psychiatrist and a psychologist believed the child's statement of child molesting. The question is not what they believed, hearing only part of the version and not knowing the background or the full factual situation: *the question is what the petitioner believed, and . . . court firmly believed the petitioner . . . caused the child to make statements, knowing full well the falsity thereof*" (italics mine).

And so we witness here, for the first time I am aware of, the tactical shift from implicating the child (as an accomplice-witness) and thus exonerating the offender, to the focus on the mother as the source of all lies (thus exonerating the offender). With this result for Alice:

"The custody of the minor child may be and is hereby transferred from the petitioner to the respondent, effective immediately, such being in the child's best interest. . . . The petitioner is found and adjudged to be in contempt of court for her willful, flagrant, and various violations of the orders of the court. As punishment, the petitioner shall be confined to the County Jail for a period of 90 days."

Could this have been taken, back then, as a premonition of the later backlash against child-protective women? Yes—if we could also have read at the time the impending change in social context, the vigorous efforts to once again silence women, to repeal their so-recently-gained rights.

One burr in Judge Cain's saddle, as it turned out, was that Mary Lou worked at that time for an outspoken feminist and writer, whom the judge referred to as a man-hater with a poor opinion of marriage, and who he said was brainwashing Mary Lou. This southern judge would seem to have been punishing Mary Lou for, in his view, having fallen among persons with seditious ideas.

At Harry's request, Judge Cain further embellished his decision by restraining Mary Lou from all communication, direct or indirect, with the child Alice—even by use of tape recordings or through third parties.

A great deal of legal wrangling followed, but the upshot is that Mary Lou has never since heard from or been allowed to communicate with her child (now, of course, no longer a child).

In light of her unwitting role as a pioneer in this vicious game (which would only see filigrees of refinement in cruelty over the coming years), it is interesting to look back over some of Mary Lou's documents. ("Document everything," her attorney had told her. "Write down whatever the child tells you.") And it is wearying to find these documents informed by the same desperate disbelief that would overwhelm mothers coming after her. ("This is America. This must be a mistake." It would all be all right if she could just get the judge to listen, to hear the child as she heard the child, and to understand not just what the child was saying about the sexual abuse, but about the other things her father was embroiling her in—group sex, drugs.)

In March 1977, Alice said (as recorded by Mary Lou):

"Before we went camping, my father, Jane, Rob and Aunt Martha took me to the hospital. We went up the stairs, the outside ones. Aunt Martha had a key. We went to the third set of stairs and Aunt Martha opened the door with her key. We went in and there was another door and that door got opened and then there was a medicine cabinet but it was up high. My father said he would give me a candy bar only if I crawled in the medicine cabinet and got the medicine. Rob lifted me up and my father gave me a key. He told me to hold it and turn the key and open the cabinet. Then he said, 'Alice, crawl in and get that little thing of medicine where the arrows are pointing to.' I got it and handed it to him. He told me to close the cabinet doors. I did it. Then we all went camping where all the bad things happened.

"I don't go with my father to get the medicine anymore. But I used to go with him and Johnny and Lou and we went to an apartment building on Reese Highway, all the way to the top. There are hippies in there with bushy beards and bushy hair and it smells like cigars and peppermint. The man gives my father and Johnny the medicine in a plastic sack. Now they go someplace else and get the medicine—anyway they don't take me. My father said I would have to learn about the medicine. He said it was good medicine. But I should have known better than believe him because when I tasted it, I came back to my mother's house with a bad stomach ache and I was sick. They keep some medicine on the third shelf above the refrigerator and the needle shot but I don't know what that medicine is either. The medicine I took is what they eat. My Aunt Martha puts green stuff in the shot needle and gives people flu shots at my father's house. Jane breaks up colored tablets and dumps them in a bowl. I don't know what it is. But I don't like to remember going to the hippie place to get the medicine because it makes me remember about my father telling me to touch myself where my mother said I shouldn't touch myself."

At the bottom of the pages Mary Lou transcribed, in a childish print-scrawl: "A L i c e."

There's a whole lot about the sexual abuse/rape. ("My father puts his penis between my legs. My father didn't say anything. He just did it. I had a Kleenex in my hand and I put it around his penis to keep the sticky stuff from getting on me. I didn't say anything. My father put his penis between my legs. Then I pulled back when he was pushing in inside against what he calls my lips. I pulled my pants back up. He pulled my pants back down.

Then he started again. . . .") But maybe you don't want to hear all that.

I remember how difficult it was to listen to this, the intensity of knowing that this was a child in the *now*; the sense of helplessness (which would become a dogged companion later). I remember thinking (hoping) well, this is one case, so far an anomaly, and it's in the *South*. . . .

It was 1981 when I first encountered a woman I will call Jan Samuels.

Although Jan was also divorced from her husband, she tried a different door to begin with: not the one marked Domestic Relations Court ("Justice is served here"), but the one marked Child Protective Services/Juvenile Court ("Help is available.") Jan was herself a social worker.

Jan wrote:

"I was married for eight plus years and left my now ex-husband in late February 1980 and filed for divorce. I have two children, Sheldon (b. 1976) and Kim (b. 1979).

"(Before I left, I had the uneasy feeling that my son was being fondled during bath time given by George. I could not determine that this was the case and, of course, really did not want to think it was so. I shared this feeling with my attorney, who thought I was crazy; or vindictive, probably.)

"We had stipulated to joint custody with the children residing with me. George had them alternate weekends, although Kim was brought home Saturday nights as she was still nursing in the A.M. and P.M. By the end of March, Sheldon was reporting that he and Dad fondled each other during visitation.

"I reported this to the Child Abuse Registry. I am myself a social worker, and I am mandated to report."

Sheldon was taken into state custody and placed in a child-care center. Jan accompanied protective service workers to have Sheldon examined at an emergency room. The records show that then-three-year-old Sheldon had told his mother that he'd been playing with his father, mutual masturbation, and the mother claimed the child told her that he took his father's penis in his mouth and they were playing and sticking fingers in each other's anus. The mother claimed the child told her that the father threatened to shoot him and cut his penis off if he told. He also talked about his father putting a screwdriver in his rectum—Jan would later tell me, with some relief, that Sheldon had told her it was the *blunt* end of the screwdriver. Such are the little good newses in this neighborhood—and about his father hurting his baby sister Kim in her vaginal area and making her cry.

The medical examination showed both kids had pharyngeal gonorrhea.

Protective services took this information to court. And the judge, perplexed that such a nice-seeming man was alleged to have done all these gross things, did what judges so often do: He turned to psychiatrists; he ordered an evaluation of George.

The evaluation found George somewhat aggressive and rigid, but found that readily understandable given what his wife was putting him through. In fact, "Save for the charges, there appears no reason subject is unfit for child custody; and to the degree his description of his wife's behavior is accurate her emotional stability is questionable."

Other psychologicals on George also found him well within normal limits; found him, in fact, completely realistic, practical, with respect for the facts, conservative, consistent, responsible, stable, painstaking, hardworking, systematic.

Interviewed (yet again) by psychologists, Sheldon said he'd been removed to foster care because of what his father was going to do to him. Asked to elaborate, he refused (he'd already *told* them). That psychologist recommended giving Sheldon to George.

Jan, of course, was evaluated as well. They found her overly sensitive to sexual issues; preoccupied with sex, sexually frustrated. And, most damning, she had been sexually molested by her stepfather when she was a child. Verdict: Give Sheldon back to George.

More psychologicals, more psychiatrists, more psychologists . . . Calendar pages were turning, as in a 1940s movie, denoting the passage of time. One expert, harking back to his Freudian training, addressed the issues of Sheldon's fantasies of abuse. Another, Jan Samuels's projecting of her unresolved problems onto Sheldon. Yet a third said Sheldon should remain in the custody of the court and foster care placement be more permanently arranged.

As psychiatrist Roland Summit wrote to me then, about this and the flood of other such cases hitting the courts:

"A normal child's complaint may be taken as valid if he happened to be molested by a disturbed adult.

"A normal child complaining against a 'normal' adult has no basis for complaint.

"A normal child seeking intervention from a normal mother against a father jeopardizes his mother. If the father is disturbed (capable of being seen as guilty by examining professionals) and the mother leaves him, she may be condemned for failing to stick by her emotionally needy husband. If she does not take action (report him or leave him) she *will* be condemned as responsible for allowing the abuse. If the father is not 'disturbed' and she leaves him, she is condemned for deserting a good husband. If she persists in the belief that the child's complaints are valid and that her husband is a menace, she is condemned for setting up the child's complaints and of overstimulating, confusing and traumatizing the child out of *her* need to deny the child his natural right to a loving father."

Jan's case went on and on, for well over two years. Jan regained custody. George got visitation, supervised by his own *mother* (for heavensakes). Both kids now testified to ongoing abuse despite that. Jan got angrier and angrier (and the court got more and more peeved) as she kept trying to protect the kids and could not.

She says, "It struck me that how I present myself would very much determine how effective I would be in protecting the kids—just another fucking way of holding me responsible. And it was pretty scary thinking that if I made a bad impression, my kid wasn't to be safe. That made me really angry, and I was always scared the anger showed. And I knew I was so enraged by the whole thing—start to finish—that it had to show."

You know what Jan Samuels considered doing in the end? (You will not like this, I bet.)

Staring hard at her choices—the ongoing possibility of totally alienating the court and losing Sheldon (and possibly Kim) to foster care or losing them to George—she considered reconciling with George.

What she said to me then was, "At least that way I can keep watch. At least that way I can have a *chance* at protecting them until they're grown up."

Things never let up in this zone of the war; my phone seemed never to stop ringing. I never stopped wondering: Where *was* everybody? Where were our troops? (Would there *be* any troops?)

Mother after mother after mother, many of them with the self-view of postfeminists—MBAs, teachers or professors, pediatricians, even attorneys, who believed the main battles had been won—found her life abruptly transformed, her career derailed, as she simply did what she believed society would support her in doing: believed her child and attempted to act to protect him or her. Each of these women proceeded with the absolute conviction that if the courts could hear what her child was saying to her, there would be no question that she would achieve the protection she sought. And—with two or three exceptions among the hundreds of women whose cases I would follow over the next years—each of them lost custody, and not infrequently all visitation, most often to the alleged abuser.

Those women who were still married when the disclosure occurred, were advised by protective services to take the child, leave the abuser, and file for divorce. This, of course, then placed the issue in the context of a custody dispute. And so it began to be evident that the great majority of child sexual abuse cases would inevitably wind up being argued as custody cases, and that the real issue of child sexual abuse in the present was doomed to be marginalized in the media, presented under the trivializing rubric of custody disputes.

On reporting the disclosure to child protective services, the women were told to get the child medically examined and psychologically evaluated. The women did so, and *secretly hoped there was some mistake, some other explanation.* Corroboration of even a "strong suspicion of sexual abuse" left them with no choice but to stay the course.

However, it also left them in a quandary. Where protective services caseworkers determined that the abuse had occurred, they would tell the mother not to let the child go for visitation. If because of a custody court order, she had to let the child go, the workers could remove the child from her for her failure to protect. But if, despite the court order, she refused to send the child—and the judge, defied, removed the child from her to the father's custody—the same workers would not act to protect the child by removal.[17]

And once a full-scale custody war was in progress over this issue, fathers' attorneys routinely intimidated protective service workers with threats of lawsuits. Their superiors then pressured them to drop the issue.[18]

Initial court hearings based on an allegation of abuse often resulted in an order for ongoing visitation pending determination. "According to one major study, accused parents were allowed unsupervised visitation in 39 percent of cases during investigation of a sexual abuse allegation; unsupervised visitation was also allowed in 29 percent of final orders in cases where allegations of sexual abuse had been determined to be valid by the caseworker or court-affiliated custody evaluator."[19]

When the children returned from visitation reporting further abuse, and/or with further physical and behavioral symptoms of abuse, the mothers—of course—returned to court.

The fathers, having hired pricey lawyers, now embarked on a counteroffensive: initiating a campaign of harassment against the mothers, including a filing for a permanent reversal of custody based on the mother's obvious emotional imbalance. . . .

Many psychological tests would be ordered, with the father testing out as normal and the mother as various kinds of disturbed: hysterical, obsessive about the issue, brainwashing the child. . . .

Women turned to the media, gag orders were issued by the courts.

Women refusing to comply with visitation were jailed for contempt. Women refusing to comply with the gag order were jailed for contempt.

That which had seemed inconceivable to the mothers drew closer: a full reversal of custody, with the child given to the father.

Findings came down making it explicit that what was at issue here was not possible or probable harm to the child, but possible damage to the man's reputation.

As attorney Joan Pennington, director of the National Center for Protective Parents writes, "When the first words out of a judge's mouth are, 'I'm not going to let you ruin this man's reputation,' it is pretty clear where this judge's bias lies. Or, as one judge stated, 'I knew she was crazy the first day I saw her in the courtroom.' One judge even said, on the record, to one mother who was telling the court that the child's father had sexually abused their infant daughter, 'You're a liar!' . . ."[20] Typically, these cases ran for years, throwing many of the women half a million dollars into debt, leaving them both broke and grievously bereft.

Marching under the banner of False Accusation Syndrome, the backlash gained power for several reasons—not least of which was the absence of any hint of historical context. Nowhere were people reminded (or informed) of how recently won were women's rights to keep their children following divorce, nor of the role economics had played in that winning. Most important, nowhere was it made plain what would have befallen these women had they *refused* to listen to the child.

Nor was any question raised or explanation offered as to what these allegations were doing being framed as an issue of custody in the first place. And this in itself served to cast doubt in the public's mind. Having been schooled in the phrase "crime of incest," it was only reasonable to think that if the allegation had merit, the issue would have been framed in the context of crime, in courts dealing with criminality. The fact that the cases were in a custody court gave credibility to their being just custody "disputes."

The backlash also gained power from judicial bias against women, most particularly against women as *mothers*, and most especially against mothers outrageous enough to allege sexual abuse.

A California task force noted that "it is much easier and more in accordance with our images of the world to regard a mother as crazy or hysterical than to recognize an otherwise seemingly rational and caring father as capable of the behaviors described."[21]

A Utah task force found that sexual abuse allegations were viewed as "emotional," not "factual"; and that women raising such allegations were presumed to be acting "solely to gain an advantage or restrict the father's visitation rights."[22]

A Massachusetts task force found much the same thing.

And what, if not bias, could account for the fact that the courts' judgments were so overwhelmingly punitive? All around the country, women began to be jailed for contempt. They lost not only custody but, sometimes, all visitation.

And yet. From the public's viewpoint, the women's credibility was endangered precisely because all this seemed so preposterous.

How could a judge deliberately give custody of a child to a rapist? On the other hand, how could it be that so many judges were making such egregious mistakes?

Women, reading of these "custody" cases, were loath to entertain what was clearly implied. That in that one moment of your child's disclosure, everything you had believed to be true—about your husband (or even ex-husband), and about your access to fairness—could be stood on its head.

All this confusion aided the father's-rights activists who, by now, had established an organization that pretended to populism, and invigorated semi-informed protest in communities throughout the country. These groups gained power from available money; from historical male right; and from the unambivalent sense that a display of might would continue to secure that right.

Their sense of insult and injury, and their profound knowledge that this was a political war, a war to safeguard their rights, left them less than susceptible to qualms about making claims that might be just a whit hyperbolic.* They had none of Jan Samuels's concerns that a display of anger would make them vulnerable to charges of hysteria or vindictiveness. In men, sheer rage can be taken for reasonable outrage, for righteous indignation: for a sign that their circumstance is indeed demanding of remedy.

Fronted by "experts," they came up with "validity" tests of transparent bias and questionable validity.

In 1987, Dr. Richard Gardner, clinical professor of child psychiatry at Columbia University, media commentator, and child-abuse theoretician, proposed his Sex Abuse Legitimacy Scale, or, SAL Scale ("an instrument for differentiating between bona fide and fabricated sex-abuse allegations of children") in conjunction with an emotional disorder he called Parental Alienation

---

* Passion apparently inured them, as well, to aligning themselves with authors like Paul and Shirley Eberle (*The Politics of Child Abuse*, Secaucus, N.J.: Lyle Stuart, 1986), who "edit a soft-core magazine in California called the *L.A. Star* that contains a mixture of nude photos, celebrity gossip, telephone sex ads, and promos [for the book]" (*Ms.*, December 1988, 92).

Syndrome (PAS).[23] As Gardner reportedly described it: "In PAS, the mother and children are so intent on driving away the father that they launch a campaign of disparagement that can include falsely accusing him of sexually abusing his offspring."[24] Although reports are that Dr. Gardner no longer endorses the legitimacy scale psychological test, it was nonetheless quickly embraced at the time by numerous evaluators, and continues to be employed by many who seem unaware that Gardner has abandoned it.[25]

There are a number of disclaimers offered preliminary to using this diagnostic tool. One that strikes me as interesting reads: "The SAL Scale is not designed to be used as a questionnaire, wherein the examiner asks the interviewee his or her opinion regarding whether or not a criterion is present. If direct input from the interviewee is elicited, it is very likely that the conclusions will be contaminated by the bias of the respondent. Rather, the scale should be used *after* the interviews with the child, accuser, and accused have been completed."[26]

If I am not misreading, what this means is that if you ask the "interviewee" whether, for instance, he/she is "very hesitant to divulge the sexual abuse," you will be soliciting *her* opinion. But if you privately decide as to that subsequently, you will be (properly) soliciting only *yours*. In this way (evidently) you will be avoiding bias.

Okay. (This is going to get a little confusing, but bear with me.) We are now instructed by the rules of this test that the greater the number of *yes* answers, the greater the likelihood that the result is no—the sexual abuse has not been fabricated. (And the more no's there are, the likelier it is that the answer is yes—the sexual abuse allegation has been fabricated.)

Under the "very valuable" list of differentiating criteria, here is what you must ask the child:

• Whether she is "very hesitant to divulge"
• Whether she fears retaliation by the accused

- Whether she is guilty over what may happen to the accused
- Whether she is guilty over having participated in the sex acts
- Whether she can provide specific details
- Whether *you* find these specifics credible ("Description of the sex abuse credible")
- Whether the child can describe in unvarying language the abuse over repeated interviews*
- Whether the child is often sexually excited apart from the abuse encounters
- Whether she considers her genitals to have been damaged
- "Desensitization play engaged in at home or during the interview" (whatever that means)
- Whether the child has been threatened or bribed by the accused not to tell

In the next questions, the scale's designer shows understandable signs of some grammatical wear and tear from all this yes/no-ing: "If a parental alienation syndrome is *not* present, check *Yes*." (Yes, a parental alienation syndrome is not present.) "If a parental alienation syndrome *is* present, check *No*." (No, a parental alienation syndrome is present.)

And finally (for the child): "If the *complaint* was *not* made in the context of a child custody dispute or litigation, check *Yes*. If there *is* such a dispute, check *No*."

When it comes to very valuable questions for the *accuser* ("Especially when the accuser is the mother"), you are to decide for her:

- Whether she denies and downplays the abuse
- Whether the complaint was made in the context of child custody litigation
- Whether she feels ashamed at revealing the abuse

---

* This one is interesting because such an unvarying description is often used as proof that the child has in fact been programmed.

And, along the same line of neutral questioning: "If she does *not* want to destroy, humiliate, or wreak vengeance on the accused, check *Yes.*" Continuing on: "If she has *not* sought a 'hired gun' attorney or mental health professional, check *Yes.*" And, "If she does *not* attempt to corroborate the child's sexual abuse description in joint interview(s), check *Yes.*"

It has been said by critics of this scale that it has absolutely no basis for credibility, but it seems to me that, if *credibility* is the issue, it *does* indeed have that: its credibility derives from the messages that have been arduously promulgated for years: that the child doesn't tell (whether she is "very hesitant to divulge"); and she doesn't want her daddy punished (whether she is guilty over what may happen to the accused). That the mother doesn't want to believe her child (whether she denies and downplays the abuse); her goal is to keep daddy in the home; that any mother who leaves the guy on discovery of the abuse or has left him previously, is therefore automatically suspect (whether the complaint was made in the context of child custody litigation)—because she has not done what incest mothers do.

Jon Conte, associate professor at the University of Chicago's School of Social Service Administration, called the sex abuse legitimacy scale "probably the most unscientific piece of garbage I've seen in the field in all my time."[27] Ann Haralambie, a Tuscon, Arizona, lawyer and past president of the National Association of Counsel for Children, faults Gardner for using a "misapplied legal principle"—that it's better to allow 100 guilty men to go free than to wrongly convict one innocent man.[28] As Haralambie points out, "That principle comes from the criminal justice arena and has no legal application to a custody dispute. Put in proper context, the principle could be stated: it is better that 100 molested children go unprotected than one molested child have the parent-child relationship inappropriately interfered with."[29]

As for me, it reminded me a lot of the science that dictated the dunking stool, a test (scale) also informed by preexisting mythology: You tie the lady to a long pole resting on a central fulcrum. Lower her into the pond or lake and if she doesn't drown she is guilty, and if she does drown—well, what's the difference, she's dead.

Indeed, your basic Witch Detector Scale might not look too awfully different from the SAL Scale.

- Does not talk to animals (yes, she is not a witch)
- Attends church (ditto)
- Takes walks in the moonlight (no, she is a witch)

It would certainly *seem* as though the guys crying witch-hunt were in fact the ones hunting witches.

———

For all the cries about men being branded and hauled off in leg irons, there is, of course, no question of a "conviction" for men in a custody proceeding—any more than there is for women accused of unfitness or, in a family court setting, neglect. What is being weighed is the significance of possible or probable abuse as against the reputation of an otherwise upstanding man.

How can one adequately convey the insanity loosed here—the sense that somewhere, some higher power was clutching his ribs, overcome by sidesplitting laughter, looking around at what had befallen uppity women who had dared, finally, to confront the core of sexual politics, of male right. It served them right, these women who had not only had the nerve to challenge licensed male physical assault but were now complaining about a little harmless nooky with the kids (which, hey, we didn't do anyway, and she's crazy—or venal, or vindictive, or hysterical—if she thinks we did).

The most astounding feature of the lunacy that had been loosed lay in the fact that all of the claims made by the backlash groups crying False Accusation Syndrome were constructed entirely of sand, smoke, mirrors: Couched in the language of psychiatric science, they had never been validated as science. They were not based on anything in the vicinity of the reality of children's or women's experiences, nor were they validated by empirical studies (in fact quite the opposite).*

Some whole-cloth assumptions that were proffered without any evidence were

- that mothers were so enchanted with the idea of having a child sexually abused by her husband or ex-husband that they would embrace and elaborate the slightest hint. Or, more tellingly, that the mothers themselves may have been molested. "The latter may often render them hypervigilant to the possibility [of] the same fate befalling their daughters."[30]
- that the mothers made these allegations with a fair certainty that visitation would then be denied the accused.
- that, "In most cases, the initial and immediate response of the judicial system is to suspend any visitation between the accused non-custodial parents and his children." That, in fact, "crying wolf"—the making of allegations of sexual abuse—"is a sure way of getting the judge's attention and suspending visitation in situations where parent was dissatisfied with the custody arrangement."[31]

There was absolutely no evidence that fathers were more than rarely denied visitation *under any circumstances*, including allegations of abuse. And there was certainly no evidence that what

---

* It is simply not true that charges of sexual abuse are more prevalent in custody and visitation cases than elsewhere. It is the backlash's unsubstantiated claims that are, in fact, the False Accusation. See Nancy Thoennes, "Child Sexual Abuse: Whom Should a Judge Believe? What Should a Judge Believe?," *Judges Journal* 14 (Summer 1988): 14–18, 48–50.

motivates women to go through the tortures involved is the glee of "crying wolf," nor that they could have any reasonable expectation of anything other than dark troublesome waters ahead. "Mothers who make claims of sexual abuse in the context of divorce proceedings often lose custody as a result. The courts in these cases find the mothers to be the real abusers for making the allegations and for forcing their children to undergo the physical and psychological evaluations necessary to prove their claim."[32]

But if the backlash experts felt no need for scientific rigor, neither did they seem to feel the need to bother with any disguise of neutrality, or restrain from unbridled supposition as support for their conjectured hypothesis. As Richard Gardner writes, "I believe that the reluctance by sex-abuse workers to recognize and accept the increasing frequency of fabricated sex-abuse allegations relates to certain psychological factors operative in their career choice. . . . I believe that people who have been sexually abused themselves in childhood are much more likely to enter this field than those who have not had such childhood experiences."[33]

Well, that is pretty candid: It is what he *believes*, based only on his psychological analysis:

"They vent their pent-up hostility on present-day offenders [sic] in a work setting that provides sanctions for such pathological release. And some of these workers operate on the principle that there will never be enough perpetrators to punish, so great is their desire to wreak vengeance on those who sexually molest children. Concluding that an alleged perpetrator is indeed innocent deprives them of their vengeful gratification."[34]

It is interesting that the missile chosen to be lobbed at those professionals seeking to expose "present-day offenders"—as a form of "pathological release"—is that they were themselves sexually abused. This marries well with the widespread notion that women who have been sexually abused marry abusers. It marries well also with the proposed truth that women who have been sexually abused are prone to hysterical allegations about their children's abuse. And it contrasts nicely with the fact that psychologists studying such matters explained that men who have been sexually abused naturally became offenders because they are simply helpless to control themselves: They are not accountable; their experience drove them to it. Thus has childhood sexual abuse been invoked for convenience—as cause for vengeful gratification in women and as a plea of mitigating circumstance in men.

Let it not be said that there was anything very subtle going on here.

Gardner also states that "my experience with children who have genuinely been abused sexually is less than that with children who have fabricated sex abuse. This relates to my deep involvement in custody litigation in which the vast majority of children who profess sexual abuse are fabricators."[35] Yet he elsewhere claims to fully appreciate that "genuine sex abuse of children is widespread and the vast majority of sex allegations of children (from *all* of the aforementioned categories combined) [i.e., including those made during custody disputes] are likely to be justified (perhaps 95% of them)."[36] How is it, then, that he so magnetically attracts only those cases he is certain are false?

In a letter published in the September 6, 1993, *National Law Journal* in response to an article by Rorie Sherman ("Gardner's Law"), Dr. Gardner wrote:

"Ms. Sherman refers to 'prosecutors who generally see him as an ideological witness for the defense.' The implication here is that I am a 'hired gun' and do not testify for the plaintiffs who are alleging sex abuse. It is true that I most often testify for the defense; however, I do designate sex abuse perpetrators as such when I identify them. They, however, do not bring me to court to testify against them."[37]

One could only watch and wonder: If we had been wrong about incest as the cradle of sexual politics, why did everything that was happening continue to make it seem that we were right? Why did it seem impossible to look at all this and see in the ferment and fulmination any other, more plausible, explanation?

What was there to be seen was sheer slaughter. Because political understanding had been so completely masked, the women who stumbled onto the front lines of virulent warfare did so without any reason to believe there was even a war going on, and with no premonition of what might lie ahead. They had for the most part cooperated with visitation prior to the child's disclosure. Indeed, often it was the fathers who had commenced harassment with abrupt and arbitrary demands and reversals concerning times, and even with petitions for reversal of custody.

Despite much of the fathers'-rights rhetoric about angry radical feminism, the women had not been politically informed or motivated before the child's disclosure: Most had been involved in their dailiness—be it full-time mothering or mothering plus high-powered career.

The mothers all believed that in acting protectively they were doing not only what they felt they had to do but what they should do and what they believed the law demanded; and they staunchly believed that the courts would share that primary goal. One by one by one, they received shock after shock after shock. As gag orders were issued by the courts, forbidding them to talk publicly about the case; as they were threatened with indefinite jail sentences for contempt of court; and as they networked and learned theirs was far from a unique situation, it only then began to come clear to them that what they were caught up in was nothing less than a full-scale civil rights struggle in a world in which they had believed their civil rights to be assured.

Abruptly, they found themselves instead in a universe shot through with prejudice, stereotyping, and a prevailing view of their value as zilch and their rights as nothing, in combat with those doubly endowed: *men* who were *fathers*. They did not, as blacks in the civil rights struggle had, have any suspicion going in of what it was they were getting into, or any way of anticipating the level of viciousness and rage that could be turned on them (and then turned upside-down, and alleged to be the proper result of *their* viciousness, their rage).

It is no wonder that, with cases like this, all following this pattern, in every state in the country an "underground railroad" was formed (so dubbed by the media). It was an interesting appellation, connoting as it did rebellious slaves making their way through a network of safe houses north to freedom. The only problem was that, for these women and children, there *was* no north. Women and children from Canada were similarly seeking escape by coming *south*.

The Canadian publication *Jurisfemme*, published by the National Association of Women and the Law (NAWL), tells us that "in November 1987, the British Columbia Continuing Legal Education Society sponsored a seminar on sexual abuse allegations in custody litigation. The mood and theme of the conference were distressingly typical of a backlash stance increasingly adopted by the press and a number of lawyers, mediators, bureaucrats, fathers' rightists and at least one teachers' organization."[38] Quoting Dr. Summit: "The bias against mothers who complain is so bad that a woman who is aware of it is often told that she may do well not to bring it up because it will only bring trouble on herself."[39]

The article continues, "NAWL noted (to no avail) in 1985, that the 'friendly parent rule,' by giving legislative endorsement to the *pre-eminence* of continued contact with the non-custodial parent, might only serve to reinforce the difficulties that parents have in protecting their children from sexual abuse.

"At the B. C. [British Columbia] Continuing Legal Education conference, the interest of many participants lay in examining strategies to protect accused parents. And it wasn't simply the right to a fair hearing that they wanted to protect. The goal appeared to be to silence the accusers.... Some participants called for special criminal sanctions against accusers and their lawyers whenever 'unfounded' allegations are made."

Faced with the question of whether this might make it somewhat difficult for women attempting to protect their children from what they honestly believed was harmful behavior, "it was suggested that unless there was irrefutable medical evidence of the abuse, the custodial parent should not raise the allegation."[40] Not only is *irrefutable* medical evidence, of course, in the eye of the beholder, but an entire secondary system, the child protective system, would be most intolerant of women who expressed a demand for that level of proof before acting.

In the Canadian meeting there was one person present who offered up candor. It was his expressed opinion as a lawyer who acts for accused parents, that sexual abuse was not the paramount issue here. Rather, the *serious* issue was the preservation of the parent/child relationship. Resorting to history, he suggested that "sexual activity between children and adults is something viewed differently at different times and in different places." He asked, "If the incidence of sexual abuse has been accurately determined ... how is it possible that it went undetected? Has there been a conspiracy of silence in a society in which men habitually abuse women? Or is it possible that there is no universally shared view as to what conduct is appropriate and what is not?"[41]

In other words, he was asking that which so many men had for so long been asking: What makes everyone think child sexual abuse by a *father* has to be such a big deal?

A family law attorney summarized her impressions of the conference:

"The message throughout this conference was loud and clear: Despite our knowledge that sexual abuse often begins at the point of separation of the parents; despite our developing awareness of the frequency of sexual abuse in our society; despite the acknowledged rarity of false allegations in custody litigation, women are being advised not to raise their concerns, because they risk losing custody to the abuser."[42] And they risked losing custody because, contrary to general assumption, there was no abiding consensus that such abuse was "abuse," or at least was abuse anywhere near comparable to what men would suffer from such a challenge to their rights, from such a blot on their reputation.

Once again, but in a new context, that which we had said proved true: Incest was not the taboo, talking about it was. Only it was not adult survivors talking about it that was proving catalytic: it was women as mothers *now*, trying to protect children *now*.

An underground railroad, then, was not only a reasonable response. Since not acting was now fraught with danger, and acting within the system was fraught with equal danger, it was the only possible response.

―――――

Meanwhile, the False Accusation folks had found themselves a figurehead: a real living Morris County, New Jersey, man, Dr. Lawrence D. Spiegel, who had actually been arrested and charged with sexually abusing his young daughter. A man who had been exonerated, who wrote a book that tells his story, *A Question of Innocence*. A man who'd actually been *handcuffed*—there's a picture on page 55 of his book—booked, fingerprinted, and released on bail. The press picked up the story: As Dr. Spiegel, offended by some of the coverage, says, "The newspaper articles did not mention that this was a family matter. It sounded as though I had molested some strange two-year-old baby."[43]

As Dr. Spiegel recounts events, he was surely the victim of a miracle. Neither a mental health professional, Dr. Walter B. Frankel, nor a pediatrician to whom Spiegel's wife had taken the child, found any evidence that the child had been abused. Yet New Jersey's Department of Youth and Family Services not only turned the case over to a prosecutor, but the prosecutor agreed to take the case. (Perhaps due to the fact that a third physician found that "something had happened," based on the child's nightmares and genital-area redness.) According to a newspaper report, "The prosecutor's office notified the family's doctor who confirmed the girl had been sexually assaulted, said the police."[44]

It is an extremely emotional story, as told by Dr. Spiegel. "When I thought of Jessie spending Christmas so far away and having no explanation as to my absence, I sunk into the deepest depression yet. I really did not want to live, but my logical mind would not let me carry out my fantasies of suicide."[45] His was a degree of emotionality that—in a protective mother charged with unfitness and denied contact with her child (even at Christmas)—one suspects would have been taken for pathology.

Things grew even more dramatic as the clinical director of the institute of which Spiegel was executive director not only sought to have him ousted but actually cooperated with the prosecutor. In response to which (in blind anger) Spiegel shouted, "I'd like to kill you for all that you've done to me!"[46]

Whereupon, the next day, "Suddenly with no warning, police officers and members of the Prosecutor's office burst into the building with guns drawn. Two of them broke into my office, told me to face the wall and spread my arms and legs. One of them held a gun to my head and demanded I give him the keys to [Spiegel's girlfriend's parents'] camper." He was patted down and heard the sounds of police officers raiding offices and dragging terrified therapists out at gunpoint.

He had to raise ($1,000) bail, in addition to hiding out in case other charges were pending.

On the whole, it would seem Dr. Spiegel could have felt more confident in his eventual exoneration early on. The judge is on record as saying, "What if it turns out that this is a totally fraudulent charge trumped up by an angry wife using this deprivation of visitation as some sort of leverage? . . . Let's just assume . . . that you have an evil, venal woman who has put up her child to make scurrilous, unfounded, totally untrue charges against her husband or ex-husband . . . ?"[47] Rather, Dr. Spiegel found his cause for hope while watching the Phil Donahue show—as those accused in the Jordan case, along with Ralph Underwager, Ph.D., announced the formation of VOCAL and discussed the railroading of innocent people.[48] VOCAL encouraged Dr. Spiegel to form a New Jersey chapter. He did, and they went on the offensive, filing a class action suit against the state of New Jersey.

Dr. Spiegel recounts the increase in media coverage; more stories of men, accused of molesting their children, now turned into "overnight activists," challenging protective services intervention.

One cannot doubt that threats of suits directed at protective service agencies across the country were overwhelmingly effective. These agencies have never been able to stand much scrutiny; finding organizational shortcomings and mismanagement in them is like shooting fish in a barrel. An organized group of middle class, often professional, *respectable* men (albeit some who had been accused—falsely, of course—of molesting their children), men who had the wherewithal to sue and media credibility as middle-class citizens, were a formidable enemy—a far cry from the complaining poor, minority, single mothers who had heretofore been the agency's focus of specialization.

Meanwhile, the judge was giving Dr. Spiegel still more reason to feel optimistic. In explaining that he had ruled the child *competent* to testify in court (on closed-circuit television), he took pains to explain that competency is a different issue from *credibility*. Indeed, he is quoted in the *Daily Record* as saying he recognizes there were indications that the child had been, if not programmed then *encouraged* by her mother, and that the child's terminology in private interviews suggested she was being influenced ("whether maliciously or sincerely") by the mother. But of course that determination would be up to the jury.[49]

The jury's verdict: Not guilty.

Dr. Spiegel, who had been working on his manuscript all through the trial, announced that the proceeds from his book would go to VOCAL.

In family court, Dr. Spiegel now filed for full custody. In the event, he gained joint legal custody, liberal visitation in his home, and full parental rights.

The case of one man's acquittal, paraded across TV screens throughout the country, gave weight to the allegation that hundreds of men's parental rights were being abruptly severed as they were dragged off to jail in handcuffs, following women's false accusations and the brainwashing of small children.

Even as, in another part of the country (as they say), the mother of one small child was in hiding and about to die.

Chapter 7

THE GREAT INCEST
MASSACRE II

THE HOUSE WAS EMPTY.

The streets were deserted.

The phone was dead.

It was, in short, the perfect atmosphere in which to spend time with the haunting figure of a young woman, recently dead, Dorrie Lynn Singley. It was in this house that Dorrie had hidden for what would prove to be the remainder of her life: on the run, attempting to protect her young daughter, whom Dorrie said she had seen being sexually violated by her husband. She had left and divorced him. He had then sought the custody of the child.

The door to the room Dorrie had stayed in, upstairs, remained closed, as it had since her death—at once a shrine and a gothic grace note.

This was the New Orleans home of Judy Watts, director of Agenda for Children, an advocacy group. Judy, along with other activists and mothers from Louisiana and Mississippi, had become enmeshed in Dorrie's struggles, along with those of another young mother, Karen Newsom, similarly situated.

Now, gone off to work, Judy has left me with a copy of the journal Dorrie had kept over the last two months of her life.

A modestly educated girl from the rural South, Dorrie was an unlikely tragic heroine—martyr, if you like—in this struggle: a young woman who liked to sew, iron, cook, sing to her kids; who had most likely never had a political thought before falling victim to what she could not fail to know was a deliberately enacted display of raw power, designed to silence her—though perhaps not to sentence her to death. ("Dear lady," said the judge, Sebe Dale, Jr., to a reporter on learning of Dorrie's death. "I am extremely sorry to hear that she has expired. I don't wish that on anyone I know or don't know."[1])

"The saddest day in my life," Dorrie wrote in her journal, discovered the day following her death, "was telling my 8-year-old-son goodbye, and my 7-month-old son. And then came my 5-year-old daughter, whom I've tried and will continue to protect, goodbye. They know I love them. I hope God helps each one through this horrid time we're going through."[2]

It is historically fitting that the first two cases to clearly illuminate the issue as one of *civil rights* took place in Mississippi, locus of so many earlier civil rights struggles. These two 1987 cases were firsts in other ways as well: They were the cases that threw up our first combat fatality; the cases that triggered the start-up of what the media billed as the "underground railroad" for mothers (now, I am told, being called, alas, for mothers in "protecting flight"). And the cases triggered the first attempted disbarment of an attorney advocating for the children and mothers (again reminiscent of earlier combat tactics employed against civil rights attorneys). Also, these cases witnessed the first truly massive lawsuits against anyone and everyone who was involved or active on these mothers' behalf.*

---

* Tim Foxworth, the father of Dorrie Lynn Singley's child, Chrissy, filed a lawsuit, first for $6 billion, then reduced to $156 million, naming every person who had been in any way involved in the case since its beginning. The case was eventually settled out of court for four thousand dollars. (Testimony of H. Joan Pennington, Esq.,

Dorrie's is also "the only case in the history of Mississippi and in the country, where a Chancery Court Judge and a Youth Referee have been found guilty of having violated a child's constitutional rights of access to the court and procedural due process."[3]

And still, in the end, the custody of both Dorrie's and Karen's children—all of whom had spoken and spoken of abuse, for which there was strong psychological and physical corroboration—was given to the fathers because the judge did not believe or value that evidence. In that most critical way, then, these two cases were no different from hundreds of other such travesties enacted in every state of the nation, throughout the 1980s and into the 1990s—and for god-knows-how-many years to come.

Karen Newsom and Dorrie Lynn Singley were very different women (Karen was described in the press as articulate, intelligent, a teacher), but they shared the same judge, and they shared with hundreds of other women across the country the same eventual resolution.

———

It was the summer of 1984 when Dorrie said she saw her husband, Tim Foxworth, kiss two-year-old Chrissy in the vaginal area as the child lay on Dorrie and Tim's bed. But she said it was when she later observed him in the bathroom, having Chrissy play with his penis, that she took the child and left.

Filing for divorce on the grounds of habitual, cruel, and inhuman treatment, Dorrie got custody of Chrissy and Tim received visitation one night every other week.

Following the divorce, Dorrie took the children and moved to Texas. Tim filed a motion for contempt in March of 1985, claiming denial of visitation. Dorrie did not receive notice, so she did not appear. The hearing was held in her absence that August.

Executive Director, on Behalf of the National Center of Protective Parents in Civil Child Abuse Cases; Before the U.S. House of Representatives Judicial Committee, *Re* The Judicial Training Act, August 6, 1992.)

And—for the first time—mention was made by the father's witness, Tiffany Sears, that the reason Dorrie would not allow Chrissy to visit with her father was because Dorrie believed Tim was sexually abusing the child. First time it was ever mentioned; first time it ever came up.

It was paid no mind, and an order was entered for Dorrie's arrest for contempt of court-ordered visitation.

Dorrie knew about none of this.

It was May of 1986, when she moved back to Mississippi, that she first learned about the arrest warrant. She retained an attorney, James ("Buddy") Hayden of Hattiesburg, to represent her at a court hearing, and immediately complied with Foxworth's visitation on July 4.

Despite this, on July 8 she was arrested for contempt and was jailed for the next ten days.

Released from jail, Dorrie sought help from the district attorney of Marion County, Richard Douglas, who told her that before any criminal proceedings could occur, Dorrie had to have physical evidence of the sexual abuse. Still complying with visitation, Dorrie took Chrissy—now four—to the Hancock General Hospital emergency room. The examining physician filed a "Report of Suspected Battered Child" with the Hancock County Welfare Department, noting the physical symptoms he observed and suggesting Chrissy may have been sexually abused. He then sent Dorrie on to meet with the Hancock County Welfare Department, where a caseworker recommended an examination by a pediatrician experienced in child sexual abuse cases.[4]

A week later, the worker and Dorrie took Chrissy to Dr. Bryant McCrary, who examined Chrissy and *also* filed a "Report of Suspected Battered Child." He stated that his findings were "very suspicious of child abuse." In addition, Dr. McCrary notified Margaret Alfonso, assistant district attorney for Hancock County, of his finding of possible abuse.[5]

Alfonso interviewed Chrissy the next day. Chrissy was explicit about the sexual abuse that had occurred during the November visits, and Alfonso was convinced that the evidence was strong enough to warrant advising the district attorney to go forward with criminal prosecution.[6]

Alfonso also recommended attorney Garnett Harrison to Dorrie, suggesting Harrison file for modified visitation to protect the child from abuse.

In light of what was to follow, it seems almost cruel that, up to this point, Dorrie had been given nothing but corroboration that what she was doing was just and right, and encouragement to proceed.

Had Dorrie any knowledge that at roughly this same time, Elizabeth Morgan in Washington, D.C., was found in contempt of court and jailed for similarly trying to protect her child? Or that Virginia LaLonde had shortly before been driven to flee Massachusetts rather than comply with the demand that her daughter visit with the father the child said had abused her? And, if she had had such knowledge, would it have changed her outlook? Probably not. Each of the mothers in these cases believes not only the child, and the physical and psychological corroboration she receives, but believes she is following a societally endorsed imperative that she protect the child. It is, after all, an imperative that certainly looks and sounds and feels like it's authentically there.

Jeannine Athas, another mother who fought long and lost, reminds me that, when she first came to see me, I tried, somewhat diffidently, to explain what might lie ahead, based on all I had seen. And—an MBA, a successful international businesswoman—she had nonetheless not been swayed: Such a right thing to do must be do-able. If anyone can do it, *I* can. My case is different. My documentation is clear. I will not be defeated.

In other words, each of the mothers begins by believing that this is about no more than the protection of a child who states unequivocally to her and, at least initially, to medical doctors, psychologists, and caseworkers, that he or she is being abused. It is only over time that the mothers discover that systematic and deliberate vilification, denigration, punishment, and mockery of *her* has become the only significant point: The child is the trophy, to be ceremoniously awarded to the man whose paternal right the mother has so recklessly elected to challenge. Far from being male-defying radicals, these women are then radicalized by indomitable events—one by one by one. Each, however, would formulate her defiance not in terms of her *own* rights, but in terms of the rights of her child.*

As Dorrie, addressing Judge Dale, would write in her journal: "No child deserves to be raped and no child should have to live with her rapist."[7]

The next bit of dithering in Dorrie's case was simply over which county would handle it, and in which court it would be heard. When it was determined that Judge Dale would handle the case in chancery court, the welfare department closed out its case.**

In December of 1986, Tim Foxworth again petitioned for custody of Chrissy. It was determined by Garnett Harrison and Foxworth's lawyer that, pending a court decision, visitation would be supervised by Foxworth's mother. Now Foxworth retained a neuropsychiatrist to evaluate himself, Dorrie, and Chrissy. So Garnett Harrison advised Dorrie to take Chrissy for a further evaluation by Gulfport psychologist Catherine Meeks.

According to Harrison, "During this period of time, Chrissy was extremely reluctant to say anything about what was occurring during the visits. She stated to Dr. Meeks that her father 'had hurt her in the bathtub.' "[8]

---

* It is interesting that, although the conversation was often put in terms of the fathers' rights or the children's rights, no mother ever made mention of her own rights, and indeed—when I suggested such a phrase—each rejected it out of hand. "It's not about *my* rights," Jeannine Athas said to me recently. "It's about the protection of my *child*."

** It is common when a case heads into custody courts for the child welfare/protective service system to bow out of the picture.

Nonetheless, evaluating professionals on both sides said that they could not rule out sexual abuse. For the next seven months, until July of 1987, Foxworth continued to exercise supervised visitation.

———

Karen had been divorced from Eugene Newsom in April 1986, with the father receiving visitation every other weekend and one month during the summer.

According to Karen, it was after a July visitation that her daughter, Katie, told her mother about sexual intrusions by the father. Karen retained Garnett Harrison as her attorney and filed a complaint, hoping to restrict visitation.

Eugene countersued for custody.

Over the next eight months, Karen would continue to send Katie and her son, Adam (age one) for visitation.

During this time, Katie began masturbating, developed night terrors, and was no longer potty trained. But it was only after visitation in February when Katie came back extremely red in the genital area and complaining that her "booty" hurt that Karen consulted two local physicians. They said that Katie's genital area was badly swollen, in such a way that the child could not have caused it herself.

During the summer of 1987, the Newsom and the Singley cases came together in Judge Dale's court.

Karen's trial lasted from July 23 to July 24. Despite expert testimony, Judge Dale refused to restrict visitation rights even temporarily. And in his August 3 opinion he found that Karen had been abusive and committed a "witch-hunt." He said:

"The assertions by Karen, together with the supporting assertions by the expert witnesses, particularly by Dr. McCrary, M.D., and Dr. Meeks, Ph.D., are expressions of suspicion and are, at best, their personal conclusions which are not supported by any factual basis. Indeed the fervor exhibited by these persons to condemn and convict Gene with no more to sustain them than the present leads the court to exclaim 'Shades of Old Salem.' "

The children had indeed been abused, he said, but by the *mother*: "Karen has subjected them to numerous unwarranted doctor's visits/examinations, and especially is this applicable to Katie. Katie has been compelled by Karen to attend at least 15 sessions with Dr. Meeks, a psychologist, virtually all of them having been of 60 minutes' duration, during which Katie has been subjected to subtleties of psychological interrogation and cross-examination, much of it revealed to have involved inferences and suggestions to the child albeit veiled."[9]

Dale transferred full custody of Katie and Adam to the father.

Just one day later, Judge Dale rendered his opinion in Dorrie Singley's case. Noting that she'd had two children out of wedlock, he found her an unfit mother. He said:

"The living circumstances and lifestyle of Dorrie Lynn shown to exist since her return to Mississippi are sorely lacking in stability and are reflective of lack of maturity and sense of responsibility on the part of Dorrie Lynn as it pertains to Chrissy, and subjects Chrissy to influences and environment which the court finds to be detrimental to the best interest of Chrissy."[10]

He transferred full custody of Chrissy to the father.

Both Karen and Dorrie decided independently to evade the court order at least long enough to have the children evaluated at Children's Hospital in New Orleans by Dr. Rebecca Russell, a pediatrician specially trained in the use of the colposcope—a diagnostic device that can see what the naked eye cannot.

Dr. Russell concluded that both children had been harmed in ways that could only have been caused by molestation, not by some self-inflicted injury. About Chrissy, Russell wrote that she had found "physical evidence of old, well-healed trauma to the hymen and perihymenal area consistent with repeated penetration by some object." She explained, "Several of the genital findings could *only* be caused by molestation, and not from vaginal infection or self-stimulation by the child."[11]

Harrison filed an appeal for a new hearing based on new evidence on behalf of both children with the Mississippi Supreme Court. Both petitions were denied.

Richard Ducote, a New Orleans attorney then becoming prominent for representing mothers trying to protect their children, became Harrison's cocounsel. His advice was to go public, and so on August 14, after both Karen and Dorrie had sent their children into hiding, a press conference was held at the Mississippi Children's Defense Fund in Jackson, Mississippi. "Mothers Defy Court, Keep Children," front-paged the *Sun Herald*.[12]

"Moms Will Brave Jail to Protect Allegedly Sexually Abused Kids," cried the *Clarion-Ledger Daily News*.[13]

Both the *Sun Herald* and the *Clarion-Ledger Daily News* recorded Foxworth's attorney's position: "This is a classic example of a mother crying child abuse where there is no child abuse." But they simply did not know what to make of Dale's grandiosity, the spectacularly punitive act of severing the children from the mothers. "Judge Dale dismissed as unconvincing the expert testimony that resulted from [the children's psychological and physical examinations], saying the conclusions those experts reached were 'not supported by any factual basis' and were even reminiscent of the Salem witch trials. . . . But for the judge to go far beyond that and accuse the mother of abusing the children, then take custody away from her, is incomprehensible. This is especially so since the psychiatrist Judge Dale, himself, had appointed as a special advisor to the court had recommended some of the very psychological sessions the judge found abusive."[14]

Both Karen and Dorrie stated that they had now hidden their children in defiance of a court order awarding custody to the fathers.

" 'I don't intend to turn them over,' " Newsom said of her children, Katie 3½ and Adam, 2½. " 'I'm sure I'll be found in contempt, which I am in contempt. I'll stay in jail.' "

" 'And I'll follow in right behind her,' said Singley. . . ."[15] (Although no contempt order had yet been issued against Dorrie, Foxworth filed for one only two days later.)

And so a movement was born: a group of outraged mothers whose children had been victimized met and organized as Mothers Against Raping Children (MARC).

On August 20, Karen Newsom presented herself at the contempt hearing, refused to state where the children were, and was ordered to jail by Judge Dale, "until she has purged herself to the satisfaction of this court and by compliance with the August 3, 1987, decree of this court [to turn the children over]."[16]

Karen was quoted as saying, "I think the judge felt like: How dare the mother accuse the father of such horrible acts? I don't want to be here. I don't want to be anybody's hero, I don't want to be a martyr. But, I didn't have a choice. My kids would have gone back to being abused, and they would have looked at me one day and said, 'You knew, how could you send me back?' "[17]

Dorrie's hearing was set for the following week. She did not show up. Instead, she sent a statement, exonerating Garnett Harrison and taking full responsibility for her decision. She said, "I am certain as I am preparing this statement that I will be put in Marion County jail if I were to appear at my hearing." And, "I will not turn custody over to the father of my child who I honestly believe has sexually abused her."

And, "It seems to me that one mother in jail protecting her children from sexual abuse is one too many." And, as though with uncanny prescience: "To go to jail for me means a life sentence."[18]

An order was issued for Dorrie's arrest.

The day of her hearing, Dorrie wrote, "I've chosen not to go. . . . How dare Judge Dale order me to jail for protecting what God gave me to love and protect, Chrissy." The next day, she wrote, "I'm glad I didn't go. I think they intended to lynch me. . . . I saw the news coverage. . . . Back to Custody Battle. How do you call *rape* a custody battle."[19]

On October 4, after forty-three days in a Mississippi jail, during which she was limited to one roll of toilet paper a month, furnished with only a mattress, wakened at all hours by the noise, and given maggot-infested food,[20] Karen broke. While still incarcerated, she gave a five-hour deposition in which, to "purge herself," she was forced to tell everything she knew or might know or suppose about the time the children were in hiding—even though she did not actually know who was with her children during that time, or where they were.

Later, Karen would explain her ambivalent behavior, first hiding the children, then caving in: "I know I was in contempt," she said. "I know I broke the law. I know that was wrong. But I don't regret what I did. At least when they get older, I can say, 'I did all I could.'

"But my children were confused. They hadn't seen me. They didn't have their mother, they didn't have their father. Finally, I thought, 'Even if they're abused, at least they'll have something, some security.' They were thinking, 'Mama doesn't love me.' "[21]

Karen was, however, asked to incriminate not only herself, but others, including Garnett Harrison. Thus began what came to be known locally as the "lynching of Garnett."

Following news of Karen's deposition, about thirty women stepped forward to "confess" to their participation in the protection of Karen's children.

As for Dorrie, for a month now she had suffered what she thought were severe migraine headaches. Early in September, she was brought to Judy Watts's home, where, Judy Watts told me, "Dorrie was sick off and on through the time she was with me. When she wasn't in pain, though, she kept busy around the house. She cleaned, washed dishes, did laundry. She sewed and cooked. She'd have dinner waiting for me when I came home. She read magazines and books."

Dorrie's journal, through this period, testifies to chronic torment, acute isolation, misery at being apart from her children— and to the abysmal dislocation experienced by someone who has suddenly stepped outside the world as she has always known and believed it to be. Dorrie's experience of individual men—certainly her experience of Foxworth—might not have been sublime. But her journal describes her complete shock that so much deadly force would be brought to bear against her simply for doing what she couldn't imagine anyone *not* doing, what she no doubt would have expected anyone—male or female—to do for a child who was testifying to having been sexually abused.

And—virtually without relief—there were the excruciating headaches.

On September 15—the very day that Karen broke down and talked—Dorrie's ability to speak was impaired. She had insisted vehemently from the time she came to Judy Watts's house that she would not go to a hospital. They'd learn who she was, and she'd be sent back to jail, and she'd probably stay there the rest of her life because she would never, ever tell where Chrissy was.

However, the severity of the attack left her no choice. She was examined at Charity Hospital in New Orleans and told her physical condition was good: She was simply suffering from nerves. (That certainly seemed credible.)

Now, for Dorrie and Chrissy, the screws began tightening. Foxworth's attorney started threatening to bring kidnapping charges against the women who had confessed. Garnett Harrison's phone records were subpoenaed, and she was threatened with prosecution. She was certain her phone was bugged. The Federal Bureau of Investigation was soon to be called in on the case. A federal grand jury was convened.

Dorrie missed most of this. On October 13, she was stricken by the brain aneurysm that would rupture and kill her. She was taken to the hospital, where she died the next day.

Her last journal entry is dated September 21. It reads, in part:

"Judge Dale, Honorable, isn't that what they call you? Honorable, isn't that what you're supposed to be? I find this hard to believe.

"An honorable man would protect the innocent rather than the accused. At least that's what I always believed. I thought justice was what protected the victim. How wrong I've been for 27 years. . . ."

The entry is signed "A Loving Mom."[22]

———————

By mid-November of 1987, the hunt for five-year-old Chrissy or, apparently more paramount, the hunt for those hiding her, had begun to rival any all-systems-alert for an escaped desperado. Along with the threats of kidnapping charges against the people she was with, there were rumors that subpoenas had been readied for anyone who might know of her whereabouts. The county sheriff's department and the Mississippi Highway Safety Patrol were on the search. The FBI was now on the case, launching a full-fledged effort to find Chrissy.

In early December 1987, Chrissy surfaced in San Francisco. Donna Medley, director of the San Francisco Witness Assistance Program, was contacted, and she, in turn, contacted attorney Sheila Brogna. An abuse petition was filed, alleging that Chrissy would be at risk if returned to her father, and Chrissy was placed in the temporary legal custody of the California Department of Social Services, although she continued to reside with Donna Medley. Foxworth was notified of Chrissy's whereabouts.

On December 14, Judge Daniel Weinstein, a San Francisco juvenile judge, ordered physical and psychological evaluations of Chrissy, and then agreed to take temporary jurisdiction over the child.

Back in New Orleans, spirits rose. Perhaps protection would prevail after all.

Judge Weinstein spoke directly with Judge Dale, and with the Mississippi commissioner for public welfare, to determine the conditions under which Chrissy would be returned to Mississippi. Both assured Judge Weinstein:

1) That Chrissy would undergo physical and psychological evaluations in Mississippi

2) That she would be placed in a neutral environment, not with maternal or paternal relatives
3) That a youth court petition would be filed on her behalf
4) That a guardian ad litem (GAL) would be appointed to ensure the child's interests were legally protected.[23]

The Marion County district attorney traveled to San Francisco on December 15 to bring Chrissy back to Mississippi, assuring Judge Weinstein that the conditions would be met, and that there would be no contact with the father until further order of the Mississippi court. On December 17, however, Chrissy was returned to Mississippi and spent that night in the district attorney's custody.

Six days later, Judge Dale declared that he intended to give legal custody of Chrissy to the father.

Fewer than three months later, Judge Dale declared the Mississippi court would not consider any directions, instructions, requirements, or conditions imposed by the California court to be of any legal significance.

Meanwhile, a full-scale assault was being mounted against Garnett Harrison. Some fishy testimony had been brought before the court by a person with the alias "John Ireland," who was claiming he had seen Garnett and Karen in a Hattiesburg restaurant, and had heard Garnett tell Karen to put her thumb in Katie's vagina and press in order to get fresh evidence of sexual abuse. Ireland turned out not to have a driver's license, or even a social security number—but Judge Dale did not require proof that he was who he said he was, or proof that he knew what he said he knew. The fact that four witnesses subsequently came forward from Ireland's condominium association to testify that, as far as they knew, Ireland's real name was Jeb Wilkins, did not shake Judge Dale's faith in the witness. He found "Ireland's" testimony entirely credible.[24]

By now, there was no doubt in Garnett Harrison's mind that

she was being cornered: that someone or someones were determined enough to destroy her to come up with what clearly seemed to be perjured testimony. Harassed, derided, and herself threatened with arrest for contempt, Garnett was starting to feel the kind of terror that's augmented by historical déjà vu.

She'd grown up in the state of Mississippi. She knew about Mississippi jails. She knew how easy it would be for good ole boys to secure her commitment to a psychiatric institution. And she knew about the 1959 case of Charles Mack Parker, one of the last men lynched in the United States. In that case, the judge, disregarding rumors, had refused to grant Parker, a black man accused of raping a white woman, a change of venue. Somehow a lynch mob got the key to Parker's cell, and he was found mysteriously dead the next day. The sheriff's deputy who reportedly gave out the key to the cell became Judge Dale's bailiff.[25]

Many appeals have been filed on Chrissy's behalf since then, raising hopes—only to dash them again. As Harrison describes it, it was a roller coaster of bad news/good news:

"After a federal judge dismissed the case in the summer of 1988—because it was intertwined with a custody decision that had already been ruled on—the case was appealed to the Fifth Circuit.

"Then in the spring of 1989, the federal district judge found error in that: You cannot dismiss a lawsuit concerning a minor child without a finding *in the suit itself* that the child's best interests are protected. So that was great. We were very hopeful. A hearing was ordered on Chrissy's interests.

"And at that hearing the judge found there was indeed a conflict of interest between the father and Chrissy. And he appointed Donna Medley as GAL.[26] And that was great. We were very hopeful.

"Well next there had to be a decision on whether or not Mississippi public officials could be liable, or whether they had sovereign immunity. And that went on a second appeal to the Fifth Circuit.[27] And the ruling there was—maybe under some circumstances they could be liable. That was hopeful too.

"So now that went to court. And a federal judge heard the whole case—beginning to end—I believe it was ten days of testimony. And the judge's opinion was: Yes, Dale and Upton had violated Chrissy's right of access to court.[28] That was 1991. Well, that was great.

"But then *that* was appealed. The case went to the Fifth Circuit *for the third time now*. And the judge said—after all this, the judge said—the court had no jurisdiction to hear the case.[29]

"So now we're three appeals later, six years down the road. *And now* the court says they don't have jurisdiction."

The Supreme Court was all that was left. They denied the case a hearing.[30] So that is the end of the matter in law. The thing is, Chrissy is now heading into adolescence. (It is the nature of these cases that they can come to encompass a childhood, leaving even eventual justice an empty win.)

Complaints against Garnett Harrison, which had been filed with the bar tribunal by the natural fathers, alleged that she had been instrumental in getting her clients to disobey court orders, that she had aided and abetted; and that she'd used publicity to attack the fathers' reputations.

Garnett denies this. She appealed. As of this writing, there still has been no hearing on that.

She is now practicing law in St. Mary's, Georgia.

Dorrie's handwritten diary remains—for some a warning, for others a rebuke.

Back when I was visiting Judy Watts that spring of 1988, she said, "The depressing thing is that nothing we do seems to make any difference. We had a rally the Saturday after New Year's and it was cold and one hundred people turned out. And it was great—and the press was there in force, and we marched and we marched—and there were fifty to a hundred letters and we stamped them and mailed them to the attorney general. And the woman who was the attorney in California, and the woman who was the foster mother in California came, and that was good. And then they met with the attorney general, and got nowhere in particular. And then, of course, we found out later that he had already given custody to the father. And we're having a meeting Wednesday night and one of the things we've got to do is decide— what are our options at this point? Because people are starting to waffle.

"Like—maybe we can't win this one. And it's too early to give up."

Was it, then? (Is it, now?)

———

November 1993. I am sitting across from Garnett in the restaurant of a Newport, Rhode Island, hotel where a conference of the National Association of Rights, Protection, and Advocacy is in progress.

We've been talking about how things have gone, about the depoliticizing of the incest issue in general, the takeover of the therapeutic ideology in particular.

"I can only tell you," Garnett is saying, "if I hadn't been able to see myself as a victim of political oppression—similar to other lawyers in other movements, I would have assumed responsibility. I would have assumed guilt. I would have internalized my pain. When I saw it as a political act, it freed me. I knew that it wasn't my fault. I was one of many who had fought against the system—and been hurt.

"If you don't have a political analysis, it's domesticated. It keeps the pain internalized. So you're singled out, not one of many.

"And you know? I keep thinking—what's going to happen as these kids grow up? They'll need a connection. They'll need a movement.

"My story? I'm in it for the long haul. I just hope there's a movement there for Chrissy. To tell her who her mother was. That's the key. What's gonna be there for these kids?

"I never thought therapy was a part of this movement. Or lawyers. The movement to me is women and children. Common people. And men. That's who organized about these cases in Mississippi, common women, black and white—and men. But I don't believe men lead this movement. Women do."

But—for the time being at least—things have sure conspired to make change less than certain.

Not long ago, Alan Rosenfeld, an attorney who represents protective mothers (and who received a six-month suspension in the state of Vermont) called to ask me to be an expert witness at the upcoming trial of April Curtis, a mother who had gone underground with her child and eventually been caught.

I'd met April several times, once while she was underground. And what was peculiar about that was I met her at—I believe it was—the Geraldo show (or was it Sally Jessy?). I remember it was hard, then, to fathom the idea that I was appearing on national television with a young woman who was in hiding. It wasn't too much *more* peculiar than a lot else that was happening, but it was decidedly strange. April was eventually caught by the FBI. And, as Alan is telling me, she now faced criminal charges on the "kidnapping"—despite the fact that custody had, at least temporarily, been returned to her.

"Why?" I ask Alan.

"Why what?"

"Why is the prosecuting attorney prosecuting?"

"What?"

"Why is he prosecuting? Evidently they now think the child actually was molested; evidently they now believe her. So why is he prosecuting? Doesn't he think she should have protected the child?"

"He thinks she should have protected the child, but within the bounds of the law."

"How?" I ask.

"What?"

"*How?* Are they ever going to tell us *how* to protect a child within the bounds of the law? I mean, if they can't tell us how, don't even know how, how are the women going to do what we tell them they must do, and protect the child, if nobody knows how they can do it? How?"*

---

* April Curtis was found not guilty in the fall of 1993.

Chapter 8

THE GREAT INCEST
MASSACRE III

I AM TALKING ON THE PHONE with Sage Freechild, a rape-crisis-center-based feminist therapist who works with adults who suffered sexual abuse as children.

She has just returned from her sky-diving training, and is describing what sounds to me harrowing and life-threatening—her passion, her avocation. In what seems to me like excruciating detail, she relates one training session, called, I believe, a "live water" experience, in which she had to jump into a swimming pool in her parachute, which of course immediately entombed her and, while other swimmers yanked at the strings to simulate river current, she had to try to extricate herself from the strangling, suffocating mass of nylon chute and the overwhelming confusion of tangled wire strands which fought her and tightened and . . . (aagh!)

"Sage," I say, "*Why?* Why do you choose to *do* this? What can this *mean?*"

A pause, then—audibly grinning—she says, "It *means* that,

these days, I'd rather jump out of an airplane than talk about incest."

I know the feeling. Well—*almost.*

———

Data didn't help.

We could show that false allegations of sexual abuse were *not* more prevalent in custody and visitation cases than in any other cases. And that it is simply untrue that there is any explosion of false allegations of sexual abuse in custody and visitation cases.

We could show that recent studies found that the vast majority of fathers were awarded sole or mandated joint custody where the custody was contested. And that where *sole* custody was sought and awarded, fathers won in most cases, including *one quarter* of all cases where they were either proven or alleged to have physically and sexually abused their children.

We could elucidate the absolute lack of empirical evidence in the published claims of certain professionals trumpeting an epidemic of false accusations.

We could show that the protective parent was treated with appalling contempt and punitiveness simply for attempting to do what she was everywhere told to do: believe and try to protect her child.

But that didn't help.

Evidence didn't help, either.

As in Chrissy's case, forensic evidence was often simply denied admission in court. But even where the evidence was allowed, courts overwhelmingly seemed to be finding that it was not conclusive, not shifting the balance to greater than 50 percent. Or else, we would find judges saying that they would require *proof beyond a reasonable doubt* before damaging the father's reputation.

Or else they would flatly say, as one judge did in a finding I have seen, "The court is again reiterating that it is satisfied that there has been sexual abuse perpetrated on this child by her father. The rationale as to why or the prognosis as to when Mr. (X) will be 'cured' is beyond the court's ability to predict at this time." However. That was not sufficient reason to deny the child the right to a loving father.

Nor, we could show, could women appeal to a federal court. Chrissy's case was the only case ever to have been granted such a hearing. The others were all denied based on the "domestic relations exception"—the idea that domestic matters did not require the same levels of recourse as matters of *serious* law. Thus, the women could only keep going back to the same courts, the same judges, which did nothing to decrease the judges' impressions that these women were harassing *them*.

Speaking out didn't help.

Even Elizabeth Morgan, whose case received a constant blitz of publicity, wound up spending two years in jail.

Yet mothers *kept* speaking out, often in defiance of orders by the court that tried to force them into silence. Having been failed by the law, they took their case to the people (at least those who watched daytime talk show television) by way of Phil or Oprah or Geraldo or Sally Jessy Raphael. But so did the fathers, who appeared to have an edge in the believability sweepstakes—if only because their testimony reassured the largely female audiences that it was not necessarily true that there existed this degree of rage and injustice awaiting a woman who simply did what everyone believed should be done.

In the end, this testimony and countertestimony, within an entertainment forum, seemed to have a decidedly antipolitical effect. The women's testimony played out as personal stories in a framework that was constructed to emphasize emotionality over rationality; to *contain* personal stories, not to extend them to include larger meaning.

In the end, it gave the public a way out of seeing all this as an overarching political injustice; a way of being reassured that it was an individual, personal issue, with reality a matter of personal opinion.

Yet for the mothers, there was little left besides the belief that speaking out, being heard, could, by itself, help; that within these national televised forums the public could be enlisted on their children's behalf. But increasingly, it was evident it could not.

By the late 1980s, the daytime airwaves were becoming a deluge of talk shows: a day-after-day onslaught of people suffering overweight, or underweight, or in conflict with their husband's ex-wives or their mothers-in-law; competing side by side or preceding or following a display of adults who not only elected to wear diapers but thought we all should know this. Talk shows aired trivia alongside discontent alongside tragedy: inflating the small and diminishing the great into one huge watery soup— offering passive observance of virtual reality.

Talk shows, which, in their early days, had appeared to be a medium through which issues could be aired, became, in effect, a medium through which issues could be encapsulated and neutralized. The shows' very structure was diminishing: those presenting their stories were bracketed by experts, invariably including a psychologist or psychiatrist, who were present to advise or comment, or explain pathology to us.

By the nature of the format, all context was absent, and the absence of context alters content. There was nothing to lend the issue coherence or connection with any other issue, nothing to signal significance or intent. The stories were framed as misfortune. And so as mothers losing custody appeared on this, that, and the other, and fathers claiming false accusations appeared on the which and the what with who—all that was generated was heat and noise, and mail from others in similar circumstances, each individually seeking help.

More serious journalists faced other impediments. The fact that the fathers had no findings against them, and had received the implied exoneration of full custody, made presenting the mothers' stories legally perilous. And it was always precisely the women whose cases had placed them in this predicament who were eager to be heard.

Those few women who, legally, *could* have spoken out and had their stories reported fully, those rare cases where mothers had—after years of Trial by Ordeal and the Hue and Cry—achieved the protection of their children and been granted sole custody, nonetheless could not speak out. They were under a different kind of constraint, in some ways even more powerful: an internal sense of threat.

In keeping with the irrational nature of what had rained down on them, the god-like powers that had devised their torments, silence was their act of prayer for invisibility.

Knowing what her response would be, I nonetheless asked one of those mothers—let's call her Susan—why she has since kept silent. An attorney, she is now once again practicing her profession. Both her daughters were sexually abused by her ex-husband. One is now in college; the other is thirteen. Her trial by fire lasted four years.

Susan? Why?

"I think," she says, "it's a number of different things. The whole process is so shaming. You're the one on trial. It is not a pleasant experience.

"Even if we won, there is still such a tremendous sense of loss. The whole experience goes to the very root of your security. Your faith in the justice system. And you feel—having lived through it and survived—it's just bad luck to mess with it.

"For years, whenever I would drive by a courthouse, I would feel like vomiting. You can understand that's a problem, given what I do. When I tried for a while to stay with the issue—talk to people about it, women looking for help—it was very draining. It took willpower.

"Over the years, any number of those acronym groups that have formed asked me to be public. But—so many people know my family—I just shuddered. I was so personally vilified. And it was out of the clear blue sky—that's what's so devastating. It just strikes out of nowhere, as though for no reason—I just didn't want to be out there.

"I lost four years of motherhood. My children lost four years of their childhood. I couldn't be there for them in important ways, take them to the zoo, be class mother. I was constantly besieged with the legal stuff, and completely obsessed with each current assault. Constant anguish, constant terror, constant crisis.

"It's as though you've taken a really horrible bloody beating, and somebody says, 'Come out in the courtyard again.' You don't want to be out there.

"It's sudden and it's vicious and it's random.

"And—I have two daughters who were molested, and I didn't want to tell people. I experienced how clearly the problem is attributed to the victim. How people look at her as though there's something the matter with *her*. That happened to me.

"And—even if you win—it feels fragile. Evidence doesn't matter. Nothing makes a difference. You look back at your winning and it seems like pure luck. Like it could just as well have gone the other way. And if it struck again—this thing from the blue, this thing that had no reason, this thing that brought down all the forces of society and of law against you—it could still go the other way."

It does not seem implausible to suggest that, if unreason is loose in the land, if—in the language of the backlash—"witches" are being hunted and hounded, the target of the witch-hunt is not men accused, but the women who have the audacity to do what they are everywhere told they must do: believe their children.

––––––––

The backlash's weapon of choice was the blunderbuss.

Aimed at women as mothers, its select ammunition was spleen, interspersed with pellets of the gender-shot traditionally packaged for uppity female targets: hysterical, vindictive, jealous, delusional. . . .

Aimed at professionals willing to listen to and hear the children and the women who sought to protect them, the backlash forces alternately loaded the 'buss up with differently derogatory epithets; scattershot libel suits; and dum-dum pellets designed to destroy professional accreditation. They also went in for spray-paint graffiti: *Zealot* was a favorite, along with the ever-popular allusions to Salem and the commie-baiting hysteria generated by Senator Joe McCarthy. . . .

As a result, fewer and fewer attorneys were willing to take the mothers' cases (it did not help that the mothers were seldom independently well-to-do).

As a result, diagnostic professionals, unhappily labeled "validators," grew increasingly cautious. And in an increasingly high-stakes game, a smattering of rogues appeared to fill the gap. Women were desperate. Women make good marks.

One mother took her son to a psychologist for evaluation for an agreed-upon fee. The evaluation was that the child had been abused. The psychologist then abruptly doubled the fee, threatening that unless she paid, he would reverse his testimony.

As a result of widespread attack, however, a kind of bunker mentality set in among many professionals. Those accorded the status of A-tier "expert," under constant siege and being treated with the same kind of arrogant dismissiveness as the women and children, began to see themselves as victims.

The backlash forces had taken control of the issue, had taken power in rhetoric; they were not only defining the terms of the war, but also operating under the relaxed strictures of war, far looser than those dictated by academic rigor. Their certainty that this was war left them unconstrained by any rules of either science or the Marquis of Queensbury. They were the principal actors, they chose the stage, they set the tone and the volume.

Constantly taking the offensive, they were never forced to confront the fact that, by at least *some* of their own determinations (they often contradicted themselves elsewhere), the hullabaloo they were raising made no kind of sense.

Take, for example, Dr. Gardner's statement that he fully appreciates "that genuine sex abuse of children is widespread and the vast majority of sex abuse allegations of children . . . are likely to be justified (*perhaps 95% or more*)." Nonetheless, he says, "the focus of this book . . . is on the false accusations for which there is absolutely no basis in reality" (italics mine).[1]

Well, but wait. If all of his impassioned writing and testimony is based on (possibly less than) 5 percent of cases, and if, as one study showed, nearly 30 *percent* of fathers are winning custody even (or, I would say it seems, *especially*) when there is evidence they have been sexually abusive of the children[2]—then where should focus more properly be placed in terms of injustice?

But wars are not fought for truth and justice (whatever the slogans may be). They are fought for dominance, and to win by whatever means.

Faced with the backlash experts' tactics of blanket assertion, the A-tier professionals—committed to their disciplines: psychiatry, medicine, or sociology—were at some considerable disadvantage. They had signed up for science, for research and discovery, for an emerging specialty: They had not signed up for the indignities of a shooting war.

Rarely did their professional literature address the issue as a political one, or position it within any political analysis. And yet, oddly enough, they knew that history contained ample precedent for severe backlash. But though they knew it factually, they didn't seem to fully take into account the implications of the present as replay. (As we had, perhaps they failed to see in history the future's blueprint.)

Freud, of course, had originally believed his female patients' testimony of childhood sexual abuse. He certainly knew that his patients were, if not all his colleagues' daughters, then the daughters of members of the same social class. He was surely aware that his colleagues depended for their professional valuation, their *business*, on the approval and patronage of that governing class. He himself said his theory would disturb "the sleep of the world." Yet, overwhelmed by the thrill of his discovery, he evidently did not infer from his social knowledge the fury and derision such a disturbance-of-sleep would unleash, or that it would result, for him, in the threat of professional exile.

In his high excitement over his discovery, he did not stop to think that neither his colleagues nor the ruling gentry were apt to be good sports about his raising public suspicions about their own private behaviors. He did not stop to think that what he was posing was a challenge to privilege, a political assault on the socially worthy.

Freud had achieved, briefly, an important understanding, but lacked the one other that was crucial. He had achieved insight into the powerful impact of childhood sexual abuse on women. But without the benefit of a female understanding of the rights arrogated to male power, he lacked the wherewithal to anticipate or plan for combat. Simply put, Freud did not have the critical benefit of being an informed feminist. (God knows there are few enough such benefits.)

So he charged forward. And when he saw what he'd done to his own credibility, when he saw he was derided and snickered at— he embraced a position of total reversal.

As Jeffrey Moussaieff Masson recounts in *Assault on Truth*, thirty-five years later, Freud's favorite student, Sandor Ferenczi, "advocated a posture of tenderness and reassurance to 'free the tongues' of patients who were afraid to recall and so resolve traumas associated with childhood sexual assault."[3] (And was then derided by Freud himself, who had by this time regained his own respectability, and was not about to truck with *that* foolishness again.)

But surely, given Freud's experience, Ferenczi must have known the powerful forces he might be bringing down on himself? Alas, he also was denied the advantage of political insight. Ferenczi died in disgrace, stripped of his status as a serious male, dismissed as a nut case.

"To the present time," psychiatrist Roland Summit writes, "those who call attention to the hazards of child molestation and those who develop techniques identifying the signs of sexual abuse have been ridiculed and disgraced. When methods or concepts are sound, people are attacked for their eccentric style or for their inferior credentials."4

Summit points to Dr. Bruce Woodling, "a family physician who began correlating sexual victimization with previously unnoticed traces of vaginal and rectal scarring." And who was then called before the California Board of Medical Quality Assurance "to defend against charges that his observations were not based on adequate research." And to Dr. Ann Burgess, professor of nursing and noted authority, who was "denounced to her employers for her unscientific collusion with police officers and other zealots," and was censured by the Board of the Kinsey Institute of Human Sexuality.5 And when Jeffrey Masson published his exposé of the suppression of the truth about incest by psychiatry in 1984, he was lambasted with attacks meant to discredit him.

But while Summit's recounting certainly points out the historical consistency of what has been happening, it does not clearly identify the profoundly male-protective force driving it, now as before. He identifies attacks only as "conservative doctrine." And he lays the force driving professional ridicule at the feet of "adult discomfort." Certainly, on the evidence, it might better be laid at the doorstep of male rage.

As Summit describes to me now his own view of the issue's evolution, he might well be talking from a hundred years past: "Psychiatry and mental health professionals—as an interest group, as a training block, as a professional proprietary interest— never got it. It isn't as if they got it and dropped away. They never got it."

Summit describes to me the scope of his field:

"There are four competing and often mutually antagonistic professional groups in the psychotherapy or the psychological realm. And there are many schools of theoretical thought, distributed irregularly among those professional segments.

"And, more or less, everyone who is conservative has avoided any meaningful awareness of child sexual abuse. And American psychiatry, and even more worldwide psychiatry, has been even more inattentive to it than most.

"Child psychiatry has been downright antagonistic at the organized level. You have [psychiatrists] who are teaching other psychiatrists how to recognize false accusations and discredit mothers who think their husbands or ex-husbands buggered their little kids. That's the money-making, authority-promoting arm of American child psychiatry. And that stereotypes a lot of things, because those people are political and vocal.

"And there are vast numbers of workaday clinicians who are doing a balance of good stuff and attending to sexual abuse if they see it. But they're not being taught to understand it.

"So what has happened in the professions is that each of the professions has its minority cadre of people who are disproportionately concerned about child sexual abuse. Disproportionately, because they have the whole load to carry, and they're working against a backlog of hostility and indifference among their peers."

What is odd is the idea that one could have anticipated anything else; that one would be surprised at the virulence of this resistance, even if one is limiting focus to the history of psychiatry. Psychiatry has, from the start, been power-aligned and power-protective: It has traditionally aimed its diagnostic machinery at the powerless, finding defect in them by setting a health standard determined by the prosperous dominant class and the dominant gender. Benjamin Rush, the father of psychiatry, named as a disease (drapetomania) the peculiar desire of slaves to escape. Most of psychiatry's most celebrated diagnoses have been directed toward the deficits of women, most particularly of women as *mothers*, who have been said to cause, in their children, everything from autism to poor homework skills to—interesting in light of the subject at hand—incest.[6]

Much has been written, over the years, about psychiatry and its role in social control, its usefulness in medicalizing and individualizing social issues that might otherwise lead to outcry. Its superior positioning to act in the political arena derives precisely from the fact that—because it is cloaked in the language of expertise—psychiatry does not *seem* political. Factoring that in, it does not seem surprising that—on the issue of incest—psychiatry is the ideal Trojan Horse designed to carry the backlash to triumph. *Not* factoring it in can lead only to perplexity.

However. The opposite can also be correct. That psychiatry and psychology *on either side*, believing or disbelieving women and children, defuses the issue by medicalizing it. That, in removing it from the political sphere to that of individual pathology, it is an excellent vehicle for problem management rather than for social change.

So within psychiatry we are offered here two less than ideal choices: On the one hand, there is an aspect of psychiatry that would adopt and co-opt sexual abuse/incest as medical specialty, rendering its victims patients or inmates. On the other hand, there is a segment that would minimize its prevalence. Whichever faction wins, feminism—and women's interest in social change—loses.

Summit says, "There never was a resolution among influential clinical people, in the same way there was a revolution among influential women: There never was an agreement, as there has come to be across society, that rape is a crime that has no excuse. A crime that results from the arrogance of men in a variety of ways. That's a successful take."

Yes it is (although I do not think it can be claimed that that consensus is yet even halfway accomplished, nor is it by any means a point irrevocably won). But rape as an issue did not make headway even to the extent that it has, as Summit points out, by the resolution of "influential clinical people." The issue did not make progress spearheaded by any segment of the mental health industry. It made whatever headway it has because of a political understanding on the part of women, one that triggered a grassroots movement.

Incest has been unique among issues of violence against women in its instant adoption as a professionals' issue—an issue of psychiatry and mental health at all levels, and that has largely contributed to its separation from the political realm. And so we wind up in a loop here: Having adopted the issue as one of objective study and removed it from the political arena, professionals found themselves trying to fight on the level of objective study that which is heartily and fundamentally a matter of power.

Even the issue of rape has not been immune to the same kind of depoliticizing assault, the same kind of large-scale effort to defuse the political by redefining it as personal. Sociologist Nancy Matthews, "who traced the evolution of the anti-rape movement in Los Angeles, has documented the ways in which the 'feminist political agenda of relating violence against women to women's oppression was marginalized, ridiculed, and suppressed.' "[7] *Marginalized, ridiculed, and suppressed* are words that describe the goal of the backlash assaults on professionals, as well as assaults on women. (Perhaps the difference is that women, as a political group, are more accustomed to those assaults.) With the issue of rape and with that of battered women (which also had a few years' headstart as a political issue), funding agencies have increasingly come to be used in support of programs and procedures that emphasize psychology/social work and individual rehabilitation over collective understanding and outreach for action.

Summit is, however, entirely correct when he says, "People are still arguing, the subject is still open to argument, whether it is a good or bad thing for a child to experience sex with an adult. And I would have hoped—our idealism of the seventies was that pretty soon we would be outraged at the presumption that anyone could do that to a child and get away with it."

Yes. But that is, alas, still in the air surrounding rape and battered women as well (and our hopes for them were idealistic in the 1970s as well). The difference is that political knowledge on those issues had ten years of play, and the issues were clearly identified as aligned: as forms of long-permitted violence against women. Feminist understanding of incest, placing it on that violence continuum, was squelched virtually from the start.

———————

"I understand HOW," Winston Smith, protagonist of George Orwell's *1984*, scrawled in his most secret diary. "I do not understand WHY." Perhaps that is at least a part of the why; a part of what gives the issue its increasingly fishy smell: gives it the kind of did-too, did-not character of highly articulate bickering. In more practical terms, that is what underlies the failure of all of the aggressive public information campaigns and the interventions built up over the past dozen years. The interventions are built on the assumption that there already is, among those whose opinions count in such matters, a consensus that child sexual abuse/incest is, in fact, "abuse"; camouflaged by that assumption is the question of how much weight that abuse (if it is such) should carry when poised against any possible penalty to otherwise upstanding men.

"Why not simply remove the father?" it was asked when the issue of state intervention and the punishing removal of the child from the home first arose.

Well, because. Men have overriding rights.

The problem is that while that question of just how serious paternal child rape is can be evaded by the rhetoric of dysfunctions and disorders, it cannot be avoided in circumstances of reality. And the unaddressed question lurks as a booby trap underneath all the goodhearted imprecations that children tell and that women act to protect them.

In the attack/counterattack game, a good deal of the play has taken place outside the public arena, in the pages of professional journals, or in convention presentations. More illuminating than every detail of each study and each rebuttal is the clear difference in style between those who saw themselves on a journey of intellectual discovery and those who sought to abort that journey.

Since Roland Summit has been with this issue since the 1970s, it is not surprising that he generated the first sign of heat.

It all began, innocently enough, back during the 1970s when, as he says to me, "we were together, thinking it was pretty wonderful that people were waking up to undiscovered sexual abuse."

From his listening, his experience as a community psychiatrist specializing in sexual abuse consultation, he put together a list of what he saw as the most common characteristics of children who had been abused. In so doing, he unwittingly became the progenitor of whole generations of checklists in books and magazines, syndrome detectors, and the like.

Simply put, what he described as characteristic were (1) secrecy, (2) helplessness, (3) entrapment and accommodation, (4) delayed, conflicted, and unconvincing disclosure, and (quite reasonably, in the face of the ensuing furor) (5) retraction.

This was, really, no more than a way of encoding a common chain of events: Kids are told not to tell *or else*; they can't do much about the situation; they manage to live with it; they maybe try to hint at what's happening; and then, when they see the frenzy of adults trying to figure out what to do about it, they say, "Never mind, guys, I take it back."

When he tried to translate this presentation—which he says was conceived to enhance or corroborate the understanding of mental health professionals—into a formal paper, he was turned down by professional journals ("not because it was radical or unsubstantiated, but because the reviewers felt it was so basic that it contributed nothing new to the literature!"[8])

Finally, in 1983, the paper was published in the *International Journal of Child Abuse and Neglect*.

Carried into court, a forum for which Summit denies it was intended, by expert witnesses testifying on behalf of children (largely because there was so little else), this descriptively conceived paper was now asked to bear undue weight. And was attacked by experts for the defense, using the simple techniques of distortion and mockery common to many defense strategies.

Summit and his Child Sexual Abuse Accommodation Syndrome became the paper target of the False Accusation Syndrome backlash. Speaking before VOCAL, psychiatrist and defense expert Lee Coleman refers to Summit's stated purpose in writing the paper: "to provide a vehicle for a more sensitive, more therapeutic response to legitimate victims of child sexual abuse, and to invite more active, more effective clinical advocacy for the child within the family and within the systems of child protection *and criminal justice*" (italics mine).9

That last was all the debunkers needed (if they even needed that much). It was difficult, then, to deny you were speaking of advocacy, and within legal systems.

"Well," Coleman says, "that all is fine, if we knew we had a legitimate victim. . . . Unfortunately, people who are getting trained in these ideas start off with the assumption that they have a legitimate victim, and then everything they do goes in this direction. 'Now it is my job to advocate for this child! I'm not going to be one of those people that fails to protect the child!'"10

It was but a butterfly step from there to characterizing professionals with whom the backlash took issue as *child advocates, child abuse finders, validators*. The image was created of a hyperemotional cadre of crusaders, stomping through the world, proselytizing like an army of Major Barbaras, banging their drums, and calling the world to redemption with the slogan *Believe the children*.

The concerned professionals (it is difficult to escape the "pro-child" characterization) had not, as the backlash had, reached out to a constituency, mounted a public relations effort; they had formed no populist alliances, done no outreach.

And so, as events spun outside their control—and they were called into preschool and day-care mass-abuse allegations, allegations about cult abuse and satanic ritual abuse, allegations of the seemingly preposterous involving space ship travel and buried infant sacrifices—collectively, theirs became a reactive stance.

More and more, they convened among themselves, wrote papers for one another, tried to match fiery accusations that gained major national attention with studies, which did not. Tried to combat hyperbole with scientific decorum. Tried to balance their own understanding and belief about many children's reality with concern for professional standing.

As they became involved in a dizzying play/counterplay, sight was lost of the critical, but unaddressed, question, which remained: How much weight are we willing to give children's testimony—even where we believe it testifies to real experience—when it fundamentally challenges the historical rights and privileges of a patriarchal structure? When, precisely because the sexual exploitation of children by men has for so long gone uncensured, challenge to this presumed male authority will loose outrage?

Therein lay the crux of the war; all the assaults and counter-assaults were diversion and decoration.

It could only get worse when the professionals were pulled into the custody fray as experts, and were seen to be saying believe (not only the children but) *the women.*

On that one, unquestionably, professionals took and continue to take a full dump of contemptuous derision and continuous personal and professional threat.

Muriel Sugarman is an estimable child psychiatrist, who has been called to testify as such in a number of cases where the credibility of the child and the protecting parent are in question.

In 1988, Dr. Sugarman led a study conducted by Harvard and Massachusetts General Hospital. That study found that 75 percent of the children who said they had been sexually abused by a divorced or separated parent were not believed.[11] Not only had these children told of the abuse, but they suffered from physical symptoms, regression, post-traumatic stress. None of the fathers were ever prosecuted, and 60 percent of the children were forced to visit the alleged perpetrator without much supervision, often overnight.

In two cases (out of nineteen), judges and the guardian ad litem (GAL)—an attorney supposedly acting on the child's behalf—

recommended, despite the evidence, a transfer of custody to the father.

Let me echo some journalists' bewilderment when witnessing the unfolding of the Singley-Newsom case: Even if the judges (and GALs) were unconvinced that there was a preponderance of evidence, doesn't a full reversal of custody seem a somewhat draconian response?

In one case, a doctor's testimony that semen had been found in the child's vagina after a visit with the father was discounted as insufficient evidence.

Importantly, the study found that in these post-divorce cases—where the sexual abuse had begun after separation—the offenders tended to be less decorous in their assault; far less concerned with incest "manners" than were offenders where the mother was still around.

Sugarman said of the findings, "Those who describe the vindictiveness or vengefulness of divorcing mothers never consider that divorcing fathers might be vindictive or vengeful enough to abuse the child in order to hurt the child's mother." They did not, in other words, understand sexual assault of children as on the continuum of *violence against women.*

Since she clearly did, I asked her: What was her view? What had she seen happening here?

"The question," she says, "is where to start. Because one very interesting thing is that when I first began with cases like this—1981, 1982—moms whose kids were abused were fighting the battle about visitation, mostly, not even custody at that point—they *had* custody. And what was interesting was that the first two cases I had, which had no more evidence than any of the later ones, went well. In one of them, the father's rights were completely terminated. In the other, the judge said, 'I don't even want to hear testimony on this. You will have to refer to criminal court.' He read my report and he said, 'The father will not see the child until Dr. Sugarman thinks he should.'

"And that was that. Both of those kids were severely enough abused, so . . . I've followed them over the years, and they've had no contact with their fathers."

That, of course, was before the backlash had begun to organize.

"And then, all of a sudden . . . the next few cases I had were completely different. It was, 'Mothers make this up to be vengeful.' And, 'They're malevolent.' And, 'This is the new ploy in divorce.' And all of a sudden, no matter how much evidence there was, no matter how much expert opinion there was, nobody was going to believe these kids or these mothers.

"I distinctly remember a case up in New Hampshire, 1986. The little girl was born in 1983. And over the course of the next year, the mother stopped visitation twice because the kid was coming home with allegations of sexual abuse that were pretty believable. She was irritated, red, had all kinds of symptoms.

"And the second time it happened, the judge found the mother in contempt.

"And she wouldn't turn over the children. So he actually said that she needed to be punished for her contempt by having temporary custody given to the father, until the final divorce hearing.

"Now every legal treatise I've ever heard of says you're not supposed to do that. No matter what the custodial parent does, you don't punish the custodial parent by taking the children away. But that's what the judge was going to do. The mother wouldn't turn the kids over, so the judge put her in jail for a week.

"And I remember testifying then on the statehouse steps in Concord, New Hampshire. And there were fathers' rights activists there.

"And the LaLonde case came down around the same time."

Virginia LaLonde, a Massachusetts mother, spent over six months in jail in 1987 for refusing to divulge the whereabouts of her eight-year-old daughter, Nicole. Her ex-husband had been ordered to have unsupervised visits with Nicole, even though experts had offered physical and psychological evidence that the child had been sexually abused by her father.

Nicole was finally found by authorities, and was placed in foster care. Eventually, Virginia lost legal custody to the father. Why?

According to a July 1989 report in *Sojourner: The Women's Forum*, the judge's ruling "despite its twists and turns basically finds that sexual abuse . . . can not be firmly established by the court." It continues, "From there to awarding sole legal custody may seem like a leap, but one [Judge] Fitzpatrick makes through a series of attacks on Virginia LaLonde. . . ."

"The closing paragraph of Fitzpatrick's decision," we are told, "reveals her reasoning on the custodial decision: 'As much as Nicole has learned that she can say "no" to sexual abuse if her father initiates such, the court believes that Nicole has yet to learn to say "no" to the emotional pressure her mother has placed on her to see life and Stephen through her mother's eyes.' "[12]

About the decision, an editorial in the *Boston Herald* opined:

"Virginia LaLonde and her daughter Nicole prove not only that the system does not work, but that the system punishes those who don't play by its rules.

"Virginia LaLonde was not the shy, reticent mother the system would have liked. She spoke to the press. She spoke out for her daughter. She defied the system and made a public mockery of it by fleeing with her daughter, hiding Nicole and brazenly choosing jail rather than divulging her daughter's whereabouts. She did all this to protect Nicole, to keep her child away from a man Nicole said had abused her. . . ."

According to the *Herald*, "Virginia LaLonde did what she should have done. She went to the courts for help, but then found herself embroiled in a nightmare. She fled the state originally because the court ordered that Nicole, despite her allegations that her father had sexually abused her, spend three unsupervised weeks with her father. Virginia LaLonde ran then with the child, away from the courts and her daughter's father."[13]

Dr. Sugarman is saying, "Elizabeth Morgan went to prison right around that same time. And there were those cases in Mississippi.

"So within that period—1983 to 1986—there was tremendous reversal."

"What," I ask, "did you suspect was happening?"

"To me," Dr. Sugarman says, "it was a gender bias issue. That the first few cases, the judges were quite properly horrified. And then they started saying, 'Well, gee, there's an awful lot of this happening. Could it be that all these nice daddies are doing this? *Most* daddies are nice. So these must be bad *women*.' And it's gotten no better. If anything, worse."

"Why do I sense that the professionals at your level are in a bunker mentality?"

"That's 'cause we're sued up the wazoo. I'm going up before the board of registration—all because I tried to protect the kids. I said what I thought was going on. And when I went to the APSAC [American Professional Society on Abuse of Children] conference in San Diego, half the presenters said, 'We're all being sued, too. Keep your malpractice insurance payments up, because you're going to be sued.' "

"And the suing is being done by . . . ?"

"The fathers. Let me tell you an interesting pattern that I see in at least a few cases. First, the fathers go through the whole divorce thing with the probate court, and they spend a lot of money and get custody of the kid. They completely defame the mother and make the allegations look phony, and they get custody of the kid.

"Then they go and sue everybody that said they did it—willy-nilly. Why?" Dr. Sugarman believes it is "because some of those people will settle, and that will give the fathers enough money to pay for their lawyers' fees." (The fathers, of course, claim they are suing because they were wrongfully accused.)

"So not only am I being sued by Mr. LaLonde, but Mr. LaLonde tried to sue the premier pediatric gynecologist in Boston, who is probably the only person in town who knows how to do sex abuse exams with the colposcope.

"He's suing the doctor in Michigan who examined Nicole

LaLonde while she was in hiding. He's suing North Shore Children's Hospital, who are the people who filed the original report. He's suing the mother's boyfriend—saying he was an abuser.

"And the mother's boyfriend's insurance company settled with him—against the mother's boyfriend's wishes. So now *he's* suing his insurance company."

(I ask you: Is this what makes America great? Or what?)

What emerges from this picture of frenzied legal assault—the use of courtrooms as stage sets for Wild West–style shootouts by (dare I say it?) vengeful fathers (maintaining their innocence)—is a fair certainty that far more is at stake for a father whose child has made an accusation of incest than the right to an ongoing close relationship with his child. At stake, of course, is implicit exoneration (surely a court would not award a child to a rapist). Nor is suing only a satisfying outlet for anger at would-be detractors. It is, if you will, an act that (in the language current to the issue) promises healing and recovery: financial healing, financial recovery.

Not least, it is a way of striking a blow for the cause: scaring off those who would speak up to make or support what the fathers claim are false accusations.

Dr. Sugarman continues: "The whole point is to make money to pay off the legal fees. They figure if they make themselves obnoxious enough to enough people who have malpractice policies, sooner or later one of the insurance companies is going to say, 'It's going to cost us too much to fight this. So we'll just settle.'"

"So that's why professionals have kind of split off?"

"I don't think I would describe it as being split off, but rather as being much, much, much more cautious, because their necks are in the noose. Not only are their necks in the noose with the courts, but their necks are in the noose with other professionals, with attorneys. It's an interesting phenomenon, because you have to watch that you don't get a reputation for being an 'advocate'—with judges and with the lawyers."

That *is* interesting. Because, unless I'm mistaken here, the experts who routinely testify for the defense are proudly and loudly advocates—for fathers who, collectively, they see as being victimized by false accusations.

"I mean," Dr. Sugarman says, "I have gone into court and had the father's attorney bring in transcripts from other cases in which I've testified—to use against me. So far, it hasn't worked. But when you know that kind of thing is going on—where there's clearly a network of fathers' attorneys who are sharing the transcripts and sharing these cases and sharing information—you feel like you've got to be so much more careful not to be an advocate, and not to look biased, if you're going to do good for anybody."

And yet, I wonder . . . Once you begin to censor yourself in this way, have you not begun to concede defeat?

"And yet," Dr. Sugarman says, "at the same time, you realize that taking that stance means that you can do less good for fewer people. But you feel like if you're gonna do anything for anyone, you have to take this stance."

That, certainly, is reasonable. Worrisome, but reasonable.

"Funny," I say. "I somehow thought that the whole premise of these civil courts was the 'best interests of children,' the chance that there might be harm to the child."

"That's in the family court/juvenile court, where the evidentiary requirement is reasonable cause to suspect. In probate (domestic relations) court, the standard is preponderance of the evidence. Which is 51 percent. Remember in the Elizabeth Morgan case, where the judge ruled fifty-fifty, 'It's in equipoise'? I could have killed that man. Even if that were true, that's a 50 percent chance that this man is sexually abusing this little girl. And they want her to go and have two-week vacations with the father.

"But see, they can say that unless the evidence is 51 percent or more, it is not in the best interests of the child to stop any contact with her beloved father. The assumption is that the best interests of the child are that they must have a relationship with both parents, no matter what the parents have done."

Well, not both parents, actually. Some mothers have completely been denied visitation.

"It's sexual abuse," Sugarman says. "It's abuse by the judiciary. These kids are being sexually abused by the judiciary system—because they're being sent to live with abusers."

"Is it your sense," I ask, "that what drives some of these men is rage at women?"

"Yeah!" (My spirits soar with the sense of validation.) "Oh yeah! Particularly in the divorce cases. Because they're pissed off as hell at these women for leaving them. In the group of cases I originally had—I think it was 60 percent of the men were beating their wives up, because they wanted to be in control. And then their wives got up and left them. And so how could they abuse them anymore? So they had to find a way to abuse them through their kids. I don't think these are people who are even particularly turned on by children. I don't think that's the issue."

So much, then, for your carry-on plethysmographs.

"Do you think," I ask, "that kids intuit this? Do you think that might account for the general impression that the kids' rage is greater at the mother? Knowing the child is a stand-in?"

"I think that's a piece of it. But the other piece of it is, the kids are often able to get angry at the parent they trust the most. It's safer. And then there's this feeling of, 'Why is my mother so impotent?' I watched this one family where the father—every other week they went with him to be abused. Yes, they were angry with him. But the little boy in particular was taking a lot of his anger out on the mother. Because he couldn't understand why she was so impotent."

Question: If sexual abuse of female children is a way of socializing them to accept later, further abuse—is sexual abuse of boys a way of ensuring ongoing delivery of that abuse? That sounds, I agree, a bit conspiratorial. But put it differently: If sexual abuse of female children *most likely results* in socializing them to accept later, further abuse, then does sexual abuse of boys *most likely result* in socializing them to later perpetuate that abuse? Is this part of what drives the perpetuation of male rage at women, particularly in their role as mothers? (And is *that* what the cryptic cycle of violence has been code for all along?)

"Mother's supposed to be the adult," Dr. Sugarman says. "She's supposed to be the protective, nurturing person. And then the courts have absolutely stripped her of any power to do anything. And it's very difficult to tell a little three- or four-year-old child, 'Well, I have to do this because the judge says I have to.'

"And even kids like Nicole (LaLonde), whose mother fought for her and ran away with her, are angry at the mother because she went back to Massachusetts and got put in jail. And virtually abandoned this child.

"How are you going to tell a kid, 'I abandoned you because the judge made me do it'? The child knew at some level that this is what happened. But it's hard for you to forgive your mother for letting somebody do that. Just like kids whose mother die and they're angry because they died. It's not logical, but it makes a certain terrible kind of sense."

So does this whole thing, actually—make a terrible kind of sense.

We do not yet know what we will be looking at when these kids reach adulthood. Numerous counselors and others who have pondered the issue of incest suggest that we may never exactly know: that these kids, having told and told and been believed and disbelieved all at once, and with the result of ongoing court-licensed abuse, may actually welcome retreating into a safer silence (the silence from whence all this came).

I think of Alice—the child in that earliest case in the late 1970s—and the psychiatrist's more recent words: "She is lost to us now." And I think of what Dr. Sugarman has said about the rage at their mothers, and by extension at all women who bear the appellation of "mother." And I think of the Doctrine of Equal

Culpability and the grim fact that, in the end, as things go, this transmogrifies, on the part of the abused kids, into the Assumption of Greater Culpability.

And I think of Garnett Harrison, saying, "I keep thinking— what's going to happen as these kids grow up? They will need a connection. They will need a movement. I just hope there's a movement that's there for Chrissy. To tell her who her mother was. That's the key...."

"How," I ask Dr. Sugarman, "did we lose the important piece, activism? The issue of battered women, of rape—they've all been medicalized to some extent. Once government funding becomes involved, so do 'protocols' and neutral language and professionalizing. But those issues never got quite so medicalized, quite so diverted from, 'Hey, guys, you're not supposed to do this.' And, 'We need *laws*, seriously enforced.' Why, at the barricades, as moms head off to jail, are survivors, for instance, so little in evidence?"

"You know, that's interesting. I think one of the problems is that survivors are a very mixed group of people. And now probably most of them are survivors of sexual abuse in intact families— not survivors of divorce/custody battles.

"And it's so much *safer* to blame it on women, or pick on the women, or not see it as political. Just see it as an interpersonal issue. You know, if you say you were abused, and you say there was an interpersonal family dysfunction, that's okay to say. If you say you were abused, and it was because of the system that allows men to do this kind of thing to children, then you can be in a lot more danger and a lot more trouble.

"Because then, even the men who aren't abusers are mad at you. And, 'Why are you saying this is a male activity?'

"Well, because 99.9 percent of the time it is. The sexual abuse is a 90 percent, 95 percent male activity.

"And my take on the female sexual abusers is that many, many, many, many of them are teenage girls who have been sexually abused by males. Or are women who are in relationships with abusive men, who do it because they would get abused for not doing it. Or they do it because they're in a relationship where they're very dependent on some man. And I think it's a very, very small percentage of women who are sexual abusers out of no-where. They were abused by male relatives.

"So it still comes back to being initiated by males. I don't think we should lose sight of the fact that it is done by some women, and they need treatment, and they need identification—but that doesn't change the patriarchal part of it."

Will anything? I wonder. (Change the gender-inequity part of it, I mean.)

"If," I say, "the criminal justice system is not the answer; if this is not to be treated as a crime. And if it doesn't belong in the court that deals with domestic disputes. And if the court that is dedicated to issues of abuse and neglect is only going to fault the mother—what kind of animal *is* this? Where *does* it belong?"

"The thing is," Dr. Sugarman says, "it *should* be a crime. But it should be enforced as a crime just like wife-beating. Because when the battered wife kills her battering husband they're pretty good at enforcing that as a crime."

True. And when kids kill their fathers (or arrange to have it done) they do a pretty good job with that too. All the while scratching their heads about why the child didn't tell, didn't get help—oblivious (as the kids are not) to the significant power differential between themselves and their respectable fathers; oblivious (as the kids are not) as to the real nature of the intervention that describes itself as "help."

"Do you think the American public just doesn't want to hear this?"

"I'm not sure they don't want to hear it," Sugarman says. "I think the real question is, who prevents them from hearing it? How is it that they are prevented from hearing it? Even people who are saying it—the press doesn't find that exciting enough to report."

I suspect you may have noticed, but I will mention it anyway:

So far, we have learned that incest/child sexual abuse does not really belong in the criminal justice system—for reasons of evidence, the age of the children, and for an assortment of other proposed reasons beyond enumeration.

It does not belong in the juvenile justice system—because mothers are punished there for having failed to protect, and because middle-class men will hit the ceiling at this invasion of their privacy and of their property.

It does not belong in custody/probate court—because this court is designed for compromise and for working out equitable solutions between separating adults. And it is dangerous because it's a court in which fathers are once again gaining overwhelming superiority—in the name of gaining equality.

All this not-belonging reminds me of something (perhaps you remember it too):

Once upon a time, several years ago, there was a proud little barge. Designed to carry garbage, it stood staunchly in the Islip, Long Island harbor, as it was loaded. (Just as its mother had taught it to do, if you must know.) With solemn grace, it bore the weight and the stench of its cargo as it was sent off to fulfill its mission: to unload its refuse.

At the first stop, its refuse was refused (and, putting its chin up, it thought to itself, 'Well, that's okay. I'm new at this. If at first you don't succeed . . .')

But then it was rejected again, at its second stop. And at its *third . . .*

For months, the brave little barge chugged on—all down the Atlantic Coast, across the Gulf of Mexico, past the Carolinas, Florida, Alabama, Mississippi, Louisiana, Texas—meeting nothing but dismal rejection from landfill after landfill after landfill.

Still, on the little orphan puffed, through rain and wind and broiling sun (which improved neither the disposition of its cargo, nor its cargo's potential for disposition)—from Mexico, to Belize, to the Bahamas. . . .

And everywhere it stopped, at every single place, people held their noses with one hand and carried banners and placards with the other, which said (and not very nicely either) things like, "Go back where you came from!" And, "This is *our* landfill. Get out!" Not to mention, "NIMBY" and, "You stink!"

Sort of like the story of incest in search of a law court, don't you think? Obviously, to the father-protective court systems, the issue of incest—forcing a collision between men and their children who claimed severe violation—was toxic waste.

Chapter 9

THE INFANTILIZATION OF WOMEN I:

A Place Called Recovery

I HAD BEEN REREADING some of the "I-story" books—survivors' accounts of childhood abuse, often including their journey toward recovery. I'd been trying to put my finger on why it was that these accounts had such a contrary, numbing quality; trying to formulate in my mind how the change in the context of the times had changed the impact of the narratives, their very nature. . . .

I looked at my watch. After 11:00 A.M.! I was missing the show!

I should explain. Every day in the past few months, I'd been going through the daytime TV listings in the *New York Times*, reviewing the talk show topics of the day in order to keep current with the media presentation of the topic of incest, along the way making note of other issues television deemed gripping for women.

Today at 9:00 A.M., Jane Whitney has "Single Mothers Who Can't Get Dates." Montel Williams is doing "Death Row."

At 10:00, Joan Rivers has "Fashion Models," while Bertice Berry has "Misdiagnosed Illnesses" and Les Brown has "Fertility Breakthroughs."

Then—at 11:00 A.M.—Jerry Springer has the "Beavis and Butt-head Controversy" and the Mo Show has the "Growing Popularity of Marijuana."

But Richard Bey—he has "Parents Accused of Incest."

Belatedly tuning in, I am greeted by what appear to be three people on the panel, at least two of them women. It is difficult to tell, however, until they speak. Because the entire screen is filled with blinking squares and oblongs, blinking squares and oblongs, blinking oblongs and squares. . . . (Are they squares or oblongs? They look like squares. Wait, some look like oblongs, but I can't be sure. Maybe if I focus on one patch of the screen . . . How would I describe the color of those boxes? Magenta? No, they're too pale. Dirty purple? Muddy brownish-pink mixed with gray? Why do I keep thinking I discern a face I can almost recognize there? Now it's gone. Maybe I am too close up—like you can be to a pointillist work or a wildly enlarged dot matrix. . . .)

A woman's voice seems to emerge from the squares and is recounting her daughter's accusation of sexual abuse when she'd been a child; *horrible* things, the woman is saying: "Satanics." And it was all the therapist's fault; her daughter had been programmed by the therapist. . . .

A title flashes, the topic of the show, "Mommy Touched Me."

Ah. A real picture. Richard Bey, microphone in hand, striding the audience aisle, saying, "Is it possible to have vivid memories of things that *never—took—place?*"

Now he says to the studio audience they should close their eyes and imagine the letter A. I do it too. Now, he says, we should slowly rotate the letter A until it is upside down.

I'm doing this, but I've only achieved a quarter-turn before he says, "You see? It looks like a W!"

Does it? Immediately, I see a W. But did it come from the A or the Bey? Is this suggestibility? Which is the suggestion? Having the A turn into a W all by yourself? Or seeing W because he said W?

But he is moving quickly.

Now, he asks us to visualize the ears of a Doberman pinscher.

Suddenly, inexplicably, I block Dobermans and get a white dog with spots—no, that's a dalmation. Dobermans—the dogs in World War II movies when the German militia is searching fields for the downed U.S. flier . . .

"You see!" Bey has already said.

Hey, no fair, I didn't get the ears yet.

That, he tells us, is the power to conjure images.

The gist seems to be that it is possible to believe you see something that can't be there. If I get it right, therefore it is possible to "remember" something that wasn't there if it has been suggested to you vividly, maybe under hypnosis. . . .

(I think there is something wrong with the logic line here, but he's moving right along; he's already ahead of me.)

Now we meet Eleanor Goldstein, author of *Confabulations*, and another recent book about accounts of false memories, called *The True Stories of False Memories*. She looks a grandmotherly sort of woman; her style is thoughtful and measured.

I remember getting a flier for her new book, which promised me that the women speaking out in the book had already spoken about their horrendous experiences with false memories on Oprah, Donahue, "Prime Time Live," CNN News, Maury Povich, Tom Snyder, "Hard Copy," and "Front Page." "Now they write their stories in *True Stories of False Memories!*"

The times, I remember thinking: You used to have to write the book *first*.

Eleanor Goldstein's books have been promoted through the *False Memory Syndrome Foundation Newsletter*, so I am familiar with her work. Now she is saying to us that a lot of educated women are being programmed by therapists. But she is being mellow; she is saying it is not *all* therapists, just *some* therapists.

We hear questions from the audience addressed to those who, for me, lurk behind blinking squares (How old was your daughter when she went into therapy? . . .). One woman in the audience stands to suggest that the blinking-square people—whose daughters, they claim, have been destroyed by therapy—should maybe seek counseling. Counseling and therapy are the Ur-talk-show solutions, preferred whether the problem is siblings or cellulite. In the context, however, the suggestion is stunning.

Now I am looking at Mel Fein. His title says he is president of the National Center for Men. He appears to be stockily built, intense eyes, and with curly red hair flowing down past his shoulders. He speaks very loudly. He seems to be angry. I gather he's angry at women, but I can't be sure. I do catch the words "anti-sexuality movement."

Now Bey asks for a show of hands of those in the audience who think the blinking boxes are guilty. This is the court of public opinion. Hands go up, I can't tell how many.

My doorbell rings. It's United Parcel. (Oh, good—it's Jan Raymond's new book, *Women as Wombs*. I've read part of it in manuscript and it's a wonderful analysis of reproductive technology as a high-tech fuck, taking control of women's bodies.)

On the TV they keep talking about therapists taking control of women's minds.

Bey approaches a black woman in the first audience row. That probably means she's an invited participant. I gather she's already let people know she's an incest survivor. Bey is asking her what she would say to those mothers onstage.

What will she say? I wait.

Why does she seem to be hesitating, staring fixedly at the women on the panel? Here, after all, is an adult survivor with an opportunity to speak to this issue of false memories, maybe at least to respond to the passions of the gentleman from the National Center for Men. . . .

She is silent.

Bey is urging her.

She finally speaks.

What she says is, "I see your pain. . . ."

By the late 1980s, the issue of incest had so successfully been carved up into different areas of specialization that it was difficult to recognize it as an *issue*. You had the state interventions with children and the mental health professionals doing therapy with them; you had mental health institutions—therapeutic group homes and residential treatment centers—for those children because they were defined as "emotionally troubled." Separately, you had mental health professionals believing or disbelieving children of mothers trying to protect them. And lopped off from both of those, you had thousands and thousands of mental health professionals whose specialty was adult survivors.

Indeed, by the late 1980s, you could not tell that which the survivors were calling the *survivor movement* from what everyone else was calling the *recovery movement*. All women with symptoms of any discomfort were equally admonished to have courage, take power, end denial, and heal. You could not really tell the books apart either. They virtually all had adopted the tone of twelve-step fundamentalism, issuing calls to personal salvation.

Survivors' "I-story" books continued to appear, all hailed for their bravery and honesty. All hailed as breaking the silence. "We-story" books had begun to appear as well, true stories of women with multiple personalities caused by abuse, often as-told-to, in which each component was personified, and all fought it out as, in therapy, the struggle was on to integrate and become one. In these, we were introduced to new language: the language of "alter" personalities, of "splitting," of "integrating." There was even something called "mapping," in which you drew elaborate diagrams of the population of alters comprising (inhabiting?) you and marked those which you had, so far, integrated. Often, these "we-story" books replicated the difficulties of Russian novels—replete with more characters than one could comfortably keep track of, it was hard to be certain where one was.

Always, the entire focus was on the journey to recovery. I am not, here, asserting any skepticism about the existence in some discrete and limited number of people of a phenomenon that can be labeled Multiple Personality Disorder, or that such a phenomenon can result from horrendous childhood abuse—(although both definitions and identified populations have become absurdly delimited as fashion and financial reward have kicked in). What I am remarking on is that, deprived of all social context, informed only by the process of healing, the stories were bereft of any larger point. The offenders, the grotesque offenses, were background to a medical curiosity.

More and more, breaking the silence—having come to be an end in itself—had come to seem bankrupt.

Amazingly, at the same time, it was obviously increasingly *bankable*.

By the late 1980s, the networks had discovered the draw of women's pain and pathology as a daily event, and discovered, since production costs were low and the victims came free (or for travel expenses), that the shows were cheap. By 1993, in the northeast, you could choose from seventeen talk shows between nine in the morning and six in the evening. It was now a rare day when incest was not on the menu.

Variety came from different elaborations on the suffering or on the treatment recommended, or from the obliquely presented shouting matches about False Accusations, False Memories. As a topic, incest had everything. The women's stories appeared to bare all, but always, demurely, there was the fig leaf of cause, of larger meaning—tantalizingly offstage. Appearing to tell all, the stories nonetheless teased real revelation. The stories told *what*. They told *how*. They did not, in other than psychological terms, attempt even to ask *why*.

As a public issue, incest defied the usual interest curve. And not just on television.

In 1991, *Time* magazine headlined incest as "Coming Out of the Dark." "Crucial to recovery," the article said, "is the act of breaking the silence."[1]

On the very same day, *Newsweek* spoke of "The Pain of the Last Taboo." This article contained a picture of Marilyn Van Derbur Atler, who had come forward as having been sexually abused as a child. In the accompanying picture, she is "cradling a therapeutic doll." Thus adding the wrinkle of showing a former Miss America *infantilized*.²

I had not been alone in wondering, from the war zone of women losing custody of their children, where everyone was; what had *happened*. Muriel Sugarman, speaking from that battlefield, had said to me that she was angriest at feminists for not being there. Joan Pennington said she was angriest at survivors for not getting involved. Florence Rush, on different days, blamed the therapists and the media.

But did looking to assign fault even matter? As you poked your head out from the foxhole, you could not, any longer, always tell the feminists from the survivors: all seemed to be suffering some disorder within, and to be in therapy and, as victims, were willing guests on the media. And everyone, survivors, feminists, therapists, and talk show hosts included, thought they were championing progress in breaking the silence, telling women they were not alone, and extolling the value of healing.

Somewhere along the way, what seemed to have happened was a gigantic Acquisition and Merger.

Somewhere along the way, rather than feminism politicizing the issue of incest, incest-as-illness had overwhelmed and swallowed feminism. The result was the mass infantilization of women.

Women who were not defining themselves primarily as in pain because they were incest survivors were defining themselves as adult children in pain because of some other parental "toxicity," or as co-dependent: as love-addicted, sex-addicted, food-addicted, relationship-addicted, substance-addicted.

Arguments erupted about whether or not feminism had driven women to a victim mentality: the occasion for the argument was the issue of sexual harassment on campuses and the nature of date rape. It was kind of remarkable, really: in not even twenty years, we had covered the issues of rape, of battered women, of pornography. These continued to be issues of the same, if not greater, magnitude (albeit wafting in and out of public discourse). Now we were focused on sexual harassment and date rape. It was as though, unable to get society's attention on the core issue and unable to diminish the incidence of any of the abuses, fresh aspects of the issue kept being tossed up and taking the spotlight. This struck some as carping: "And another thing I've been meaning to tell you . . ." It struck some as harping on women as victims (but what is the choice? To be good sports?). Not only men, but women, seemed to be getting fed up.

Now, the challenge was put forth that if everyone is equally a victim, regardless of the degree of insult, then the word *victim* itself becomes meaningless: It is all the same. So. Now not only was the word *survivor* being rendered bogus, so was the word *victim*. What we seemed to be suffering, here, from all this speaking out, was a kind of aphasia: a loss of words, the material of speech itself.

If the recovery movement reigned supreme, it can plausibly be argued that incest survivors, a huge, available group of potential consumers, drove it. Virtually everything women would be adjured to recover from was something to which incest survivors were said to be prone. Strangely enough, given therapists' descriptions to me of the survivors' fragility and unreadiness to engage with anything outside their own private orbit, within the recovery movement survivors were the *leaders*. Well, they were the leaders as *followers*.

Searching for the support and solace and healing and *belonging* promised by a community designed for their recovery, and drawn by the promise that what they were seeking was freedom, liberation, empowerment, survivors were persuaded by the *therapeutic ideology*, a comforting blend of feminist language and mental health credo.

It is important to be clear. It is the therapeutic ideology, in apposition to the feminist worldview, that is at issue here. Feminist understanding (in my understanding) opens the personal to the political and to a comprehension of the larger issue. The therapeutic ideology—whatever its language—raises the personal to the paramount, placing the individual as the hub of her own claustrophobic universe; putting her "in recovery," as though that were a geographic location. For all the exuberance of the collateral language—healing, and so forth—to be *in recovery* derives from the disease model of alcoholism: thus, to be "in recovery" suggests a rather permanent placement. (There is no such thing, we have long been told, as a *recovered* alcoholic.)

The distinction I'm making is not between seeking, or not seeking, emotional help as a private enterprise, but between "the personal is political" and the "personal is all."

Much therapy was deemed to be *feminist* therapy. This designation derived from rape crisis centers and battered women's shelters, where women in crisis required counseling and support: it derived from the pragmatics of helping women to pick up the pieces and get on with their lives.

As Sage Freechild, whose background is in the rape crisis movement, says, "Once it became evident that there were literally millions of survivors, the mental health industry took notice. They identified a vast land of economic opportunity. We got tons of services for survivors, self-help books flourished, and conferences on survivor issues were sponsored by *professionals*, who were *experts* on the needs of women who'd been abused. Rather than lending support to grassroots, survivor-led existing services and fueling the already growing movement against abuse, therapists with the power of the mental health industry behind them took over. They *seem* to embrace the movement against violence against women and children. But their clinical focus works against any political agenda."

Borrowing from feminism, therapists rapidly came to speak of the goal of their specialty as "empowering" women. But what does this mean? As with the "empowering" of children by telling them to say no to rapists, it would seem to mean the creation of an illusion of power where the social reality is otherwise, and the consequent victim-guilt when all of that power does not quite do the trick.

Within the orbit of feminist therapy and female recovery, "speaking out" was sometimes referenced, in rebuttal to challenge, as still a political act. But as defined within the therapeutic universe, it was first and foremost a "stage" in recovery; something survivors needed to do by way of *healing*.

Laura Davis and Ellen Bass, in their now highly controversial best-seller, *The Courage to Heal*, write, "Speaking publicly— doing outreach to other survivors, working on child assault or rape prevention programs—is a powerful way to transform shame into a feeling of personal effectiveness and power." It is, they explain, "a way to let go of shame."[3] The primary goal is the goal of the self.

I have heard prominent professionals, addressing other professionals, similarly frame speaking out as something survivors need to do on the path to recovery, and actually call it a stage they "go through." (Something like the "terrible two's.") It is this that has worked to transform speaking out from the political into no more than the public confessional.

This understanding of speaking out is fixed in the therapeutic firmament. And because it is a phrase hijacked from feminist understanding, it is unequivocally asserted to be feminist. As is the purchase of the entire therapeutic package.

As Celia Kitzinger points out critically, the argument goes that, "The supposedly 'personal' activity of therapy is deeply political because learning to feel better about ourselves, raising our self-esteem, accepting our sexualities and coming to terms with who we really are—all these are political acts in a hetero-patriarchal world. With woman-hating all around us, it is revolutionary to love ourselves, to heal the wounds of patriarchy, and to overcome self-oppression. If everyone loved and accepted themselves, so that women (and men) no longer projected on to each other their own repressed self-hatreds, we would have real social change."4

Would we?

Some women and some men have, throughout history, found peaceable accord and it has not meant *bubkes* in diminishing paternal child rape or wife-battering or the rape of adult women. It is not now, any more than it ever has been, *all* men who choose these violences. But there is now, as there always has been, something that generates these violences in *men*. To shift the focus to women's self-rehabilitation can only lead to a victim-blaming theology that says that those who (allow themselves to) suffer violences need only learn to love themselves.

As my friend Tracy, who blew the whistle on her father when she was thirteen and was coerced into therapeutic encounters for the next four years, says, "They kept saying it was not my fault. But *I* was the one who had to be in therapy, where they kept saying it was not my fault. Fine. *I* knew that. If *I* knew and *they* knew it, why did we have to keep talking about it?"

The therapeutic ideology readily leads to, not change but imaginary change. Not to assault on the root cause of rape but to the building of endless treatment centers for a predictably endless supply of the wounded who, in their public display of anguished neediness, are taken to suffer from *diminished capacity*—to be humored and offered warm milk and medication. But who are not themselves to be taken seriously. Their *illness* is what is to be studied, debated, named and renamed; their defects are focal.

Once speaking out was transformed into confession, survivors were perceived exclusively in terms of their wounds, and began to see themselves that way.* As would become clearer and clearer, they were entirely marginalized. And the saddest of all the sad things to see was that they did not want to be. They deeply wanted to see themselves as a force.

---

* I am speaking of survivors collectively here, as a perceptible group. A heterogeneous lot, a goodly number have worked out what bothered them and gone on their way, thank you. Clearly, they are not, as survivors, part of the picture.

It bothered them greatly when I said, "Adult survivors, speaking out in this way, do not threaten the status quo." But—it was true.

And so survivors followed the therapeutic ideology along diagnostic trails—up the embankments of dissociation, through Multiple Personality Disorders; down gullies to Post-traumatic Stress Disorder, across raging currents to trauma disorders; they followed it to camps, to retreats, to Outward Bound programs, to psychiatric hospitals.

If incest drove the recovery movement, it also pervaded it. Because every single addiction or disorder addressed by "recovery" was said to be a symptom of possible childhood sexual abuse, it was probably inevitable that a certain amount of bleed-through would occur, a certain muzziness as to who was and who was not sexually abused. A proliferation of checklists of symptoms led to assumptions about who *might* have been abused, to undifferentiation, a welcoming of all into the "community." In *The Courage to Heal*, Laura Davis and Ellen Bass write, "If you don't remember your abuse, you are not alone. Many women don't have memories, and some never get memories. This doesn't mean you weren't abused."[5]

Laura Davis writes in her workbook, "Many survivors call me to ask permission to come to workshops because they're afraid they don't qualify. They don't have clear memories of their abuse, only an icky feeling or intuition. . . .

"When I get these kinds of calls, I reassure the survivor. I say, 'Yes, come.' "[6]

But why would women *want* to *qualify* for a sexual abuse workshop? (And isn't "qualify" a strange term in the context?) As a recovery issue, incest had become *fashionable*.

From being an aggressor's act that, along with other violences, served to socialize women, one by one, to acquiesce to larger male power (and in that subjection to become obsessed with weight, to feel distrust, to have—in the ubiquitous phrase—low self-esteem), incest became focal as *the* isolated, personal event that lay behind (or might lay behind) symptoms not uncommon in a great number of women—as well as women who had been sexually violated in childhood.

We had entered a land of circularity sufficient to blow brain-cell circuits. The nature of the pathology, the survivors' complaints, were in most ways identical to the complaints most women could recognize—vulnerability, bad relationships, dependency (co-dependency). . . . And these were the very complaints that feminists had identified as politically determined and politically derived. The very real and very rotten and very prevalent fact of paternal child rape now was the therapeutic substitute for political consciousness. Incest had crossed a boundary into a very dangerous neighborhood—that of metaphor.

It was an astonishing turn of events.

What we had hoped was that feminism would adopt and strengthen the issue of incest by insistently putting it forward within the larger issue of licensed male violence and working toward *change*. Instead, feminists, following not their own logic, but their own purloined *language*, followed—almost trance-like—as that language was snatched from them and dangled before them by psychology and therapy: words like *liberation* and *power* and *choice*. Instead of survivors being drawn to feminist-designed solutions, feminists were drawn to solutions designed for the defined pathologies of survivors.

Well. I cannot argue that that is not *change*.

Feminists, survivors or not, began enjoying lengthy ill health and even lengthier recovery, and calling it *confrontation*. The *struggle* had been entirely reframed.

––––––––

If all this focus on incest-as-illness did not strike me as healthy for survivors, it certainly did not seem to be healthy for feminism.

Wendy Kaminer has written, "The marriage of feminism and

the phenomenally popular recovery movement is arguably the most disturbing (and potentially influential) development in the feminist movement today. It's based partly on a shared concern about child abuse, nominally a left-wing analogue to right-wing anxiety about the family."[7]

But that, of course, is precisely the brilliance of the therapeutic ideology. By defusing the political content, it serves the status quo, and it offends no one. In the view of the left, *help* appears to be liberal. In the view of the right, it diverts people with justifiable complaints from protest. Given that, it appears to be something outside of politics itself. After all, who can be against "treatment"? Who can be against healing or recovery?

This shift from the feminist analysis to the therapeutic understanding (supported by feminists) inevitably changed the nature and the meaning of women's narratives, and of speaking out, itself. As Carol Tavris writes, "It was part of the larger cultural shift away from collective political action to an individualizing mental-health movement. Each battered or raped woman, each molested or raped child, was regarded as an instance of rare and bizarre family pathology."[8]

And so the net effect of the parade of out-speakers and recoverers was—no matter how much the press played the widespread incidence, the routine commonality of paternal child rape—that the public's perception of paternal child rape was nonetheless as a one-by-one, peculiar, *aberrant* event.

It is unsurprising that, as the embrace of illness and need for recovery was extended exponentially to include virtually all women suffering from virtually all the miseries long-associated with female complaints, a pain-competition would develop, as survivors sought to distinguish themselves in what had become a densely populated field. So it is not surprising that survivors began to speak of their suffering in ever more elaborate terms.

Nor is it surprising that feminists would bring to their passions for the reigning therapeutic ideology some of the same energies and political issues they had brought to activism, and encounter challenge on those fronts.

Kaminer says, "There's an emerging alliance of anti-pornography and anti-violence feminists with therapists who diagnose and treat child abuse, including 'ritual abuse' and 'Satanism' (often said to be linked to pornography). Feminism is at risk of being implicated in the unsavory business of hypnotizing suspected victims of abuse to help them 'retrieve' their buried childhood memories. Gloria Steinem has blithely praised the important work of therapists in their field without even a nod to the potential for, well, abuse when unhappy, suggestible people who are angry at their parents are exposed to suggestive hypnotic techniques designed to uncover their histories of victimization."[9]

This may be somewhat overstating the case and oversimplifying it. (For a word-turned-epithet, *feminist* has been claimed by a surprisingly large number of women holding astonishingly disparate beliefs.) But it does point up the degree to which many feminists have been seduced away from questioning the lure of the therapeutic ideology.

And it is certainly worth examining what happens when unhappy, *isolated* people see acceptance and the embrace of their suffering, understanding of their *feelings*, in a community of misery. "You are not alone"—meant initially to assure survivors who had grown up under a world-blanket of secrecy and silence—had proved a much more powerful, a virtually irresistible, draw. It was, of course, the same kind of draw to community that had energized activist feminism.

If there is any question as to whether early second-wave feminists were correct in posing consciousness-raising and therapy as antithetical, one need only glance around the world as customized for incest survivors to discern the answer. (By comparison, the universe in which mothers were fighting on behalf of their children seems a model of lucidity.)

To me, it seems like this: You emerge onto a large field, bathed in unnaturally bright light. From left, from right, from center, wafts a mix of calliope music, occasional portentous but disconnected musical phrases, and the drift of a trivial tinkle of Muzak.

All paths promise to lead to Recovery. Along them, many rides and tents are set up. At some, you can fingerpaint. At others, win teddy bears. Under klieg lights, a rotating stage is set up. A sign marks it as the Speaking Out Stage. From it, talk shows are being perpetually broadcast: The lines of women eager to get on the stage stretch as far as the eye can see.

Alongside one path is an elaborate enclosed construction with tracks running through. Rail-cars are constantly filling up. With a single toot, one after the other leaves to enter the tunnel chambers. A large sign bills this as the Tunnel of Alters. Underneath which, in quote marks, is written, "Multiples Are Not Alone!"

Outside the booth at which you pay for your ticket (and receive an insurance form in receipt), a barker, in constantly changing voices, delivers a pitch about this as the ultimate trip toward Recovery, during which, one by one, your Multiple Personalities Will Make Themselves Known! At the exit is a large stand selling T-shirts and sweatshirts and books on how to stencil on the shirts maps of your alters, indicating, by colors, the ones who have, during the ride, agreed to be "integrated."

As you amble along, on each path you encounter numerous billboards with lists on them, such things as feelings of moodiness, difficulty concentrating, poor relationships, occasional fearfulness, poor self-image . . . and congratulating you on your courage in choosing this path!

Along some paths, tents have been set up—ones especially for your "Inner Child," others for your "Inner Toddler," and "Inner Adolescent." There are yet other tents, marked "Bodywork," and "Dance." And platforms covered with foam rubber mats, lined with foam rubber pillows and foam rubber bats, each called a Rage Stage.

Each path is crowded with women, some going one way, some another (but then on each path, in either direction, the arrow points to "recovery," so it appears not to matter). The mood of the crowd seems to be at once one of teariness and of complete absorption. The women move indeliberately, without haste or urgent purpose, as though here to stay, not just to visit.

Pausing to sample each offering, they purchase a book here, a tape there, a button somewhere else. Occasionally, someone bursts into tears, whether overcome by all this that has been set up just for her, or from the exhaustion caused by all this work on her "issues" you can't be sure. Counselors then appear and, making soothing noises about the woman's progress on the path, lead her off to one of the frequently placed metal structures marked PORT-O-SAFE ("A Safe Space").

This was what life had brought us, then: An Incest Recovery Theme Park.

It was a theme park with a decidedly spiritualist dimension. More and more, the promise of *treatment* and of *healing* had come to sound indistinguishable from the promise of Lourdes. The promotion had come to sound evangelical. And the materials used, to seem Revivalist. From the very outset, the cajoling to recovery had sounded like the call to conversion.

"By now it should be clear," therapist Beverly Engel wrote in 1982, "*recovery is possible*. A new life is possible. But neither is possible without a commitment to begin and complete the journey. *It is the single most important thing you can do to assure your recovery*. A commitment is your promise to yourself to go through all the steps required in the recovery process and to stick with it, no matter what. The agreement is *not* 'I will work through the trauma of abuse *if* I can.' And it is also not 'I'll do it unless it gets too painful.' It is saying with conviction, 'I will continue working through the effects of the abuse until I reach recovery.' "[10]

In much of the literature, the directives seem designed to reduce women to the childish and the infantile.

"Do you remember the wonderful warmth and security you felt by holding your special childhood toy?" Engel writes. "Your inner child needs that comfort once again. Take your inner child to a store and spend lots of time choosing just the right stuffed animal or doll for her recovery process."[11]

One woman quoted in *The Courage to Heal* gave herself birthday parties. "Starting with my 'fifth' birthday, I have been counting down to my first. I celebrated my 'fifth' over children's stories and chocolate cake. Friday I'll be celebrating my 'third' birthday. . . . I'm going to build a tent out of bed sheets and we'll sit inside and read stories by flashlight. There will be glow-in-the-dark stars on the tent ceiling. Oh, I love being little!"

Another woman, we are told, "set up whole playrooms for the injured children within her."[12]

While, again, I have no interest in doing other than assuming there is such a phenomenon as gives rise to the label Multiple Personality Disorder, it is extremely interesting that the intense reification of the "Inner Child" (and toddler, and adolescent) preceded what is now taken to be an epidemic of such disorders.* Women were actively being encouraged to corporealize the phantom child: to converse with it (her?), to comfort it, to deal with it as though it were *actual* and not figurative.

Engel writes, "While you work on each step of your recovery program, continue your dialogue with your inner child. Check with her often to see how she feels. Listen to her closely. She will tell you what you need in order to feel safer and more secure."[13]

Whatever the true incidence of persons with whatever symptoms gain them the label of Multiple Personality Disorder, in this way, women as a whole were being encouraged to create in themselves "multiples."

Some of the advice given in these books seemed dippily to deny the existence of a social universe—where there might be an audience to your behavior.

* "From 1920 through 1971, 12 cases of multiple personality disorder were reported in the psychotherapy literature. In the 1980s, more than 20,000 were diagnosed" (Kim Ode, "Issue of Memory Is Complicated," Minneapolis *Star Tribune*, October 11, 1993, 3E).

About releasing your anger, for example, Engel advises that you make these things part of your daily schedule:

" Each time you reach forward with the vacuum cleaner, call out, 'Get away from me.'
" When taking out the garbage, stomp on the egg cartons, aluminum cans, or any other garbage that makes a loud sound and imagine you are stomping on whoever hurt you.
" If you do carpentry, pound each nail with a 'Take that!' "[14]

Elsewhere, she advises that you throw unwanted dishes or raw eggs against your garage wall, back fence, or garbage can.[15]

One can only hope that the women who took this advice had no proximate neighbors.

More critical here, however, is the way in which women are being urged to *domesticate* their anger—to vent their energies in little psychodramas while vacuuming or taking out the garbage. They are not being urged to think in terms of larger meanings, to organize to act in the larger world toward any larger purpose.

———

Increasingly, I have been hearing of acute-care inpatient psychiatric hospitals preying on incest survivors in what has become a flourishing staple of their "services." Insurance-covered, these are programs women *choose* to go into.

Therapist friends send me brochures advertising Sexual Trauma Programs for all the things survivors are said to suffer from: anxiety, depression, eating disorders. . . .

One hospital even offers an inpatient program simply for *women* who, today, the brochure tells us, "face unprecedented challenges." "The inpatient program houses five to eight women at a time. Mental health care services such as treatment for depression, anxiety and eating disorders are provided: additionally, special group sessions, selected films and readings, nutrition and exercise counseling and other services designed particularly for

women are included." So now just being *female* is pathology
enough to check yourself into an acute-care psychiatric facility.

Other programs offer inpatient treatment for co-dependency,
"a disease brought on by growing up in a dysfunctional family
system." (And what kind of family systems do we know cause
incest?)

Cottonwood de Albuquerque Treatment Center offers Treatment for Sexual Trauma, which they advertise with the quote, "I
am an INCEST VICTIM. THANK GOD, I THOUGHT I WAS
CRAZY." It is signed, "by an unknown incest victim." We are at
the very border, here, of the danger of—um—confusion.

Most of these programs promise referrals to twelve-step programs upon your release.

I stare at the twelve steps for incest survivors from a 1983
Sexual Abuse Anonymous pamphlet, aghast. Here are some of the
steps:

" Admit you are powerless over your early experience and that
your life has become unmanageable.
" Come to believe that a power greater than yourself can restore
you to sanity.
" Make a decision to turn your will and your life over to the care
of God as you understand Her/Him.
" Admit to God, yourself and another human being the exact
nature of your wrongs [yes, yours].
" Be entirely ready to have God remove these defects of character
[yes, *yours*].
" Humbly ask Her/Him to remove your shortcomings.
" Make a list of all persons you have harmed and become willing
to make amends to them all."[16]

I ask you. If this were a twelve-step program designed by
rapists, could they have improved on this program of sin and
redemption (sin, yours; redemption task, yours)?

Adult women engrossed in journeys of healing and recovery

bothered no one, threatened nothing. Women, daughters, hugging teddy bears and seeking safe spaces did not discomfit fathers. Survivors, pursuing the early goal of forgiving their offenders, shared this in common with those following the Christian doctrine of forgiveness: Offenders or sinners, neither cared, one way or another, whether you forgave them or not.

It was only when survivors, operating from the safety of their cloistered therapeutic world, did something to poke the larger outside reality, that loud angry shouting could be heard: that the backlash mobilized and sent out its enforcers. Sadly, by then, survivors collectively had become so marginalized that when the marauders attacked, they were not even the targets.

Chapter 10

THE INFANTILIZATION OF WOMEN II:

A Place Called Denial

B Y 1 9 9 2 , from the hullabaloo you would have thought the sky was falling. By 1993, you would have thought the very heavens were tumbling on top of it as well.

Alarm about so-called false memories of incest and satanic or ritual or cult abuse now raged everywhere. And the most spectacular disorder the issue of incest and severe childhood abuse had so far thrown up, Multiple Personality Disorder, was everywhere those things were and anywhere they were not. And wherever MPD went it played out as spectacle, drawing oohs and ahs (but inevitably leaving some in the audience wondering how the trick was done).

This morning, November 14, 1993, at nine o'clock, Jane Whitney has for us couples; the wives suffer from MPD. The show is called "My Wife Has 100 Personalities." (If you are tiring of these reports in the media, just think: What I refer to is only .0005 percent of all that has gone by.)

First we meet Peter and Alexis. She holds two stuffed animals, one of them a Snoopy dog. Next to her sits her husband, who smilingly tells us, "I don't always know who I'm talking to!"

What we learn is that Alexis had always believed she'd had an idyllic childhood. But in reality satanic torture had shattered her into one hundred personalities, and she didn't remember it until she'd been raped and had started to see a therapist.

Gary Lefkof, M.D., is with us. He will be our expert this morning. He specializes in this disorder, and he tells us Alexis's case is very typical, that it's kind of a fight-or-flight response, only we run in our own heads and split into different parts, sometimes called "troops," or "characters," or "alters."

Of the many alters who participate in his married life, Peter says, "A lot of them hate me."

The thought crosses my mind (and so it must cross others') that perhaps these two people may be unduly medicalizing her moods. The thought also crosses my mind that Peter has said this as though he is kind of proud of the whole thing.

There is the perhaps inevitable question from the audience as to whether Peter ever finds he is really making love to a ten-year-old. The answer is elided in cross-talk.

Now we meet Sally, who explains to us the difference between being conscious and being "co-conscious." She is not, she explains, co-conscious. (This appears to mean she—whoever "she" is—doesn't know her alters.) Sally tells us that the condition makes her dangerous—who knows who is driving the car? And she sometimes wakes up with blood coming out of her arm. In answer to a question, she says the reason these alters exist is to keep the secret.

Sally will let us meet "Abby." Abby is five. Abby says, "I just want to say I am real. I live in this big old body. Where do you live?" And she (Sally, I gather) will let us meet "Crystal" as well, though she warns us that Crystal doesn't speak, she uses sign language.

According to Dr. Lefkof, the treatment is to introduce the personalities to each other until they are integrated and no longer have to dissociate, and it can be a long process, often ten years.

We meet Ron and Kay. She carries a stuffed dog, too. One of her multiples has a drinking problem. Another is suicidal. Kay says she doesn't remember any sexual abuse.

Lefkof says that is something that comes out later.

Asked about her stuffed animal, Kay says, "This is Barney. The children play with Barney."

The children won't come out for us today, though.

Smiling, Ron explains: "They're mad at her. Because she's telling about it."

Why does he seem so pleased? Why do all the men seem so happy with this state of affairs? Why do they seem absolutely proud, displaying their wives with their teddy bears and their alters?

What is wrong with this picture?

What is wrong with this *whole* picture?

Although the issues of so-called false memories and satanic ritual abuse would seem on the surface to be separate, they have both been made to conflate around the issue of memory, and allegations (and counterallegations) of mind control. According to officials at the False Memory Syndrome Foundation, 15 percent of the 2,846 calls it received its first year related to accusations against parents by adult young women that they had been victimized during their childhoods by satanic abuses.[1]

Nationwide, thousands of women are speaking about having been forced to kill and eat babies at satanic ceremonies, seeing children dismembered; about being drugged and branded with irons, raped with crucifixes, buried in coffins, being penetrated by snakes, tied to crosses, transported in cages. . . .

And so memories of routine household child-rape and truly exotic and time-consuming torture are now tossed at us in tandem with, from one side, the cry of "Believe!" And from the other side, the cry of "Lies!" And what we are looking at resembles nothing so much as a holy war.

In keeping with the oddly allied interests of fundamentalists, therapists, and talk shows, we have all now been warned that to disbelieve any woman's testimony—be it of simple childhood rape or marriage to Satan—is to disbelieve all.

To doubt or be skeptical is to live in another geographic space: This one is called "denial."

It is, of course, the linking of "false memories" and satanic abuse that so brilliantly befuddles thought. By itself, the outcry over false memories (which is itself a pejorative for delayed memories) can be parsed.

What happened was, the issue of incest went into yet another court.

Adult survivors began to sue.

And there came upon us a most unholy noise, a mixture of earnest anguish and blustering rage.

And they called the noise False Memory Syndrome.

And cries of *confabulation!* rang out through the media with a great din, as we were asked:

"CHILDHOOD TRAUMA: MEMORY OR INVENTION?"[2]

And told:

"SEX ABUSE MEMORIES IN QUESTION."[3]

And regaled with:

"A CHILD'S MEMORIES AND A FATHER'S NIGHTMARE."[4]

"Over the past several years, psychotherapists have helped thousands of people discover repressed memories of childhood sexual abuse," leads a *Mother Jones* article. "What is more disturbing still is that many of these memories may be false."[5]

In all of the stories, in all the megatons of material put out about the issue, survivors themselves were never blamed. Always, it was the therapists, who had programmed them, hypnotized them, and preyed on their suggestibility, who were held to be at fault and who were, collectively, held to be "cult-like." The women themselves were portrayed as vulnerable, gullible, *infantile* . . . and at the mercy of Craftier Forces.

Was this backlash?

Clearly, there was evidence that it was. Dr. Ralph Underwager, who had been most outspoken about child sexual abuse "hysteria" and had been an expert witness for fathers in numerous "custody disputes," was on the advisory board of the False Memory Syndrome Foundation. The foundation's attack was directed at "feminist therapists" for creating false memories.

Right in the midst of all this uproar, Dr. Underwager's interview with the Dutch journal *Paidika, The Journal of Paedophilia*, was published.[6] Also, that same year, Dr. Richard Gardner of Columbia University, who had also been vigorously outspoken on sex abuse hysteria and had also testified widely on behalf of accused fathers, published a paper in Underwager's journal, *Issues in Child Abuse Accusations*, entitled, "A Theory About the Variety of Human Sexual Behavior." This theory proposes that "many different types of human sexual behavior, including the paraphilias, can be seen as having species survival value." What Gardner hopes to demonstrate is that "even those forms of sexual behavior that do not lead immediately to procreation may still serve nature's purposes and thereby not warrant being excluded from the list of the so-called natural forms of human sexual behavior."[7]

Gardner proposes that most men are naturally promiscuous, and that children are "not only naturally sexual but that they may be the initiators of sexual activities." Thus, he places sex with children among other things psychiatry has identified as deviances from the sexual norm (paraphilias) that "in a way, serve the purposes of species survival and are therefore part of the natural repertoire of humanity. They serve this end by their ability to enhance the general level of sexual excitation in society and thereby the likelihood that people will involve themselves in activities that are more directly contributive to the reproductive (and, by extension, species survival) process."[8]

Gardner's focus is narrow—eschewing, for example, broader concerns about world overpopulation, the social costs of teenage pregnancy, sexually transmitted diseases. "Pertinent to my theory here," he writes, "is that pedophilia also serves procreative purposes. Obviously, it does not serve such purposes on the immediate level in that children cannot become pregnant nor can they make others pregnant. However, the child who is drawn into sexual encounters at an early age is likely to become highly sexualized and crave sexual experiences during the prepubertal years. Such a 'charged up child' is more likely to become sexually active after puberty and more likely, therefore, to transmit his or her genes in his or her progeny at an early age.

"The younger the survival machine at the time sexual urges appear, the longer will be the span of procreative capacity, and the greater the likelihood the individual will create more survival machines in the next generation."[9]

In short, this is a theory that would seem to support sex with children as a benefit to the very survival of our species. The fact that no note was taken by the media of either Underwager's or Gardner's publicly stated philosophical positions on pedophilia is interesting, as evidence of the degree to which the issue of incest had been successfully robbed of perceptible political significance; the degree to which politics had been obliterated from the consciousness of all but the backlash. Where a dozen years earlier, such views seized media attention, were found shocking, the proponents labeled the "pro-incest lobby" and publicly challenged—by 1993 the whole issue had been so successfully psychologized and "expertized" that it did not appear to occur to any serious journalists to look behind the debunkers' expert credentials, to rummage for even easy-to-find signs of a political/philosophical agenda.

Instead, the field was left clear for the backlash to rail on about radical feminists, by which they meant therapists, who in the greatest majority had no feminist or other political identification or agenda; many of whom were, in fact, strongly supportive of the rubric that offenders were gender neutral.

But—was there some evidence that a goodly number of therapists were using doubtful techniques, or using respectable techniques with doubtful skills, to evoke (or implant) memories?

That seemed, to me, equally clear. There were too many all-inclusive checklists of symptoms, too many therapists vested in specialization; there was too much money to be made to think there was not witting or unwitting error occurring. There was too much *historical* evidence: psychiatry and psychology have long targeted and exploited women. There were too many credible stories of mind-leading and persuasion-to-believe told by too many women. And then there was the manipulative literature itself, published by therapists. Along with all that, the voguishness and belonging that now accrued to the label of "incest survivor," combined with the fashion for the "adult child" identification, ensured large-scale susceptibility.

Was there such a thing as long-delayed memory, or repressed memory?

In my opinion and in my listening experience, definitely. Even in the mid-1970s, any number of women I heard from had a sudden surge of remembering, tripped when something overwhelming happened to them, often something reminiscent of the earlier sexual trauma—like their own or their daughter's rape. These were un-looked-for recollections and, at a time when incest was still thought a stigmatizing taboo, entirely unwelcome. This kind of sudden recall, then, was easy to account for: In a time of silence, nothing stirred memory up. In a time of silence, there was simply nothing to be done with such information: It could not be shared and it could not be plausibly integrated into all of the rest of life.

Florence Rush says to me, "People do push things aside, particularly when there is strong social pressure to put things aside, push them back. Now, however, women are being pressed into trying to remember things—things as early as six months, two years. . . ."

Now, in fact, the entire context had changed. "Incest survivor" had been posed as an acceptable defining identity; unremembered or ill-remembered childhood rape had been posited to account for all manner of later female experience. And now the stakes had been raised as well. Adult survivors who had not earlier presented any threat to the status quo, had decided not only to challenge their aging parents with sometimes no more than snatches of dim recall, but to actively confront them and take them to court. This certainly contributed to bringing down upon our heads an organized backlash which, invoking a mantle of medical authority, decided to charge forth under the banner of a newly invented disease: False Memory *Syndrome*.

At bottom, one main trigger for the backlash that brought us into this morass was that well-known emotional catalyst, money.

It was 1980 when I first began hearing about women suing or planning to sue their fathers or stepfathers for childhood sexual abuse. It was proposed, then, with an unmodified elation I could not fully share.

Unquestionably, civil suits could be an effective political tool, a tactic. But that required that they be set within a larger strategy, wherein power abuse and the demand for restitution could be clearly communicated. Not only did we lack coherent force, but we had not yet been allowed to make clear the deliberateness, the gratuitousness, of the assaults—had not removed them from the family muddle and identified the offender as a conscious agent. (Indeed, the opposite was happening, with mothers implicated and the language of dysfunction flying loose.)

At that time, we were still deep in the woods with the prevailing wisdom that children like the sex part (they just don't know yet that it's "wrong"). Or that the children take bribes for it— meaning there is some trade-off that works.

It did not seem to me that adults now suing for money damages would do anything to mitigate these myths. It was doubtful public relations.

More critically, it seemed woefully premature.

"This will get them where they live," survivors would say.

Well, yes. Precisely.

And there was nothing in place yet to deal with what I, at least, thought would be the anticipated result. Because whether the suits succeeded or failed in any particular instance, the net result was bound to trip outrage on the collective part of alleged perpetrators.

Unless they were placed within a larger understanding, civil suits risked becoming a tactic vacant of context.

As such, in the face of the backlash's passion, they were extremely vulnerable, and they rendered survivors as a whole extremely vulnerable—most particularly when the reason most often articulated for the suits was to cover the costs of therapy.

Again, I was not against civil suits as one part of a remedy. (It has been the rash of civil suits that have at last forced the churches to deal with abuse by priests and clergy.) But I was concerned by what seemed extravagant optimism in household cases where the individual suits existed in isolation. And where they were—as they increasingly came to be—framed as actions toward recovery rather than justice.

Even then, survivors spoke of lawsuits in personal terms—of taking power, of healing. But even then it seemed very much a fantasy power. It is excruciatingly difficult, in a courtroom, where all of your records are made available, where all of your feelings and past behaviors are open to question, to feel anything other than under attack. Any idea that this is power is purely delusional. And I don't think very many people who have participated in a lawsuit would describe the experience as contributing to *healing*.

Blocked, then, only by statutes limiting the time that could pass before the pressing of suit—nonetheless even then some suits were successful. One, in Utah:

"A young woman's successful $42,000 damage suit against her stepfather for eight years of sexual abuse is upheld by the Utah Supreme Court. The stepfather contended the girl had consented to his sexual advances, but the court declares a minor cannot consent to such acts."[10] The girl was nine years old when the abuse began.

As statutes of limitations were challenged in more and more states, we began to read headlines like "Incest Survivor Sues Father."[11] And "Grandfather, 96, Hit by Molestation Suit."[12] And of how "the twin daughters of a UC Berkeley associate professor of physical education charged that their father sexually abused them, in a civil suit filed against him and the university."[13]

And, "Court Orders Father to Pay $243,000 in Sex Abuse Suit."[14]

By 1993, twenty-three states had extended or eliminated statutes of limitations barring lawsuits in such cases.[15]

While the recovery literature spoke of suits in terms of growth, therapeutic strengthening, personal power, and self-esteem, by the 1990s, survivors themselves sounded bravely determined but far less certain. They seemed, rather, to take that message of litigation-as-liberation as one more challenge to their *courage* to heal.

It was as though they wanted to do something *active*. But within the hermetically sealed universe that had been designed for them, they were so mired in the personal that a personal action seemed all that was possible. To the degree that they intuited the potential impact of their aggression, they intuited it only in personal terms. What moved them seemed a mixture of some grandiose imagined good, muddled thinking, and hurt feelings.

"So why did I choose to sue?" one survivor, pseudonymed Penelope, writes. "The decision rested more on being one of millions of survivors, and standing up for us. The decision incorporated the possibility of stopping this man from molesting other children and with refusing to allow one more perpetrator to get away with this crime because incest is such a shameful secret. I felt I must stand up to empower myself, as well as to help future children and present survivors by breaking the secret."

It is disheartening to hear in this survivor's words the sound of someone whose world seems so insular: boundaried by meaningless terms and imagined heroics, entirely remote from awareness of the pedestrian realities of trying to prove in court that your father raped you fifteen years ago. Unaware, as well, that should there be a settlement, she would most likely be barred from mentioning the settlement or talking further, publicly, about the abuse at all. (Instead of "breaking the secret," she will be, for herself, *remaking* it.)

It was disheartening to hear, in this universe where "you are not alone" was the motto, the sound of someone so isolated in her search for "empowerment." It was as though, in her world, language promised reward for confused thinking.

"My decision to sue my parents in civil court was made with great trepidation," she writes. "I risked losing my parents, my siblings, my friends, and most of all, my client-therapist confidentiality. I feared physical retaliation from my perpetrator, and felt a tremendous amount of guilt because I was hurting my family."[16]

What can one *say*? Suing the offender for the funds he had earmarked for his retirement is not a gesture of reconciliation. And if reconciliation is *not* what she had in mind, why the concern about "losing" her parents? The idea that she might lose the affections of other family members is plausible, as well. Her siblings might be somewhat taken aback at the prospect of impoverished, perhaps dependent, parents.

Then why do it?

"The only two personal benefits I could perhaps rely on," Penelope writes, "were the empowerment I might gain from standing up for myself; and the additional issues triggered by the lawsuit I would have to resolve. The former would be an important positive feeling of control over myself; the latter would be important as I am finishing my Master's degree in counseling, and my issues must be resolved to be an effective counselor."[17]

What can one say?

What kind of a health-giving universe is it where everything—dance, music, art, physical activity—is part of *therapy*, including *lawsuits*. It was as though women had somehow managed to become institutionalized outside of institutions; as though they were part of a social experiment in hospitals-without-walls.

Once again, what is hardest to swallow is the fact that to do so much direct and collateral damage to survivor credibility—in the face of all this ambivalent and unformulated thought—the false-memory backlash did not have to be very swift at all.

As it turns out, I was not alone in my skepticism about this suing business. (Although I *felt* alone, jeez.)

Lucy Berliner, with the Sexual Assault Program at Harborview Medical Center in Seattle, is primarily concerned with survivors' emotional health; with the clinical, rather than the political. She says, "To my mind, that's another problem area—civilly suing for damages. Essentially, getting into that world—that legal world which is a guy world; winners and losers, adversaries duking it out, proving things—pretty standard guy type ways of solving problems and deciding on things. Well, what does it really mean?

"What's the experience of really doing that? Allegedly, the women are doing it to get a sense of justice—that's what they say. And justice means what? It means that some other people will officially say he did it. Your own internal experience of knowing that he did and having your own friends and people around you who know and love you and who know that, isn't enough. It isn't official."

"Well," I say, "but they had this certainty that they were going to get the bastards where they hurt. And when I first started to hear about this, I remember saying, 'That's exactly the problem. You folks have not organized for the kind of retaliation you're going to get.' "

"Well, if you saw that coming, you were absolutely right. The whole False Memory Syndrome controversy is almost entirely coming out of that. Almost entirely. When we started to get out of the therapist's office and dealing with our own experience. When the survivors were having these personal meetings with their family—then nobody cared. You didn't see organizations springing up around that. It was the court and the money.

"And look what suing does to the victim. First of all, you are engaging in a process in which you are—number one—agreeing to delay any possibility of feeling better for several years minimum. In order to get the money—maybe. And the accountability. But in civil suits, part of the agreement once you settle is you can't say anything publicly about it. You get the money but you can't say how much and you can't talk about it.

"But here's the thing that bugs me about it. It is: *The sicker you are, the more you get.*"

Oh dear. So here we were—in yet another court that doesn't work for us, and with another act of recovery that in fact serves to immerse the victim more three-dimensionally in her pathology.

And here we were, back once again to the problem we had at the beginning: How much damage do you have to prove to say paternal child-rape is *serious?*

Lucy says, "The question is, why can't it be awful without your having to be dead—or the walking wounded? Why can't you just say, 'It was terrible. It was an awful experience.' And you can still be a person. Why is it either it didn't really happen or it wasn't that bad? We should not want to contribute to that kind of paradigm. Where in order for it to have been bad, you have to have been destroyed."

No. We should not.

But apparently—here we are, doing just that. And here again, it is the switch from the feminist to the therapeutic ideology—with its muzzy-minded focus on incest survivors as the neurasthenics of the 1990s—that has framed a lousy and truly destructive and potentially devastating experience as an individual disease, rather than as the result of an ingrained social disorder.

And so even the potentially effective political weapon of civil suits was becoming corrupted by the therapeutic goldrush; the trolling for possible survivors; and by the alienating, individuating language of *journeying* to *recovery*. The combination of a practical threat of retaliation and the absence of a larger political understanding and force simply served to step up backlash vigor—without leading to moral engagement.

Liz Kelly, Linda Regan, and Sheila Burton write, "The notion of a 'journey' to survival, where one is 'healed' is both naïve and idealistic. It is impossible to change what has happened in the past, although that may indeed be what many children and adults wish they could do, hence the potency of forgetting as a coping strategy. . . . The medical metaphors of 'healing' and 'recovery' offer a false hope that experiences of abuse can be understood and responded to in a similar way to illness: where both symptoms and cause can be 'got rid of' if one can simply find the right 'treatment.' Thus interactional and social events which are fundamentally about inequality and the use of power-over are transformed into individual encounters equivalent to the contracting of germs or viruses."[18]

With the overwhelming sweep of victim-voguishness, the proliferation of checklist-indicators, and the escalating emphasis on horrendous pathology, it was more than conceivable that some of those appearing in news stories or on television as parents claiming their children had been programmed with false memories were more than likely correct. Just as some of those marching under the VOCAL flag might well have had genuine reason to be miffed at wrongful state interventions.

What was most astonishing to me as I followed the uproar through its escalating caloric heat was that nowhere did anyone seem to make a connection between this newest "syndrome" and the one by which the media had, earlier, been carried away: False Accusation Syndrome.

In its November 29, 1993, issue, *Time* magazine followed a piece on "Is Freud Dead?" with one on "Lies of the Mind," which told us that "repressed-memory therapy is harming patients, devastating families, and intensifying a backlash *against mental health practitioners*" (italics mine).[19] You have heard it right: a backlash against mental health practitioners.

On December 5, 1993, *The New York Times* in its Week in Review section said, "Some suggest that what may seem like memories are unreliable: feelings of oppression and resentment, whether at the hands of parents or priests, are converted through some mysterious alchemy into 'memories' of physical abuse. Others argue that the accounts of suddenly recalled incest are so prevalent because such abuse is indeed rampant."[20] While the author of the story, Susan Chira, does quote feminists Katha Pollitt and Harvard associate clinical professor of psychiatry Judith Herman as identifying this as part of a backlash, neither she nor they take the opportunity to connect the backlash against adult testimony with that against children. Evidently, by now, the issue of incest had been so completely and convincingly severed in its parts that connections were not seen or made—by the media or even by feminists—that would have illuminated what was going on as simply one more smart bomb in a planned and deliberate and across-the-board *political* war. Instead, tunnel vision prevailed.

What this narrowcast of events did was to throw the entire conversation once again into the (hardly apolitical) courts of "science" and the bickering of experts—from which this aspect of the issue is likely to emerge bedraggled (after a very long time), festooned with an elaborate aura of doubt.

———

The pattern we were presented with by the false-memory folks was that of a bright, attractive daughter; a stay-at-home mother; several bad relationships the daughter had had with men; the daughter's job disruption; her seeing a therapist—and her uncovering of memories or inklings of past sexual abuse.

Terence Stone and his wife, Colette, seem pretty typical. He is the mayor of Madlia, Minnesota. She's always stayed home, raised the kids. They are the Minnesota contact family for the False Memory Syndrome Foundation, which now claims membership of some five thousand families.

In 1991, their daughter's therapist wrote to the Stones that their daughter "always has presented her family in terms of high praise, rarely even subject to the normal frictions which are present in families. However, beginning in February 1989, she began to have confused and disturbing fragmentary memories of sexual abuse."[21] Now, the therapist told them, he was convinced that their daughter had been molested from infancy and that her eight siblings had been molested as well, and that her mother had not only known of the abuse but had participated in it.

According to the Stones, they've since learned that their daughter also alleged there were orgies in the family basement with the neighbors and their kids.

As does everyone else in this neighborhood, the Stones made mention of *The Courage to Heal*, often referred to as the "bible" of therapists, who recommended it to survivors. With a full schedule of speaking and writing engagements, as well as trainings for professionals based on the book, Laura Davis and Ellen Bass, it could certainly be argued, had made the book's language and lessons part of what amounted to a conceptual franchise.

One of the lessons included was on *planned confrontations*. The *Courage to Heal Workbook* invites the survivor to give this the kind of excruciatingly detailed thought that in itself seems designed to create ambivalence, apprehension, and anxiety:

How do I want to confront? Why have I chosen this method? If I'm choosing the confrontation, where do I want to do it? Why is it the best choice? Have I considered other alternatives? Do I want anyone else to be present? Why or why not? When will I do the confrontation? Why have I chosen this time? How long will the confrontation last? How will I know when it's over? And so on . . .

As this planning played out in the Stones' case, in June of 1992 the Stones received a letter from their daughter asking that they come to a motel in Milwaukee. "They could bring one other person. She would be there with her support group and her therapist, and a referee. She would speak for a half-hour. Terence could respond for 10 minutes; she would speak for a half-hour and Colette could respond for 10 minutes."

Would you agree to this if you were guilty?

Would you agree to this if you were innocent?

What is the point?

Once again, the point is issued in the same stew of language: "Confrontations can be incredibly empowering because you learn that you are strong and powerful. You experience the freedom of telling the truth and you break the silence that has bound you."[22]

(Once again, I ask: What silence?)

As far as all this empowerment goes—along with virtually every other family publicly interviewed as falsely accused, the Stones did not blame their daughter. They did not, by implication, see their daughter as fully adult, and fully autonomous, but rather as a gullible, child-like receptacle for antifamily bands of scheming manipulators: "We don't want our daughter to be the bad guy here," Terence said. "She's not the culprit." Colette added: "The person we're angry at is the therapist."[23]

In fact, it is their expressed hope (and that of many other families we have heard from) that their daughter will one day join them in a lawsuit against the therapist.

The new American Family Reunion.

————

If False Memory Syndrome was a reaction, driven by over-programmed confrontations and by lawsuits, there was, however, no doubt it was driven by yet other forces. And supported by still other forces. Not only did the False Memory Syndrome Foundation's organization bear the imprimatur of its advisory board member, Dr. Ralph Underwager, who had testified on behalf of those accused in Jordan, Minnesota, and been an advisor to VOCAL. But the first open testimony by a parent, "Jane Doe," had been printed in the summer of 1991 in the Underwager/Wakefield publication *Issues in Child Abuse Accusations*, the year before the inception of the False Memory Syndrome Foundation.

Jane Doe begins her story: "When she was 33, Susan had a revelation that she had been repeatedly sexually abused and raped for 13 years by her father. I am Susan's mother, and I have been trying to cope with that revelation."

The tone of the article is a mix of the coy and the soppy:

"Usually Susan planned favorites for our arrival, but this time the rice was cooked with liver (which I really should learn to like) and the chicken was served so that Alex did not get a breast. Should we have been forewarned?"[24]

"Jane Doe" turned out to be Pamela Freyd. And it was she who was the founder of the False Memory Syndrome Foundation. "Susan" turned out to be her daughter Jennifer Freyd, a professor in the Department of Psychology at the University of Oregon, who had never spoken publicly about her abuse, nor mentioned a lawsuit.

And so, with this "false memory" fandango, we are evidently looking at backlash that is both more and less than pocketbook-driven. Some of it undoubtedly driven by genuine perplexity. And some of it driven by the insult of current allegations about years-ago transgressions. In other words, some of it was driven by financial interest, some by ego interest, and some by genuine concern about error. The constituency was clearly there. All it took was leadership and organizing.

It is Jennifer Freyd's recall about the Great Chicken Breast Episode that:

"My memory of that evening is dominated by the fact that my then-two-year-old son was holding a turkey baster, and my father explained to all of us at the table that turkey basters are used by lesbians to inseminate themselves. This sort of comment was one I found very familiar, one I had always considered 'normal.' The next morning my husband, on my request, asked my parents to leave my house."

Having only that week begun to remember incest (following what was only her second therapy session), Jennifer Freyd was not up for the "normal."

She says, "When my husband asked my parents to leave they naturally wondered why. My husband answered, 'Because Jennifer remembers that Peter abused her.' My father's first response was, 'I have no memory for that' and after that he said that either he must be crazy or I must be crazy.'"[25]

That was in December of 1990. Within a year, the "Jane Doe" article appeared. Within fourteen months, Pamela Freyd had incorporated the False Memory Syndrome Foundation. As one clinician is reported to have said, "There is persuasive evidence that this organization grew out of one family's feud that's overgrown its boundaries and come into the popular culture."

So here was this haphazard admixture of real backlash, pragmatic retaliation, and sheer pique, and yet out of it came *tsuris* such as the world had never seen. The media reacted to it like a starved thing. The stock of quotable experts soared. Serious social scientists took it to be seriously about *memory* and set themselves to doing studies and publishing articles.

One study, by Linda Myers-Williams, followed up on one hundred children who, seventeen years earlier, were known to have been sexually abused, and found that 38 percent of these women had no recall of the abuse.[26] Other studies researched the potential for the creation of false memories, the malleability of memories. . . .

To convey the extent of the furor of activity FMS generated in the professional community, let me only note that one article by psychologist Elizabeth F. Loftus carried 147 citations to support sixteen pages of text.[27]

We had media hullabaloo, professional frenzy, superbowl passions.

In the midst of it all, we had that curious interview Dr. Ralph Underwager and his wife Hollida Wakefield gave to *Paidika*. In it, Underwager is asked: "Your scenario for the child sexuality hysteria is the breakdown of the social contract and a religious/mystical dysfunction. Do you recognize other causes than these?"

To which he answers, "I would add radical feminism, which includes a pretty hefty dose of anti-maleness. I think in a very real way these women may be jealous that males are able to love each other, be comrades, friends, be close, intimate, work cooperatively, function in groups. . . . This would hold true for male bonding, and paedophile sex too. The woman is jealous of the connection. She says, 'Wait a minute, we're not going to let you do that!' "[28]

Notice, please, *his* implicit assumption that we are speaking of *males* as offenders (albeit misunderstood ones). Never let it be said that the backlash is confused as to the gender-specificity of what is going on here.

To be fair to Hollida Wakefield, with this idea that women are driven by *jealousy*, she does disagree. But Underwager is unfazed, saying, "I believe that women are also violent, cruel, and hostile. Possibly more so than men. The radical feminists only express that side of femaleness against paedophilia."[29]

And—on top of everything, we had the therapists spearheading the incest-recovery movement, taking *credit* for what they were blamed for, and taking credit based on their *power*, and taking credit as though they were the central and exclusive actors on the entire issue of incest:

"It seems clear," Laura Davis, coauthor of *The Courage to Heal*, said, "that the community of survivors and those who work with them has become strong enough and poses sufficient threat to move us into the stage of backlash."

Move us *into* the stage of backlash? (Where had she *been?*) Hadn't we been looking at backlash for well over *ten years?* As though oblivious to the legions of women who had gone down fighting to protect their children, giving them neither notice nor credit, Davis said, "We have become effective enough to make an impact on people who have an investment in abusing children, hiding abuse they've committed, denying their spouse's abuse, denying incest in their families, and on a larger level those who profit from child pornography and child prostitution. And the people who don't want to believe that so many children are abused—or in such severe ways—and there's a sizable number to oppose us."[30]

And along with all this, we were overwhelmed with tales of satanic abuse, ritual abuse, cult abuse (no one even knew what to *call* it). What had begun a few years ealier with some survivors' apparently incredible but seemingly genuine recall of grotesque childhood abuses now began to pour forth as a torrent of such claims. And before anyone had had time to carefully listen to and to formulate a context in which to consider these stories, there was a race on among therapists to specialize, and a race on among competing ideologies to colonize this phenomenon and make capital of it.

And there was humongous play in the media, and everywhere, perfectly reasonable people seemed to be going nuts and having a wonderful time—all at once. The apparently manic and ludicrous material pouring out at high pitch of course was simply more kindling for the FMS, who were now able to adopt the posture of *rationalists* in a world gone amok. Clearly it could *only* be social hysteria that would lead reasonable people to conjecture rampant malevolent ceremonial doings involving exquisitely refined techniques in mind control not only throughout the land and reaching to all levels of society, but worldwide. . . .

This was horror-movie stuff presented in sense-surround. And it was weird enough to reawaken the unease planted earlier by the Jordan and McMartin cases. (Even for me it was enough to kindle a momentary flicker, a superstitious thought: Could this apocalyptic sense of chaos be the warning that had been implied all along about *talking* about incest, about breaking the I ast Taboo? Nahhhh . . .)

At last, I guess, we had achieved what reviewers had missed in TV presentations of incest early on: the sense of Sin. The sense of Wickedness.

I guess you could look at it that way—that it may have taken satanic images and triple sixes and cannibalized infants and pentagrams and chanting from the Dark Side—but we'd finally gotten the sense of something *bad* going on.

Of course you could also look at it this way: The tormenting and raping of children by ordinary familial human agency just hadn't been bad *enough*.

Chapter 11

THE INFANTILIZATION
OF WOMEN III:
The Demonic Dialogues

ACTUALLY, *BAD AS A WORD* didn't even begin to cut it. Neither, really, did *wickedness* and *sin*. *Evil* was the only word you could assign to the specter conjured up by the gruesome, gross, comic-book monstrousness being related and ascribed the proportions of a scourge. It was a truly epic distraction from the humdrum business of ordinary men allowed to molest children in the normal, everyday, routine course of events. In fact, as dialogues, speculation, and passion zoomed over what was variously called satanic, cult, or ritual (or ritualized or ritualistic) abuse, incest plain and simple was left behind to eat dust.

Actually, in the satanic ritual abuse portrayals, the sexual torment of children was not even close to the real shocker. Set in the framework of huge conspiracies, reaching to the highest levels of local, state, and federal government, of related cabals that signaled one another via demonic hieroglyphics and "triggers" by which they could recall anyone anywhere to the rule of the cult; and who, on innumerable days of the year gathered in groups to chant and eat feces and have children perform ritual sacrifices of infants, born of pubescent girls, whose blood they then drank, and whose flesh they ate—sexual violation of children was barely a blip on the larger screen.

Much was made of the fact that so many particulars of adult survivors' stories matched, and that they matched as well the stories told by children in day-care scandals like that of the McMartin Preschool. This was put forward as evidence that these doings must then be common and real. Less was made of the fact that these horrendous and terrifying events appeared to so agreeably correlate with the newly prominent diagnosis of Multiple Personality Disorder (MPD). This led to a felicitous combospecialty for a growing number of therapists: MPD-SRA (Satanic Ritual Abuse). Perhaps because of their more highly tuned sensitivity to the symptoms, these therapists seemed to find an ever increasing number of cases.

Their sensitivity, however, was not heightened by osmosis. A burgeoning number of seminars or trainings began to be staged at which leaders in the field lent their imprimatur to the credibility of an epidemic of ritual abuse and the allegedly resulting Multiple Personality Disorder. Among them was Roland Summit. At the 1987 Fourth International Conference on MPD-Dissociative States in Chicago, Illinois, he said that sufferers of ritual abuse "run a common basis for the development of MPD and other dissociative disorders. . . . The worst thing that can happen to children will turn up in MPD. . . . Sure enough, a striking finding has been the number of children speaking as alters through multiple personality, individuals who describe blood-curdling kinds of experience that have left us reeling in our incredulity. . . ."[1] One year later, he said, "Because we see it clinically, we see something we believe is real, clinically, and whether or not our colleagues or the press, or scientists at large, or politicians or local law enforcement agencies agree that this is real, most of us have some sort of personal sense that it is; at least speaking as a bias of one, and for the academics on the platform."[2]

The backlash, of course, had only to sit there, smiling, and pick up this strangely improbable fruit to lob back at us as it fell off the tree.

With no definition of or demonstrable context for the reported events, the subject was speculators' heaven. Passions were polarized in a holy-war way—believers (including most therapists and many feminists) versus debunkers (which included not only the backlash, but all skeptics).

For many of us who knew that a goodly number of fathers had used their children in pornography and involved them in drug rings without much ceremonial decoration, it was intensely awkward and more than a little intimidating. We were certainly aware that there were cases of grotesque abuse that had been uncovered and prosecuted (though most often not as ritual abuse). As Linda Regan of the Child Abuse Studies Unit at the University of North London says to me, "Of course there are some cases. You have only to read Amnesty International reports about some of the bizarre things that are inflicted on children to know that. The problem comes when we are asked to believe there are hundreds of thousands."

And, I add, to believe that the hundreds of thousands involve nationally or internationally linked groups of satanists or others with a defined, elaborated, and commonly adhered-to agenda. What is actually known on a formal level derives from the only study done so far. Titled "The Extent and Nature of Organized and Ritual Abuse," it is a report to the British Department of Health by anthropologist Jean S. La Fontaine.[3] While it generated sensational headlines in London in April of 1994 ("Government Inquiry Decides Satanic Abuse Does Not Exist"[4]; "Whitewash Claim Over Satanic Abuse"[5]), these are some of the study's findings about ritual abuse cases reported in Britain in the recent past.

- Out of eighty-four cases of reported organized abuse studied, "cases in which ritual/satanic abuse of children is alleged constitute about 8 percent."[6]
- "Three substantiated cases of ritual, not satanic, abuse were

found. These are cases in which self-proclaimed mystical/ magical powers were used to entrap children and impress them (and also adults) with a reason for the sexual abuse, keeping the victims compliant and ensuring their silence. **In these cases the ritual was secondary to the sexual abuse which clearly formed the primary objective of the perpetrators. The rituals performed in these cases did not resemble those that figured in the allegations of the other eighty-one cases"** (bold type in original).[7] Additionally, in these three cases, each group had been organized by a different man. In all three cases, material evidence was found to verify that rituals were performed during which children were sexually abused. But in each case the man had also abused children without rituals. "None of the three men concerned learned the rituals from belonging to an occult group. . . . "[8] While books related to ritual abuse were found in the three cases, they were not the same book. Objects were found in two of these cases, including altars, cloths, and candleholders with candles. In the third case there were objects, but no altar.

Further:

- Alleged disclosures of satanic abuse by younger children had been heavily influenced by adults—not infrequently by foster parents whom intervening authorities had set to documenting children's disclosures.
- Interviews with the children had often been poorly conducted. Not only had leading questions been asked, but what got written down was interviewer-interpretation. **"What is defended as 'what the children say' may be nothing of the sort"** (bold type in original).[9]
- Where a few older children described satanic rituals, no evidence was found and the children had often been victims of other abuse.

The report concludes that the Evangelical Christian campaign against new religious movements was one powerful factor encouraging reports of satanic abuse. But, *"Equally important in spreading the idea of satanic abuse in Britain are the professional 'specialists,' American and British. Their claims and qualifications are rarely checked. Much of their information, particularly about cases in the United States, is unreliable"* (italics mine).[10]

The report also concludes that "A belief in evil cults is convincing because it draws on powerful cultural axioms. People are reluctant to accept that parents, even those classed as social failures, will harm their own children, and even invite others to do so, but involvement with the devil explains it. The notion that unknown, powerful leaders control the cult revives an old myth of dangerous strangers. Demonizing the marginal poor and linking them to unknown satanists turns intractable cases of abuse into manifestations of evil."[11]

In sum, in three cases there was support for allegations of sexual abuse in a ritual context. In two other cases there was some bit of evidence that adults dressed up and abused children. In seventy-nine (of eighty-four) reported cases of organized abuse studied, there was no material evidence of any ritual found at all.

Thus, the evidence pointed to the fact that, within the spectrum of incest/child sexual abuse, a certain number of men led other adults in child-terrifying behaviors in order to secure the children's compliance and silence. Further searches, new studies, may turn up some limited number of isolated groups with ties to pornographers or to other criminal elements, or even to some unconventional belief system.

All that is as we thought, and would find unsurprising. And it is entirely credible that those women who, as children, had been victimized within any such nightmarish world might emerge fragile, agonizingly fearful, and devastatingly harmed.

And yet here we were, being challenged to believe in the existence of a whole satanic pudding replete with masters of brilliant brainwashing techniques and exquisitely refined organizational skills. We were challenged to ignore the evidence that we did have and jump on a bandwagon based on evidence no one had. The message was: You'd better believe it is all of it every bit of it true, and the reason you'd better believe it is all of it every bit of it true, is because it is unbelievable and that's what everyone had said about routine household child-rape:

"The phenomena that is going around on this issue is not unlike the phenomena round the issue of child abuse that we saw in the last decade. That somehow in the early 80s and late 70s no one believed that child sexual abuse was going on either. It wasn't until a program like 'Something About Amelia' aired on TV that suddenly people started to reach out and say that 'this happened to me also when I was a child.' No one believed those of us who are survivors in the audience and throughout the conference, who are now mental health professionals. We are perpetuating the same process of not believing again because it is too impossible to believe, there is no evidence that tells me that this is physically in front of my face."[12]

Not only is this imprecise as history: A made-for-TV movie might have been a cultural landmark, but women were speaking out, and even being believed, well before that. But it uses this history as a kind of blackmail against all open questioning— including questioning of those therapists who were the main actors in eliciting the stories, and the main conduit for conveying interpretations of them to one another and to the public.

Proof was supposed to be found in the fact that the great numbers of women speaking of satanic/ritual abuse were speaking without knowledge of one another. Yet the evidence was that contamination in the supposedly segregated world of the clinicians and specialists who were transmitting these abuses was rife.

Sherrill Mulhern, an anthropologist, has written some of the most cogent critiques of the satanic/cult/ritual abuse phenomenon. She said at a 1989 think tank of A-tier professionals, "An analysis of the content of training seminars, as it has evolved over the past couple of years underlines the fact that what we are dealing with is a rumor. This rumor has an observable internal dynamic which, as it spreads, has left the data of therapy floundering in its wake. For example, I just attended a conference where 'experts' in ritual abuse seminars 'described' at length the sophisticated mind control and brainwashing techniques which the 'cults' have allegedly used which have enabled them to remain unnoticed for so long. I heard passionate evocations of the 'Manchurian Candidate' and astonishing explanations of sophisticated brainwashing techniques which owe their efficiency to an acquired addiction to endorphins released during the violent torture of infants and small children. Another expert declared that anything and everything was a potential trigger which could set off satanically programmed behavior, and that every day was potentially a satanic holiday. I admit that this simplified the note taking process."[13]

Mulhern describes, as well, that once political, now revivalist, event—the speakout—as it was now taking place within the therapeutic context:

"For example, a recent, day-long training seminar which I attended featured an adult survivor panel. The whole thing was very tearful. As each adult survivor finished her story, she was greeted with a standing ovation. In this charged atmosphere, therapists tend to lose their critical faculties and passed over some rather extraordinary details offered by the speakers. At one point, one of the adult survivors declared that she had ovaries sewn into her so that she could breed more babies. Now I do not know how much you all know about implant surgery, but I would venture a guess that if that statement were true, satanists would be making millions of dollars with people who are having difficulty conceiving children."[14]

Satanic (or ritual, or cult) abuse hit as an instant sensation: There was an exuberance, a charge to the media attention and a quasi-messianic vigor to the treatment literature. It was hard not to get the feeling that everyone was invigorated.

And why not? Satanic/ritual abuse overrode all of the problems that had dead-ended simple incest. In these abuses, of course, offenders are spectral. Individual faces are blank. Not only are women alleged to be focal actors in these pictures, but the men's behavior is rather majestic: Gory as the proceedings are said to be, they have a certain Grand Guignol *style*—much removed from the rather sordid and somewhat pathetic machinations of every-day child-molesting dads.

Mullhern says that satanic/ritual abuse material "seems to provide perplexed investigators with missing information on the motivations of alleged perpetrators. It apparently explains the who, why and how of perpetrators' mischief.

"There is a cult, the goal of whose rituals is mind control and the brainwashing of innocent children to become future members of a religion devoted to the worship of evil . . . [that] has infiltrated society so completely that blood infant sacrifices, cannibalism and mutilation which seem impossible to corroborate have been overlooked for generations."[15]

What this who, why, and how offer, of course, is an apparent *alternative* explanation; one that—despite all the described desecration and carnage—is far less socially threatening. It does not challenge gender power relations. And for all it is said to involve ordinary unnamed police chiefs, morticians, politicians, attorneys, judges, and chemists, because of its conspiratorial tentacles satanic/ritual abuse does not challenge the "traditional" family.

It commands us to believe not that nice fathers are skulking into Susie or Johnny's room while mothers are at PTA meeetings, but that mothers and fathers and the neighbors are gathering in woods, church basements, and recreation rooms with an astounding collection of costumery and paraphernalia—not sometimes, but often; not in isolated locales, but everywhere.

Instead of trying to explain the social content of this sudden assault of stories, or to explore its context as perhaps derived from the therapeutic ideology, many professionals—treatment and otherwise—devoted themselves to filling in the blanks, constructing the imagined environment within which the narratives could be construed as literally true. What could not be explained was ascribed to the cults' use of drugs or hypnotic suggestion. (As a tribute to the nutsiness of this whole thing, the epidemic of these stories was ascribed by debunkers to hypnotic suggestion used by therapists.)

And this whole shaky edifice claimed, as its fulcrum, its moral authority, the issue of incest. It was put to us that *this* phenomenon was a continuation of *that* phenomenon: that the freedom to speak for satanic/ritual abuse survivors derived from the open conversation about incest. And that to disbelieve here was the same as, earlier, to disbelieve there.

But does this linchpin correlation between satanic abuse and incest hold? Not really.

For one thing, historically, women were not disbelieved. They were *silenced*. And that is different. Even Freud's turnaround did not hamper his followers' continuing to ruminate about how those children who spoke out had actually instigated the hanky-panky, and how they did not suffer from it but indeed actually enjoyed it. This is not disbelief. It is incrimination.

And there is the fact that for long periods of time children's sexual abuse (as we now call it) was not seen as abuse. It didn't matter. It didn't count. It wasn't valid. Great gobs of time were spent negotiating at what age it might matter. For other long periods of time, girls were implicated in any abuse they reported, and themselves penalized as participants. And, waxing and waning in prominence, always there have been with us quite respectable men who openly advocated the child's right to have these things happen. Child pornography offers vibrant testimony to the fact that many men have a more-than-surreptitious interest in sex with children. And in a world where the neighbors' kids are regarded as off-limits, safety dictates sticking with your own.

The real problem with our airing the issue of incest was not disbelief. It was (as it continues to be) the possibility that some damn fools might actually try to make change. (And look at the mess you get into then, with upstanding men in high dudgeon over state intervention in their own private and personal business, or wives turning ex-wives and trying to take their kids away from them.) Incest's continuity has both depended on and supported the dominance of men within their private realms and the devaluation of women and children. To actually do something to stop it, to prohibit it, to hold offenders accountable for it, would require breaching a tacit compact the state has always held with respectable men. Their homes, their castles; their families, their turf. Paternal prerogative; paternal privilege.[16]

Thus, when incest survivors spoke out and children now were encouraged to speak out—the backlash.

None of this carries over to allegations of satanic/ritual abuse. There are not inconsiderable numbers of people who not only believe in an epidemic of satanic/ritual abuses, but whose worldview it vindicates. And open mike on Oprah and Sally and Phil right off the bat is a far cry from being silenced. No social or legal penalty attaches for victims speaking out. (There is talk of threats from the cult, and survivor and therapist fear of retaliation, but so far, at least, no evidence I know of that anyone has actually been harmed.)

The incest–satanic/ritual abuse analogy, while powerful emotionally, is actually fragile. It appears to sustain because the dominance of the therapeutic ideology has driven out political understanding that would point up distinctions. It has rewritten history with a new mythology, and now wound up with a claim to widespread cultish oppression and stories of large-scale murders, for which there are no corpses, there is no evidence, and no motive other than antireligious obsession.

Fundamentalists, the Christian right wing, ordinary citizens . . . everyone would be more than happy to band together as one and drive from the land satanists, cultists, ritualists. So far, they just seem unable to find them. Few people are anywhere near so certain about censuring household offenders, and they have faces and names and are not at all hard to find.

People engaged in considerable imaginative gymnastics to explain the weird discordances of ritual abuse stories, all reflecting different takes on the world and its mechanisms. This conjuring of explanations to suit one's sense of how things work was something familiar to me from my mother.

Say she was on the telephone with her sister, Eve, and the connection was broken. She'd come into the kitchen; I'd say, "How is your sister?" And she'd say, "Well, fine, I think." "You think?" "Well, we got cut off." And I'd say, "Well, try her back." And she'd say, "Oh, no." And I'd say, "Why not?" And she'd say, "Well, dear, I imagine someone else must have had a more important phone call to make. I wouldn't want to interrupt them."

Whether or not satanic/ritual abuse is a rumor, it is most decidedly a cipher. A societal Rorschach test, to which different people can bring different explanations, different interpretations, depending on their view of the universe.

Fundamentalists see in it the "systematic deconstruction of the victim's personality to destroy their faith, trust and hope. Such abuse is inflicted to take control (present and future) of the individual's mind, body and soul in order to gain supernatural power and demonstrate complete loyalty and obedience to Satan."[17]

Curiously enough, in this theologically driven worldview, the prescription for fighting this evil is comprehensive mental health care, biblically based. By the end of the 1980s, psychiatry and religion—arch enemies for so long in their war for ideological dominance—seemed to be finding a common accord. This coincided oddly with the rise of reports of child sexual abuse by priests and clergy. Perhaps the defining moment was the meeting between a delegation of prominent psychiatrists and Pope John Paul II.[18] Whatever may have transpired in that meeting, the *New York Times* reported that "the forthcoming edition of psychiatry's official catalogue of mental illnesses has added a brief entry titled, 'Religious or Spiritual Problem.' "[19]

By the late 1980s, Christian healing manuals contained the same kinds of checklists of symptomatic evidence of cult abuse as did the more secular variety, with only some additions, such as, "convinced they are 'possessed' . . . Also, feeling that soul belongs to Satan . . . contempt/rage at God, Jesus Christ, Christianity . . ."[20] In one manual's construct, the satanists, using mind control, can produce lasting "triggers" such as—if the survivor was abused in a cult that conducted rituals by a full moon, she will feel compelled as an adult to seek out a cult and participate in rituals whenever the moon is full.

Those with an avowedly right-wing political agenda were also comfortable with the idea that the devil is on the prowl. Beverly La Haye has been dubbed the "Queen of the Right."[21] La Haye is the founder and president of Concerned Women of America, a large women's organization concerning itself with fighting abortion, outlawing homosexuality, and so on.

La Haye publishes magazines and pamphlets, one of which, *The New Age and Our Children*, asserts that some forty thousand to sixty thousand satanic ritual killings take place every year. Confronted with the fact that the FBI tallies only twenty-five thousand reported murders of any kind every year, La Haye says that "there are a lot of occult murders that are never reported." She explains, "There are young women who give birth to babies and those babies are sacrificed, and those murders are never reported. I've talked to some of these young girls myself."[22] La Haye is evidently comfortable with this information. I wonder whether she, or any member of the Right or Religious Right, would be equally comfortable with any statistic or fact that highlights paternal child-rape within the traditional family.

And so we have with the appearance of satanic/ritual abuse this most peculiar phenomenon: that while some people are using the stories' preposterous qualities to cast doubt on all memory, including adults' memories of incest, yet others are willing to find memories of satanic/ritual abuse *more* credible.

Within the unequivocal believers' world-scripts, all bases are covered. If a victim begins having memories and goes to the police department, a cult member on that force will relay the information and the victim will get threatening phone calls. Phone calls will threaten the victim's therapist as well. Or cult members may prevail on the victim's family to stick her in a mental hospital.

(Well, why not? If you can get wedlock between religion and psychiatry, why not between antireligion and psychiatry?)

One of the curiosities about these scripts is that they presume the very social cohesiveness and stable community life the absence of which is so widely bemoaned in American life. Neighbors are said to be involved, and local authorities, as well as court systems.[23] It does no good to question this: There is an answer to everything. Cult members have infiltrated everywhere—even into twelve-step meetings.

"They want to know everything they can. . . . It's important for them to know the latest in counseling techniques with this, for instance, so they can devise strategies to reverse and undermine the effectiveness."[24]

It could hardly be supposed that *Ms.* magazine is either fundamentalist in its editorial persuasion or driven by a theological imperative. Yet here we find the same events, written to authenticate a different worldview, in a first-person story by the pseudonymous Elisabeth S. Rose.

"My mother became pregnant a few months after I was inducted into the cult," Rose writes. "About seven months later, the cult decided she was carrying a girl child. Her labor was induced and the infant delivered prematurely by the cult doctor at our house. I witnessed the birth. The baby was born tiny, but alive.

"Two days later, I was forced to watch as they killed my baby sister by decapitation and ritual sacrifice. The sacrifice was followed by communion ritual, during which human flesh and blood were consumed. The death was never reported, because the birth had not been reported."[25]

Where theologically driven cult stories speak of Dark Forces Loose in the Land, Rose's story of her cult experience speaks of misogyny raised to orgiastic levels.

Rose remembers her uncle telling her, "When you grow up, I'm gonna kill your babies the same way we killed your baby sister, understand? Babies deserve to die. Satan wants their blood, especially girl babies because they taste so good."[26] Woman-hating reigns here to an almost fairy-tale degree. "The idea of female wickedness and depravity was pounded into my head at the impressionable age of four. I was told repeatedly that a woman's only value was her ability to sacrifice herself to Satan. If she was worthless to Satan, she would be worthless to the world. I got the message that a female child had no value to cult members, except in her ability to participate in rituals. The life of a girl was an expendable commodity. In our cult, only female infants were sacrificed."[27]

It is difficult to read this and not hear the feminist message elaborated as metaphor, as though politics had been abandoned for poetic license. With the real politics buried by a barrage of gender-neutral language and masked in victim symptomatologies, this is not surprising. It is as though the ugly reality of fathers sexually violating children in their care and trust, as promoted by the therapeutic ideology, had become unbearably meaningless. It required a larger canvas, bolder strokes, a more apocalyptic message of menace, to give it impact and point.

It is as though to just be a victim of childhood sexual assault by your father—now that it was all "understood" as psychological malfunction—was not *enough*.

It is as though "you are not alone" had backfired and been trivialized to read instead, "you are ordinary, your experience common." And, once drawn into the recovery universe, it is as though women began trying to express both their uniqueness and their anguish and their experience of being female in this society through amplified narrative and, since that was the coin of this realm, greater pathology.

Once the experience had been robbed of larger significance, once the stories had become no more than stories, then grander stories became the only vehicle for both gaining attention and finding coherence.

There is real and present danger that the to-do over satanic/ritual abuse in combination with the diversionary focus on a "science" of memory that is bound to remain ambiguous, will succeed in casting grave suspicion over the entire issue of incest. Kenneth V. Lanning, supervisory special agent for the Behavioral Science Unit of the FBI, was an early believer in stories of cult abuse. His investigations, the sheer lack of any evidence, has made him more skeptical. He says, "I'm greatly concerned that this issue is distorting the issue of child sexual abuse and is going to cause serious problems for this movement down the road and affect the credibility of victims. I'm also extremely concerned because I believe, all across this country, people are getting away with molesting kids because we can't prove they're satanic devil-worshippers."[28]

But all the focus on the exotic has already begun to take its toll, silencing even those who express skepticism about the rash of truly extraordinary claims, lumping them together with the backlash, consigning them to "denial"; making it seem, to me, more perilous to speak out on this, for example, than it was to speak out on incest in the first place.

Combined with the garish display of pathologies, replacing politics, and the florid rhetoric of recovery, the satanic spectacle is already working to re-silence many survivors. Some simply don't want to be associated with the whole thing.

My friend Mo Sila, feminist therapist and early incest activist, says, "I've stopped talking because—nobody listens. And I've stopped identifying as a survivor because—I'm embarrassed. In the beginning, to identify as a survivor meant you were doing important things. Now there's this whole group that misrepresents all of us as whiners and victims-in-isolation. I don't want to be part of that."

In Canada, my friend Elly Danica, who broke the issue there with her book *Don't: A Woman's Word*,[29] now says, "It's *weirder* now than six years ago. There's all this competitive stuff about it. 'My pain is greater than your pain.' "

And some survivors feel they just can't compete: "I feel any-more," one survivor of nonexotic incest said to me recently, "that

I shouldn't even be talking about it. I don't want to talk about it. It's like—compared—what happened to me wasn't so bad."

It is truly uncanny that incest is being used to promote unqualified belief in all stories of satanic/ritual abuse—even as reports of satanic/ritual abuse are fed into the weaponry aimed at the credibility of reports of incest. And both things are working to diminish focus on routine paternal child-rape equally well. It is astounding that therapists are being accused of sophisticated mind-control techniques even as satanists are being accused of ultrarefined mind-control techniques. And both things are working to diminish focus on routine paternal child-rape equally well.

I have to wonder, sometimes, who has been writing the script for all this.

Perhaps most critical, however, is that this re-silencing of adult survivors is only a small part of a more general re-silencing that is occurring unacknowledged and unattended across the entire spectrum of the issue, despite the ever rising decibel level.

Over the past few years, more and more sentient people—having seen all too often what happens to children who tell and are then subject to state intervention—are quietly cautioning kids not to volunteer that which will bring them to the attention of the system. As one feminist counselor, herself a survivor, said to me recently (begging anonymity for obvious reasons), "I tell the kids to stay put. I tell them what I know: 'The rape is time-limited. The system is a life sentence.' "

Those who field the imprecations of desperate mothers seeking to protect their children are similarly urging caution. At the very least, they are warning the mothers to get as much professionally documented evidence as they can *before* saying anything at all.

But there is a still more worrisome result of the triumph of the therapeutic ideology—and the concomitant failure to identify this issue as political. A far stranger and more dangerous silence can now be seen in play.

Not only do journalists and the media continue to be largely silent about feminist political views on incest, and the evidence underpinning those views, but they remain silent about the position underlying the views of some backlash professionals as well—including the published statements of some sympathetic to pedophilia.

To propose sex with children as the "natural" order of things is to restate the rationale behind the *permission* for male predation that feminists have long identified: It was our fathers, after all, who told us, "It's only natural." "It's only natural in nature."

Those backlash professionals who affirm pedophilia simply celebrate as benign and inevitable that which we deplored and hoped to change.

What is odd here is that it is the original feminist will to challenge this hoary rationale for ongoing ruthless predation that has been ignored as radical—in a society that purports to censure child sexual exploitation. *Yet it is the feminist analysis that implicitly assumes male rationality and capacity for self-control.* Meanwhile, the backlash's forthright and published apologias for its postures, which are based on essentialist views of men as hopelessly, irrationally, uncontrollably, and unchangeably predatory (and justifiably so) are overlooked, publicly unexamined, unquestioned, unreported. Feminist political views are taken as biased. Backlash opinions are taken as above suspicion, respectable, within the mainstream, on such matters as true and false accusations, true and errant memories. Backlash views on children's and women's credibility are widely quoted without reference to their philosophical underpinnings.

However, even this, alas, cannot be laid at the doorstep of demonic conspiracies. It can rather be attributed simply to the suppression of the political component, and the blinding triumph of a therapeutic ideology, which serves so many diverse interests, run rampant. By means of this ideology the personal, made public, has been remade as personal and robbed of coherence.

That this has happened despite the fact that all the evidence continues to support the feminist understanding of incest as, in fact, deeply and profoundly political is remarkable.

That such a profound silence has come to envelop this fact—in the face of all the to-do, all the thunder and roar—is more remarkable yet.

Chapter 12

ONE HELL OF A TRIP

HERE, FOR THE MOMENT, our story—stops.

Normally, in leaving a tale at this inconclusive juncture, one would expect the reader to feel dissatisfied, wanting more. Not so in this case, I think. Given the almost gothic imbroglios, the theatrical diversions, the way in which some actors have been chewing the scenery, here there is equal likelihood that, instead, the reader may now be surfeited; wanting *less*—or at least wanting less by way of carnival atmosphere.

Perhaps wanting more by way of real change?

What strikes me most as I review the evolution of this issue is how effective fifteen years of diversion and newspeak have been. How *oldthink* it sounds to say what the evidence continues to show to be true: that the thorny issue of incest, the core around which intransigence reigns, is an issue of male privilege. It is not, any more than it ever has been, an issue of what all men do or what all men want to do. It remains an issue of what those men who so choose feel is part of their presumed prerogative; at the very least, *their* business, no one else's. Denials have varied over time to aggressively meet circumstance: it doesn't happen, it's all in the kid's mind or fantasy, children are sexual and seductive; children make it up, women lie; the aggressor as victim. . . .

It is worth suggesting that just because we identified this early on as the very cradle of sexual politics—said it and said it—and went unheard, does not mean that what we said was wrong. It is equally likely, especially in light of the evidence that has subsequently accrued, that we were right—but that dealing with that fact was far too troublesome, far too socially disruptive.

Despite all efforts to gender-neutralize the issue, on the evidence, it certainly remains true that if all we were looking at were sex crimes committed against children by women, we would have something of such small scale as to not even be identifiable as a social problem, much less an occasion for massive machineries designed to palliate and pacify. And it does not seem outrageous to suggest that if we are willing to see women punished for failing to protect children (failure to protect), and if we are willing to see women in jail for attempting to protect children (vindictive mothers), scruples about punishing women as offenders would not run too high.

Virtually every aspect of the social response to the issue of incest has been crafted to divert challenge to male authority, beginning with "decriminalization" and the family dysfunction rhetoric, and extending to faulting women who "knew or should have known." Virtually every step of the way—from the allowances made due to men's own imperfect childhoods, or to their wives' claimed inadequacies—has implied a policy of appeasement toward men.

That despite all this effort there is backlash, that the policy has not entirely succeeded, is a sign only of the heightened sensitivity alleged perpetrators and their sympathizers feel on this issue. That they do not even acknowledge all the efforts on their behalf shows only their sense of privilege due.

As a society, we have defused accountability. We have identified women as causative, removed their children, even jailed them. It is enough to make one sigh: What more do men want?

We have devoted a huge amount of energy and resources to denying what is overwhelmingly apparent. We have made a huge investment in convolution in order to turn the focus of attention from male responsibility for household predation to children's responsibility for prevention.

There has been funding here.

Enormous resources have been used to turn the problems this predation causes women and children into their illness. To turn the fact that children may later be battered or raped because of this same sense of male privilege into the children's, the women's, *predisposition* to having this happen. We have made sexual and physical assault the victim's (unwitting) design, rather than acknowledging that it is to luck that any woman owes escaping such an encounter (thus shifting those issues to allow focus on *her* vulnerability).

There has been money to be made from this.

And we have gone to all lengths to avoid knowing that this lesson in permitted rage against women as wives and mothers leads to the likelihood that men will continue to express anger at women through aggressions against their own children. (What else do silly excuses for paternal child-rape like the wife not putting out enough or her being ill imply?)

Experts skilled in designing language to assist this knowledge-avoidance have been well compensated.

The issue of incest as it pertains to children now has been chopped free of the issue as it pertains to adult women whose violation was in the past. And even within the subset of children's issues, areas of specialization are sequestered from one another. Thus, when I went looking into the reality for kids of what intervention meant, I found myself in a separate universe, child welfare. Here, an entirely different set of experts holds sway, and a different set of measurements. And I found myself all but alone in asking what it was that really happened to the young victims of incest who had done what we had suggested they do: tell.

Then, as I discovered how quickly children identified as

sexually abused became targets for mental health labeling and "special needs" designations, searching for that reality in terms of children's lives took me into yet a separate world—that of children in institutions labeled psychiatric or therapeutic.* Here, again, yet another set of experts was dominant, and here yet again I was all but alone in inquiring specifically about the path designated for young incest victims. Child advocates' estimates of how many children in these psychiatric institutions were in fact incest victims ranged from "a great many" to a firm 75 percent.

It would be natural to believe that these children had been so psychologically devastated by their violation that they "needed" to be in such places—subjected to regimentation, to psychotropic medications, to restraints, and to isolation. That, however, did not prove to be at all true.

Rather, other things entirely were operating, dictating these children's placements. For one, the assumption that incest caused inevitable emotional impairment led to these kids being scrupulously scrutinized for *any* noncomformity or rebelliousness or dispute with the system. Once identified as an incest victim, the child was under surveillance for *symptoms*, and even normal responses to childhood upheaval were taken to be clinical symptoms that inhered to some individual child's disease. (Ironically, dizzyingly, this exactly mirrored the search among adults who shared *symptoms* for a past that included incest.)

For another, the child protection intervention system often had nowhere else to put the kids down. Facilities designated "therapeutic" were simply someplace.

For yet a third, during the 1980s kids were becoming the cash cow of institutional psychiatry. There was an explosion of private inpatient psychiatric facilities specializing in kids. (Again, this was reflected in the world of adults as well, as more and more private psychiatric institutions offered specialized treatment pro-

---

* A journey I describe in *And They Call It Help: The Psychiatric Policing of America's Children* (Reading, Mass.: Addison-Wesley, 1993).

grams for the panoply of adult female problems said to result from incest.) During the 1980s, the range of possible disorders in children expanded to include even Arithmetic Disorder, alongside all manner of conduct and behavioral disorders. (And during the 1980s, the number of disorders to be searched out in adult women multiplied as well.)

Identified as individual children's mental health problems, incest had enormous consequences for children—well beyond the rape itself. Yet to view those consequences meant entering different arenas, and so they tended to remain unseen by those specifically concerned with policy on incest, and by the general public as well.

The social vehicle for achieving all this succor for the status quo has been the therapeutic ideology—which has gone all but unchallenged. There is no question that consolation and an understanding outside presence offer some individual children and women benefit. Nor is there any question that change in the future cannot mean ignoring those damaged in the present. But the dominant emphasis on the language of pathology, treatment, and therapy as the primary social response to incest, actually isolates and marginalizes victims—even while announcing that "you are not alone." It is an emphasis on pacification, on deflecting attention from all larger social meaning.

Astonishingly, even this has had unwitting side effects greater than what the backlash can bear—and the backlash activists have reared up and raised fists, and railed against "overzealous feminists" engaged in a "lifelong vendetta . . . a campaign of vengeance that will involve the destruction of every man who has the misfortune to cross their path and whom they have an opportunity to destroy."[1]

Encouraging women to regress and obsess is anything but feminist. Indeed, the dominance of this ideology is counterfeminist and anything but radical. But given the emotional plane on which the issue has come to rest, accuracy here is not required—any more than it was during the commie-bashing McCarthy days to which the backlash spokespersons so often refer. Compared with the charge of "man-hating," woman-hating has never had much cachet.

The confusion generated by talking about the "crime of incest," while treating it as a psychological matter, has left the backlash free to swing allegations about wildly—of men automatically assumed to be guilty; of courts' hair-trigger reactions, severing their parental rights; of the massive and peremptory jailing of alleged offenders. . . .

The actions dictated by those who focus on individual pathology are carefully claimed to derive from no moral or political base; ordered to no social goal beyond that of patching the wounded. This has left the moral high ground for the backlash to seize, themselves posturing as the grievously wronged, as the *real* victims; declaiming the violation of their rights. No one much speaks of the child's rights; of her right to remain free of what— where fathers and stepfathers are concerned—is surely sexual slavery.

Working backwards from the diagnostic category of Post-Traumatic Stress Disorder, much has recently been made of likening the psychological effects of incest to the effects of captivity on political hostages, or the aftermath of combat.[2] While this has the considerable virtue of extricating the emotional damage from the welter of disorders ascribed to biology and female pathology, it still focuses on a psychiatric diagnostic category, on the need to prove severe and lasting injury. It still retains the medical model. And it elides important differences.

Combat takes place in the openly acknowledged context of war, with the other side clearly marked "enemy." It has the support of the state and generally is seen as necessary for some greater good. While casualties and fatalities may be labeled a *byproduct* to winning, they are expected. It is openly agreed that trampling the other side is the goal.

Similarly, those who fall victim to terrorists and are captured are the (unwilling) victims of a deliberate act openly intended to cause terror. It is considered an act of high valor to resist and to try to escape.

For all that the effects (symptoms) of "post-traumatic stress" may be similar to the effects of incest, extending that clinical analysis to routine child-rape by fathers and stepfathers has remarkable implications. Neither national enemies nor political terrorists stand in a position of trust to their victims; they are not expected to act in their captives' interests.

Within the family, we would not be willing, I suspect, to say of fathers and stepfathers the same: that, as a class, they can be expected to behave like the enemy. That is the meaning behind the rhetoric about incest as a "betrayal of trust."

While a great deal has been said about that betrayal, little has been said about the fact that the offenders are persons the children are beholden to *obey.* This is one of the prime sticky wickets of incest (as opposed to generalized child sexual abuse) *prevention.* Obedience is part of the deal. You get no medals for escape from your captor, or for running away, and certainly not for turning a weapon on him.

Additionally, the problem with the Post-Traumatic Stress Disorder model is that it masks the gratuitousness and the deliberateness of the offense, and the fact that it is so often done amidst mumblings of love.

More cogent than a combat-hostage model, which is predicated on later emotional distress, is a basic civil rights argument: that paternal child-rape is a form of sexual slavery—in a society in which slavery is emphatically illegal.

We are not talking here of a child's right to refuse to do her homework, or to clean her room. We are talking about the offender's act of sexual enslavement. He stands in a position to make both legal and illegal demands, and to do so as a matter of routine. Of course we would be back in *courts* with this paradigm, and consequently back with all the evidentiary issues and court biases and charges about protecting mothers and radical feminist therapists programming kids. . . .

But at least to see it as sexual enslavement is to more clearly name what it is offenders do (rather than focusing on later emotional disrepair in the victims). And it is to begin to speak the language of accountability. To name it "sexual slavery" would at least position incest as exploitation for the benefit of the slaveholder.

You'll remember that even as the framing of the Thirteenth Amendment was being negotiated, there were those who saw the explicit connection between the enslavement of blacks in this country and the status of children. There were those who saw the connection so clearly, in fact, that they sought to explicitly exempt children from the protections of a ban on slavery.

We have spent fifteen years enacting demonstrations to show that incest is not safe to bring up in any court. We have spent fifteen years extolling as the solution the therapeutic response, the therapeutic ideology. The kids who have been treated with all this benign sensitivity do not, in my listening experience, seem to be saying thank you.

My friend Tracy puts it well. She blew the whistle on her father when she was thirteen, spent a short while in foster care (with mandatory therapy). A psychiatric evaluation brought her three years in various mental health facilities. I asked Tracy if she saw any relevance in the response to her problem.

"I—do—not—understand," she said. "I do understand that it was important a dozen years ago for you to tell people this stuff happened. Back when nobody knew. To break the silence and all that. But we *did* that.

"Now we're just going over and over the same shit over and over again. It's kind of like, 'Okay, guys, well guess what! We've dealt with this.' At least I have. And I think it's now time to deal with how we're *dealing* with it. Fine, we know that incest is there. We know that these things exist. We know that it's happened to a lot of people. And I think . . . I think we all feel that we're not alone anymore. I mean, give me a break: I do not feel alone.

"There's groups everywhere, 'counseling' everywhere. There's so much 'treatment' out there it's not funny. But they don't discuss what *kind* of treatment it is. They don't talk about how this stuff is helping *nobody*.

"The difference between saying, 'Yo, this happened to me, too,' and going after the offenders is that all this speaking about it just makes you a patient or an inmate. It doesn't challenge power. Because if you say, 'My daddy's a big, rich man over there, and he did this. Go do something about him,' then you're challenging a higher power. I feel there's a war going on with all this who's gonna get which kids in treatment.

"And I feel in my mind that there should be a war on the treaters. Some days, I just want to go in and let all the kids in 'treatment' go free—let them out, like the animal rights groups let minks out. Set them free. But—what are the kids gonna do then?"

I think we should be unsurprised to find that the kids we have beckoned forward, told to tell, in these years—the kids then victimized by custody courts, the kids coerced into endless thera-peutic circumstances—may well have been *re-silenced*. No small number of kids suggested to me that it was harder to survive the ensuing "help" and "treatment" than it was to survive the incest.

What happened to them felt like punishment of them. It did not help to keep telling them over and over that the incest was not their fault.

Oddly enough, we could have anticipated the response from the "bad guys." What we could not have anticipated was how much ammunition would be proffered to them by the "good guys."

We could not have anticipated the degree of dominance of the therapeutic ideology. Nor the way in which a concept like speak-ing out would be transformed from a political one into a clinical or therapeutic one. The way in which the feminist concept of the personal as political would be translated to read the personal is the public. Nor the way in which the concurrent rise of talk shows would work to take the making of the personal public, and trans-form that—so that what appeared to be public in fact conveyed the idea that the issue was intensely private: a matter of individual treatment, individual wounds.

No matter how sundered aspects of the issue become, one from the other; no matter how scattered the parts become; no matter how many diversions can be thought up; no matter how many vaudeville or cream-pie-and-banana-peel burlesque turns are staged, it will always come down to the early questions. How serious do we think the sexual exploitation of children by men who hold them in power is? What are the rights of women and children in the face of victimization? (Can they, at the very least, be allowed to go free?) Does seriousness depend on proving dire injury? And—the question I see nowhere considered—is the price of proving dire injury simply too high?

In terms of present circumstance, it will always come down to the testimony of a child, with assistance from medical technology as it becomes more sophisticated. Benign rescue will always depend on the actions of a protecting parent. And that, in turn, will always depend on that protecting parent herself being accorded dignity and credibility. Social "rescue" will always come down to some challenge to the due process protections that—when it is their robust ox being gored, and not the poor bedraggled creature possessed by women in family court—men find so dear.

For adults victimized as children who would triumph, it will always come down to an act of incorporation, a way of finding coherence. And that can only be helped by understanding the larger context of the experience, its relationship to the experience of others and to different experiences (of one's own and of others). It will always be helped (I believe) by seeing incest as one among the violences against women. Personal comfort and personal change will always be private events, no matter how many talk shows and speakouts go by.

There is no final place called recovery. Among the reasons there cannot be is that any girl growing up, and any woman, is likely to encounter events reminiscent of early exploitation. (This is not a matter of women whining about victimhood. It's simply a matter of the degree to which—despite propaganda of progress—the sense of male entitlement still obtains for many men.)

As a result, there is, as well, no self-conferred thing called empowerment. A deliberate victimization is a deliberate victimization (whether incest, sexual harassment, rape, or battering). Pigs is pigs. All that can be changed is from now on.

———

What could happen from now on to provoke the kind of change we might reasonably call progress? What might we do to have an impact on the lives of kids now, and to begin to seriously reduce the incidence of incest in the future?

Women as a political force need to take mothers' issues, childrens' issues, more seriously—beyond issues like day care and parental leave. Issues of violence cut to the core of sexual politics. And there is a connectedness between assaults against women and those against children. In 1970, Shulamith Firestone wrote in her book *The Dialectics of Sex*: "Except for ego rewards in having children, few men show any interest in children. . . . So it is up to the feminist revolutionaries to do so. We must include the oppression of children in any program for feminist revolution or we will be subject to the same failing of which we have so often accused men: of not having gone deep enough in our analysis."[3]

In the 1990s, of course, we might amend this: Even as it appears that more men are embracing fatherhood, too many men continue to show a predatory interest in children. It is women, as mothers, who are obliged by the state to protect those children. And it is women, as mothers, who most often act to do so. Women, as mothers, need full feminist support in this.

Somehow fundamental connections became obscured during the 1980s by debates on essentialism, by the perfectly reasonable reaction of early second-wave feminists against the social enforcement for women of the motherhood role, by critiques of the heterosexual family. And many battles were overridden by the necessity of struggling to preserve the right to choose abortion.

Yet women who choose motherhood should be able to do so without the extreme risks they now face—almost total vulnerability in the eyes of the state (whether in the form of the child welfare system or the domestic relations court)—and lack of support by the activism of feminists, or of the very women, survivors, *who wish their mothers had acted to protect them.*

There needs to be a greater awareness on the part of adult survivors that their experience is part of a greater social problem, and that they could play a role that can make a difference to children now. This is a role with risks; it defies fashion. It is, quite simply, *undiplomatic* to identify incest as other than gender-neutral. It is impolite; it is rude; and it is not socially safe. But as recent history has shown, diplomacy is useless when the other side's position is non-negotiable. What is needed, however, is the courage to *know*, the courage to *understand*; the courage to think and to speak in one's own language, and to make that language heard in the larger world.

For many survivors, I believe, such awareness, such a role, would carry the reward of a greater kind of connectedness, and would lend greater meaning to what they endured. This would require that women reclaim their own experience, and adopt skepticism that one can find empowerment by turning power over to "experts."

Too many women have succumbed to the charm of a sales pitch that seductively promises personal salvation and offers tasks to keep them occupied until that day comes: too many have accepted as *their* failure, the failure of these tasks or steps to make much of a difference. And too many women have been lured into believing that incest *by itself* explains their adult misery—by those whose professional specialty it is to do so.

The current exposure of overeager "healers," looking for memories of incest in adult women everywhere, is not in itself necessarily destructive. It is not, in itself, *backlash*—though it draws the enthusiasm of those whose agenda that is. What it does do, alas, is come perilously close to rendering real memory of real events vulnerable, and real events befalling real children suspect. Adult survivors need to speak for themselves, out of certainty—not out of therapy.

It would make a serious difference should survivors decide to organize with the goal of supporting children now, and supporting mothers who believe their children's disclosures of abuse. It would make a greater difference yet if these mothers could find support somewhere in the system, and if alliances could be set up, networks. . . .

As a political issue, incest describes a stunning parabola. From silence to satanism in a dozen scant years. From professionals' denial to professionals' fervor. From ignominy to vogue. The focus on incest-as-illness has served as a form of pacification of an otherwise potentially contentious population.

Perhaps it is time to reclaim that contentiousness, and to set for ourselves the terms of the debate—not on the grounds of "sick" or "well," but on the grounds of a far-too-rampant sexual assault on children that continues to be quasi-legal.

For me, personally? Optimism is a stuggle. Pessimism is unbearable. To stand on neither side of an ever-tensing polarity is to feel excluded, to feel—well, yes: alone. The energy and passion that informed our early protests are now dismissed as unstylish. The clarity, the naming, is labeled simplistic. The humor that leavened the early stages of the journey is now taken for sacrilege.

Do I believe there will come a time soon when women will, on this issue, once again listen to their own voices, follow their own moral compass toward their own defined goals—independent of "experts"? I need to believe that if I continue to hope for change.

For all the talk of *listening to the children*, in a very important sense the children continue unheard. Their voices come to us through interpreters. Do I believe we will ever start really listening to the kids themselves? Again, I need to believe that if I continue to hope for change.

And of course I *do* quite profoundly hope for change.

I've been down all the fascinating highways and byways that radiate out from this issue so far.

It's been one hell of a trip.

For all the curlicues, filigree, and baroquery, however, I remain as convinced as ever that we were not incorrect the first time out in identifying incest as the cradle of sexual politics.

We gave it a push.

The bough is still holding.

The cradle's still rocking.

It remains to be seen what will happen next.

ACKNOWLEDGMENTS

It would be an overwhelming task to thank every professional whose work has informed mine or whose research has documented discovery on this issue. Those whose work has combined with invaluable personal dialogue over the years include Lucy Berliner, Phyllis Chesler, Andrea Dworkin, David Finkelhor, Garnett Harrison, Jeffrey Moussaieff Masson, Joan Pennington, Diana Russell, Muriel Sugarman, Roland Summit. . . . (I hasten to let them off the hook: My grateful acknowledgment does not mean that this book necessarily reflects their views.) The work of Liz Kelly, Linda Regan, Sheila Burton, Sara Scott, and Mary McLeod has been a special beacon. All of the survivors over the years, and each of the protective mothers, who have been part of my experience and helped formulate my understanding of this issue, have my very warmest acknowledgment and thanks.

For their support, and for helping me hold both my humor and my center through the vicissitudes, I thank Elly Danica, Mary Dean, Janet Fink, Jan Raymond, Julie Reiskin, Florence Rush (of course), and that greatest of gardeners and shoppers, Mo Sila.

First and foremost, there is Tom, without whom I cannot imagine having any humor or center intact after all this.

NOTES

Introduction

1. Stuart A. Kirk and Herb Kitchins, *The Selling of DSM* (New York: Aldine de Gruyter, 1992), 8.

1. Incest: The Early Years

1. Laura Davis and Ellen Bass, *The Courage to Heal: A Guide for Women Survivors of Child Sexual Abuse* (New York: HarperPerennial, 1988), 473.

2. Steve Meurice, "Child Sexual Abuse Not Common—Psychologist," *The Record* [Sherbrooke, Ontario] May 13, 1992, 3.

3. "Interview: Hollida Wakefield and Ralph Underwager," Conducted in Amsterdam, June 1991, by Editor-in-Chief, Joseph Geraci, in *Paidika, The Journal of Paedophilia* 3, no. 1 (Winter 1993): 12.

4. Irene Peslikis, a founding member of Redstockings, cited in Celia Kitzinger and Rachel Perkins, *Changing Our Minds: Lesbian Feminism and Psychology* (London: Onlywoman Press, Ltd., 1993), 78. Also published by New York University Press, 1993.

5. Cited in Celia Kitzinger and Rachel Perkins, *Changing Our Minds*, 78.

6. S. Kirson Weinberg, *Incest Behavior* (New York: Citadel Press, 1963), 147.

7. Loretta Bender and Abram Blau, "The Reaction of Children to Sexual Relations with Adults," *The American Journal of Orthopsychiatry* 7 (1937): 500–518.

8. Lindy Burton, *Vulnerable Children* (London: Routledge & Kegan Paul, 1968), 169.

9. Florence Rush, *The Best Kept Secret: Sexual Abuse of Children* (New York: McGraw-Hill, 1980), 27.

10. Ibid., 34.

11. Linda Gordon, "The Politics of Child Sexual Abuse, Notes from American History," *Feminist Review* [Family Secrets: Child Sexual Abuse] 28 (Spring 1988): 57.

12. Florence Rush, *The Best Kept Secret*, 39.

13. Ibid., 45.

14. Leigh B. Bienen, "A Question of Credibility: John Henry Wigmore's Use of Scientific Authority in Section 924a of the Treatise on Evidence," *California Western Law Review* 19, no. 2 (1983): 240, 249. Citing 3A J. Wigmore, *Evidence in Trials at Common Law* § 924a (rev. ed. 1970).

15. Ibid., 261. Citing letter from Dr. Karl A. Menninger of the Menninger Clinic.

16. Leigh B. Bienen, "A Question of Credibility," 267.

17. See 25 NYS 2d 602 in 74 ALR 2d, *American Law Reports Annotated*, 710–711.

18. Michael Wald, "State Intervention on Behalf of 'Neglected' Children, A Search for Realistic Standards," *Stanford Law Review* 27, no. 985 (April 1975): 324, n. 203.

19. *Sanders* v. *State* (1937), *American Law Reports Annotated*, 710.

20. Alfred Kinsey et al., *Sexual Behavior in the Human Female* (New York: Pocket Books, 1953), 121.

21. As cited in Anna C. Salter, Ph.D., "Accuracy of Expert Testimony in Child Sexual Abuse Cases: A Case Study of Ralph Underwager and Hollida Wakefield" (Commissioned by the New England Association of Child Welfare Commissioners and Directors commissioned in May 1988), 8.

22. Yvonne Tormes, *Child Victims of Incest* (Denver: The American Humane Association, Children's Division), 32, 33, 35.

23. "Counseling Incestuous Families: Method of Frank S. Pittman M.D.," *Medical Aspects of Human Sexuality* (April 1976): 58.

24. Philip Nobile, "Incest, the Last Taboo," *Penthouse*, December 1977, 118.

25. Gloria Cole, *Fairpress*, June 15, 1977, A-3, A-15.

26. Capt. Neal Lustig et al., "Incest, A Family Group Survival Pattern," *Archives of General Psychiatry* 14 (January 1966): 31.

27. M. Leary, "United States v. Bear Runner: The Need for Corroboration in Incest Cases," *Saint Louis Law Journal* 23, no. 747 (1979): 750.

28. Akhil Reed Amar and Daniel Widawsky, "Child Abuse as Slavery: A Thirteenth Amendment Response to DeShaney," *Harvard Law Review* 105 (1992): 1359–1385.

29. Ibid., 1367.

30. Sandra Butler, "Incest: Whose Reality, Whose Theory," *Aegis: Magazine on Ending Violence Against Women* (Summer/Autumn 1980): 49.

31. Celia Kitzinger and Rachel Perkins, *Changing Our Minds*, 45.

32. Melba Wilson, *Crossing the Boundary: Black Women Survive Incest* (London: Virago Press Ltd., 1993), 1.

33. Billye Y. Avery, "Breathing Life into Ourselves: The Evolution of the National Black Women's Health Project," in *The Black Women's Health Book: Speaking for Ourselves*, edited by Evelyn C. White (Seattle, Wash.: Seal Press, 1990), 8.

34. Raymond A. Sokolov, "Nonfiction in Brief," *New York Times Book Review*, August 6, 1978, 16, 20.

35. Donahue Transcript #11099, November 9, 1979 (WGN-TV, Chicago, Multimedia Program Productions), 10.

36. Kee McFarlane, "Sexual Abuse of Children," in *The Victimization of Women* (vol. 3 in *Sage Yearbooks in Women's Policy Studies*), edited by Jane Roberts Chapman and Margaret Gates (Beverly Hills: Sage Publications, 1978), 90. Also see "The Police Perspective in Child Abuse and Neglect" (Gaithersburg, Md.: International Association of Chiefs of Police, September 1977), 8. "Incest usually has taken place over a long period of time, from six months to several years. According to one study, fathers confronted with detection frequently deny the incest or if they admit it, attempt to minimize their guilt, and often express surprise that incest is punishable by law. They frequently insist that they have

done nothing wrong. Some fathers believe sexual access to be one of their parental rights."

2. *"It's A Mental Health Problem, Stupid"*

1. Terry Wolverton, "Incest," *Fuse* (July/August): 280.

2. William Wasko, Jr., M.S.W., supervisor of the Child Abuse Emergency Team in the East St. Louis region of the Illinois Department of Children and Family Services. "A Social Judgment: Involving Law Enforcement Agencies in Incest Cases," 2.

3. Alayne Yates, M.D., "Incest: The Child's Response," 3. Yates is author of *Sex Without Shame: Encouraging the Child's Healthy Development* (New York: William Morrow, 1978).

4. Carla Dowben, J.S., associate professor, University of Texas Health Science Center, Dallas, Tex., "Legal Tolerance of Incest."

5. As cited in Michael de Courcy Hinds, "The Child Victim of Incest," *New York Times*, June 15, 1981.

6. Lois G. Forer, "Incest: A Crime That Must Not Be Belittled," *New York Times*, June 29, 1981, editorial page.

7. Ila J. Schonberg, "The Distortion of the Role of Mother in Child Sexual Abuse," *Journal of Child Sexual Abuse* 1, no. 3 (1992): 51.

8. As quoted in Clare Crawford, "A Therapist Says the Hush-Hush Scandal of Incest Occurs in 'Average, Respectable Families,' " *People*, May 9, 1977, 50.

9. Georgia Dullea, "Pioneer Therapy Deals with Incest by Treating the Entire Family," *New York Times*, October 3, 1977, 26.

10. See Barbara J. Nelson, *Making an Issue of Child Abuse: Political Agenda Setting for Social Problems* (Chicago: University of Chicago Press, 1984), 58–59.

11. Benjamin DeMott, "The Pro-Incest Lobby," *Psychology Today*, March 1980, 12.

12. As quoted in "Attacking the Last Taboo," *Time*, April 14, 1980, 72.

13. Ibid.

14. Ibid.

15. Benjamin DeMott, "The Pro-Incest Lobby," 12.

16. Yehudi Cohen, "The Disappearance of the Incest Taboo," *Human Nature* (July 1978): 78.

17. James W. Ramey, Ed.D., *SIECUS* Report of the Sexual Information and Education Council of the U.S. 7, no. 5 (May 1979): 11.

18. Ibid., 12.

19. Philip Nobile, "Incest, the Last Taboo," 118.

20. Ibid.

21. Ibid., 158.

3. The Doctrine of Equal Culpability

1. Liz Kelly, "Bitter Ironies," *Trouble and Strife* 16 (Summer 1989): 15.

2. Celia Kitzinger and Rachel Perkins, *Changing Our Minds*, 140.

3. Jean La Fontaine, *Child Sexual Abuse* (Cambridge: Basil Blackmore, 1990), 107, 108.

4. Ann Jones, *Women Who Kill* (New York: Holt, Rinehart, and Winston, 1980), 300.

5. Ibid., 300–302.

6. Quoted in Susan Faludi, *Backlash: The Undeclared War against American Women* (New York: Crown Publishers, Inc., 1991), 232.

7. George F. Gilder, *Sexual Suicide* (New York: Quadrangle/The New York Times Book Company, 1973), 23.

8. Ibid., 59.

9. Ibid., 105.

10. Susan Faludi, *Backlash*, xvii.

11. *Men's Equality Now* (newsletter of the Men's Equality Now International Coalition) 8, nos. 9–10 (September/October 1982): 5.

12. Rorie Sherman, "Gardner's Law," *National Law Journal* (August 16, 1993): 46.

13. *Men's Equality Now* newsletter, 7.

14. See Nancy D. Polikoff, "Why Are Mothers Losing: A Brief Analysis of Criteria Used in Child Custody Determinations," *Women's Rights Law Reporter* [Rutgers Law School] 7, no. 3 (Spring 1982): 235.

15. Maurice Franks, *Winning Custody: A No Holds Barred Guide for Fathers* (Englewood, N.J.: Prentice Hall, 1983), 35.

16. Quoted in *The Globe and Mail*, Toronto, Canada, March 1, 1988.

17. Andrea Dworkin, "Feminism: An Agenda," speech given April 8, 1983, Hamilton College, Clinton, N.Y. Included in her *Letters from the War Zone* (Brooklyn, N.Y.: Lawrence Hill Books, 1993), 139–140.

18. Marty Friday, *Off Our Backs* (September 1983), 16.

19. Florence Rush, "The Sexual Abuse of Children: A Feminist Point of View," in *Rape: The First Sourcebook for Women*, edited by Nareen Connell and Cassandra Wilson (New York: American Library, 1974) 73–74.

20. Evan Stark, Anne Flitcraft, and William Frazier, "Medicine and Patriarchal Violence, the Social Construction of a 'Private' Event," *International Journal of Health Services* 9, no. 3 (1979): 472.

21. Michael P. Rosenthal, "Physical Abuse of Children by Parents: The Criminalization Decision," *American Journal of Criminal Law* 7, no. 2 (July 1979): 168.

22. See, for example, Glenn Collins, "A New Look at Life with Father," *New York Times Magazine*, June 17, 1979, 30.

4. Ringling Brothers and Barnum & Bailey Present . . . Incest!

1. Liz Kelly, Sheila Burton, and Linda Regan, " 'And What Happened to Him?': Policy on Sex Offenders from the Survivor's Perspective," in *Beyond Containment: The Penal Response to Sex Offenders* (London: Prison Reform Trust, 59 Caledonian Road, London N19 3U, 1992), 14–27.

2. Timothy Egan, "Therapy for Child Molesters: Many Doubt That It Works," *New York Times*, January 1, 1990, 1, 12.

3. Gene G. Abel, Judith V. Becker, Edward B. Blanchard, and Armen Djenderedjian, "Differentiating Sexual Aggressives with Penile Measures," *Criminal Justice and Behavior* 5, no. 4 (December 1978): 320, 321.

4. Louise Armstrong, *The Home Front, Notes from the Family War Zone* (New York: McGraw-Hill, 1983), 67.

5. *The Women's Advocate* (newsletter of the National Center on Women and Family Law) 14, no. 1 (January 1993): 3–4.

6. Walter T. Simon, Ph.D., and Peter G. W. Schouten, M.A., "Penile Plethysmography in the Courtroom," *Medical Aspects of Human Sexuality* (July 1991): 35.

7. The Portable CAT-600, The Portable Sex Offender Assessment System," under "The Value of Plethysmograph Assessment Data," noted as being personal communication, July 11, 1983.

8. Mary MacLeod and Ester Saraga, "Abuse of Trust," *Social Work Practice* (November 1987): 78.

9. See Jenny Kitzinger, "Who Are You Kidding? Children, Power and the Struggle Against Child Sexual Abuse," in *Constructing and Reconstructing Childhood: Contemporary Issues in the Sociological Study of Children*, edited by A. James and A. Prout (London: The Falmer Press, 1990).

10. Daniel Goleman, "Abuse-Prevention Efforts Aid Children," *New York Times*, October 6, 1993, sec. C.

11. Cited in Louise Armstrong, *Solomon Says, A Speakout on Foster Care* (New York: Pocket Books, 1989), 181–182.

12. *Kidsrights*, produced by Judith and Martin Froner, 10100 Park Cedar Drive, Charlotte, N.C., 28210.

13. *The Talking and Telling About Touching Game*, copyright 1984, Thomas G. Beck, available from Victim Assistance Games, P.O. Box 444, Akron, OH, 44309.

14. Florence Rush, "The Sexual Abuse of Children," 71.

15. Alfred Kadushin and Judith A. Martin, *Child Welfare Services* (New York: Macmillan, 1988), 228.

5. Nineteen Eighty-Four

1. James Henderson, M.D., "Is Incest Harmful?" *Canadian Journal of Psychiatry* 28, no. 1 (February 1983): 35.

2. Cheryl McCall, "The Cruelest Crime, Sexual Abuse of Children: The Victims, the Offenders, How to Protect Your Family," *Life*, December 1984, 35–62.

3. "Sexual Abuse: The Growing Outcry over Child Molesting," *Newsweek*, May 14, 1984, 30–34.

4. Nicholas von Hoffman, *Albany Knickerbocker*, January 14, 1984.

5. John Corry, "Four-part Series on Child Sexual Abuse," *New York Times*, September 14, 1984, sec. C.

6. See David Hechler, *The Battle and the Backlash: The Child Sexual Abuse War* (Lexington, Mass.: Lexington Books, 1988).

7. Declaration of Roland Summit, M.D., Regarding *People* v. *Dill*, in the Superior Court of Fern County, California, July 1987, 18.

8. Ibid., 19–21.

9. Ibid., 22.

10. See David Hechler, *The Battle and the Backlash*, 111.

11. VOCAL national newsletter (May/June 1985), 1, no. 1, 8.

12. Nicholas Kittrie, *The Right to be Different: Deviance and Enforced Therapy* (Baltimore, Md.: The Johns Hopkins Press, 1971), 59.

13. Judith Areen, "Intervention Between Parent and Child: A Reappraisal of the State's Role in Child Neglect and Abuse Cases," *Georgetown Law Journal* 63, no. 88 (1975): 899, n. 68.

14. See Barbara J. Nelson, *Making an Issue of Child Abuse*, 58–59.

15. Both the Jordan case and the McMartin case are described in fuller historical detail in David Hechler, *The Battle and the Backlash*, and John Crewdson, *By Silence Betrayed: Sexual Abuse of Children in America* (Boston, Mass.: Little, Brown and Co., 1988).

6. *The Great Incest Massacre I*

1. Anne Perry, *Defend and Betray: A Victorian Mystery* (New York: Ivy Books, 1992).

2. "Nightline" transcript, show no. 696, 8.

3. Jim MacLaughlin and Shelly Murphy, "Mom Sues to Save 'Abused' Son," *Boston Herald*, June 3, 1987, 7.

4. Eleanor J. Bader, "Court Gives Kids to Abusive Dads," *New Directions for Women* (March/April 1988).

5. Scott Shane, "Mother Cited for Keeping Child from Ex-Husband," *Baltimore Sun*, August 21, 1985.

6. Glenn P. Joyner, "False Accusation of Child Abuse—Could It Happen to You?" *Woman's Day*, May 6, 1986, 30.

7. Lee Coleman, M.D., "Has a Child Been Molested? (A Psychiatrist Argues for Reforms in the Way Child Sexual Abuse Cases Are Investigated)," *California Lawyer* 6, no. 7 (July 1986).

8. "A Bitter New Issue (Some Accusations of Child Abuse Are False)," *MacLeans*, October 3, 1988.

9. 122 NYS 2d 216, 122 Misc. 2d 276, Family Court, Richmond County, January 2, 1984.

10. 113 Misc 2d 307.

11. 115 Misc 2d 161, Family Court, Richmond County, January 3, 1984, NEXIS.

12. Tom Vesey, "Mother Defies Custody Terms," *Washington Post*, March 24, 1984, A1–A12.

13. Robert Lindsey, "A Mute Girl's Story: Child Abuse and the System," *New York Times*, May 12, 1984.

14. Release from the National Center on Women and Family Law, undated.

15. Dr. Lee Coleman, as quoted in Paul and Shirley Eberle, *The Politics of Child Abuse* (Secaucus, N.J.: Lyle Stuart, 1986), 159–160.

16. "Matter of Michael G.," *Family Law Reporter*, January 23, 1986.

17. H. Joan Pennington, Esq., "The Hardest Case: Custody and Incest," National Center for Protective Parents, Inc., 1908 Riverside Drive, Trenton, N.J. 08618 (February 1993), 12.

18. Ibid.

19. H. Joan Pennington, amicus brief, *In re* Bobbi Conner, case no. CA-1570 (filed April 30, 1993), 8–9.

20. H. Joan Pennington, "The Hardest Case," 25.

21. H. Joan Pennington, *In re* Bobbi Conner, 7.

22. Ibid.

23. Richard A. Gardner, M.D., clinical professor of child psychiatry, Columbia University College of Physicians and Surgeons, *The Parental Alienation Syndrome and the Differentiation Between Fabricated and Genuine Sexual Abuse* (Cresskill, N.J.: Creative Therapeutics, 1987), 302.

24. Quoted in Rorie Sherman, "Gardner's Law," *National Law Journal* (August 16, 1993), 45.

25. Ibid., 46.

26. Richard A. Gardner, *The Parental Alienation Syndrome*, 302.

27. As quoted in Debra Cassens Moss, "Abuse Scale," *ABA Journal* (December 1, 1988): 26.

28. As quoted in Debra Cassens Moss, 26. See Richard A. Gardner, *The Parental Alienation Syndrome*, 175–176.

29. Ann M. Haralambie, "Handling Difficult Custody Disputes," in *Using the Law for Children: New Horizons for Attorneys and Expert Witnesses*, edited by L. Michaels (NACC, 1992), 168.

30. Elissa P. Benedek, M.D., Diane H. Schetky, M.D., "Allegations of Sexual Abuse in Child Custody Cases," presented at the annual meeting of the American Academy of Psychiatry and the Law, Nassau, Bahamas (October 26, 1984), 12; included in VOCAL compendium "Divorce, Custody, and Allegations of Child Abuse," and published in *Emerging Issues in Child Psychiatry and the Law*, (New York: Brunner/Mazel, 1985).

31. Corey Gordon, "False Allegations of Abuse in Child Custody Disputes," included in *Divorce/Custody and Allegations of Child Abuse*, a compendium of papers distributed by VOCAL; also published in *Minnesota Family Law Journal* 2, no. 14 (July/August 1985): 228.

32. Sharon S. Keating, "Children in Incestuous Relationships: The Forgotten Victims," *Loyola Law Review* 34 (1988): 114.

33. Richard A. Gardner, *The Parental Alienation Syndrome*, 104.

34. Ibid., 106.

35. Ibid., 274.

36. Richard A. Gardner, *Sex Abuse Hysteria: Salem Witch Trials Revisited* (Cresskill, N.J.: Creative Therapeutics, 1991), 7.

37. "Dr. Gardner Defends Work on Sex Abuse," *National Law Review*, September 6, 1993, editorial page.

38. "Custody Litigation and the Child Sexual Abuse Backfire Syndrome," *Jurisfemme* 8, no. 3 (Winter 1988): 21.

39. Ibid., 23.

40. Ibid., 21.

41. Ibid., 23.

42. Ibid.

43. Lawrence D. Spiegel, *A Question of Innocence: A True Story of False Accusation* (Parsippany, N.J.: Unicorn Publishing House, 1986), 63.

44. Ibid., 69.

45. Ibid., 88. Photocopy of newspaper clipping marked "Exhibit A," headlined, "Psychologist Indicted on Sex Assault Charge."

46. Ibid., 84.

47. Ibid., 103.

48. Ibid., 114–115. Photocopy marked "Exhibit A," Donahue Transcript #01155.

49. Ibid., 184. Photocopy marked "Exhibit A, Brian Murray, Judge Finds 4-year-old Competent to Testify," from New Jersey *Daily Record*.

7. *The Great Incest Massacre II*

1. Quoted in Diana Hawk Woodin, "Singley Logs Headaches, Heartaches in Writings," *Sun Herald*, Biloxi, Miss., October 17, 1987, A-4.

2. Ibid., A-1, A-4.

3. *Garnett Harrison* vs. *Mississippi State Bar Association*, Brief of Appellant Garnett Harrison, appeal from the Complaint Tribunal of the Mississippi State Bar Association, No. 91-BA-1222. Sequence of proceedings: 780 F. Supplement 1127 (S.D. Miss 1991); later overturned based on lack of jurisdiction in federal courts at: U.S. Court of Appeals Fifth Circuit, No. 92-7002 (1992); Cert. denied *Chrissy F. v. Dale*, U.S. Supreme Court No. 93-754, 20 FLR 1240 (March 22, 1994).

4. Harrison appeal, 10. Citing Dr. William Bradford, "Report of Suspected Battered Child," November 18, 1987.

5. Harrison appeal, 11. Citing *Singley v. Foxworth*, CA 20098, Chancery Court of Marion County, Deposition of Dr. Bryant McCrary, June 18, 1987.

6. Harrison appeal, 11. Citing *Chrissy F. by Guardian ad Litem, Donna Medley* vs. *Mississippi Department of Public Welfare (MDPW), Judge Sebe Dale, Jr.; Garrard Upton, Richard Douglas, et al.*, CAJ 88-0340 (B) S.M.D.S. (December 6, 1991).

7. Harrison appeal, 9. Citing Dorrie Singley's letter to Judge Dale contained in Dorrie's journal, August 20–September 21, 1987, 75–77.

8. Harrison appeal, 13. Citing *Singley* v. *Foxworth*, Deposition of Dr. Catherine Meeks, June 17, 1987.

9. *Garnett Harrison* vs. *Mississippi State Bar Association*, Brief of Appellant Garnett Harrison, appeal from the Complaint Tribunal of the Mississippi State Bar Association, No. 91-BA-1223, 10.

10. Harrison appeal, No. 91-BA-1222, 14.

11. As quoted in Francis Wilkinson, "Witchhunting in Hattiesburg," *The American Lawyer* (May 1988), 108.

12. Ellen Ann Fentress, "Mothers Defy Court, Keep Children," *Sun Herald*, August 15, 1987, C-1, C-2.

13. Deborah Skipper, "Moms Will Brave Jail to Protect Allegedly Sexually Abused Kids," *Clarion-Ledger Daily News*, August 15, 1987.

14. "Chancellor's Newsom Ruling Is Bewildering," *Sun-Herald*, September 4, 1987.

15. "2 Women Refuse to Let Children Return to Alleged Sexual Abuse," Mobile (Al.) *Press Register*, August 16, 1987. Also Skipper, "Moms Will Brave Jail to Protect Allegedly Sexually Abused Kids."

16. Harrison appeal, No. 91-BA-1223, 12–13.

17. Ibid., 13.

18. Ibid., 20.

19. Dorrie Singley, Journal in Hiding, August 20–September 21, 1987.

20. Harrison appeal, No. 91-BA-1223, 13.

21. As quoted in Daniel Golden, "What Makes Mommy Run?" *Boston Globe Magazine*, April 24, 1988, 43.

22. Dorrie Singley, Journal in Hiding.

23. Harrison appeal, no. 91-BA-1222, 29. Also, 780 F. Supplement 1127 (S.D. Miss 1991), 15.

24. Francis Wilkinson, "Witchhunting in Hattiesburg," 109.

25. Howard Sneed, *Blood Justice, The Lynching of Mack Charles Parker* (New York: Oxford University Press, 1986).

26. *Chrissy F.* v. *Mississippi Department of Public Welfare*, No. 883 F 2nd 26 (Fifth Circuit, 1989).

27. 925 F 2d 851 (Fifth Circuit, 1981).

28. 780 F. Supplement 1127 (S.D. Miss 1991), 15.

29. No. 92-7002 (1993).

30. *Chrissy F. v. Dale*, U.S. Supreme Court, No. 93-754 20 FLR 1240 (March 22, 1994).

8. The Great Incest Massacre III

1. Richard A. Gardner, *Sex Abuse Hysteria*, 7.

2. *Contested Custody Cases in Orange County, North Carolina Trial Courts, 1983–1987: Gender Bias, the Family and the Law*, The Committee for Justice for Women and the Orange County, North Carolina Women's Coalition (1991). Summary, at 1.

3. Jeffrey Moussaieff Masson, *Assault on Truth: Freud's Suppression of the Seduction Theory* (New York: Farrar, Straus and Giroux, 1984), 3.

4. Roland Summit, M.D., "Too Terrible to Hear, Barriers to Perception of Child Sexual Abuse," adapted March 13, 1987, from a paper written in support of testimony before the U.S. Attorney General's Commission on Pornography, Miami, Fla., November 20, 1985, 6.

5. Ibid., 7.

6. See Paula J. Caplan, Ph.D., and Ian Hall-McCorquodale, B.S., "Mother-Blaming in Clinical Journals," *American Journal of Orthopsychiatry* 55 (1985): 345–53.

7. Cited in Carol Tavris, *The Mismeasure of Woman* (New York: Simon & Schuster/Touchstone, 1992), 315.

8. Roland Summit, "Abuse of the Child Sexual Abuse Accommodation Syndrome," *Journal of Child Sexual Abuse* 1, no. 4 (1992): 155.

9. Roland Summit, "The Child Sexual Abuse Accommodation Syndrome," *Child Abuse and Neglect* 7 (1983): 179.

10. Cited in Paul and Shirley Eberle, *The Politics of Child Abuse*, 158.

11. dar, "Sex Abuse Ignored by Courts," *Off Our Backs* (October 1988), 7.

12. "LaLonde Outrage Continues," compiled by Judy Andler and Ann Holden, Boston Briefs, *Sojourner: The Women's Forum*, July 1989, 26.

13. "Victimized Again," *Boston Herald*, June 26, 1989, 24.

9. The Infantilization of Women I: A Place Called Recovery

1. Christine Gorman, "Coming out of the Dark," *Time*, October 7, 1991, 46.

2. "The Pain of the Last Taboo," *Newsweek*, October 7, 1991, 7.

3. Laura Davis and Ellen Bass, *The Courage to Heal*, 109.

4. Celia Kitzinger and Rachel Perkins, *Changing Our Minds*, 190.

5. Laura Davis and Ellen Bass, *The Courage to Heal*, 81.

6. Laura Davis, *The Courage to Heal Workbook: For Women and Men Survivors of Child Sexual Abuse* (New York: Harper & Row, 1990), 206.

7. Wendy Kaminer, "Feminism's Identity Crisis," *Atlantic Monthly*, October 1993, 66.

8. Carol Tavris, *The Mismeasure of Woman*, 315.

9. Wendy Kaminer, "Feminism's Identity Crisis," 66.

10. Beverly Engel, *The Right to Innocence: Healing the Trauma of Childhood Sexual Abuse* (Los Angeles: Jeremy Tarcher, 1982), 59.

11. Ibid., 45.

12. Laura Davis and Ellen Bass, *The Courage to Heal*, 113.

13. Beverly Engel, *The Right to Innocence*, 46.

14. Ibid., 99.

15. Ibid., 103.

16. Sexual Abuse Anonymous pamphlet, "Survivors Reaching Out to Survivors" (Sexual Abuse Anonymous, P.O. Box 405, St. Cloud, Minn., 56302, 1983), 1.

10. The Infantilization of Women II: A Place Called Denial

1. See Leslie Bennetts, "Nightmares on Main Street," *Vanity Fair* June 1993, 48.

2. Daniel Goleman, "Childhood Trauma: Memory or Invention?" *New York Times*, July 21, 1992, C-1, C-5.

3. Sally Jacobs, "Sex Abuse Memories in Question," *Boston Globe* April 4, 1993, 1, 24.

4. "A Child's Memories and a Father's Nightmare," *Sunday Independent,* March 7, 1993.

5. Ethan Watters, "Doors of Memory," *Mother Jones,* January 1993, 24.

6. *Paidika* (Winter 1993), 4.

7. Richard A. Gardner, "A Theory About the Variety of Human Sexual Behavior," *Issues in Child Abuse Accusations* 5, No. 2 (Spring 1993): 105.

8. Ibid., 111, 113, 114.

9. Ibid., 115.

10. "No Parental Immunity in Suit Against Stepfather," 6 FLR 1190, January 14, 1980.

11. "Incest Survivor Sues Father," *Ms.,* December 1984, 25.

12. Hugh Wright, "Grandfather, 96, Hit by Molestation Suit," *Record* [Stockton, Calif.], June 16, 1984, 9.

13. Modestor Fernandez, "UC Prof Sued for Alleged Sexual Abuse," *Daily Californian,* August 30, 1984, 3.

14. Margaret Zack, "Court Orders Father to Pay $243,000 in Sex Abuse Suit," *Minneapolis Star Tribune,* April 8, 1986, 18.

15. See Kim Ode, "Studies Differ in Findings of Child Sexual Abuse," *Minnesota Star Tribune,* 3E.

16. Penelope, "Suing My Perpetrator: A Survivor's Story," *Journal of Child Sexual Abuse* 1, no. 2 (1992): 120–121.

17. Ibid.

18. Liz Kelly, Linda Regan, and Sheila Burton, "Beyond Victim to Survivor: The Implications of Knowledge about Children's Resistance and Avoidance Strategies" (June 1992), unpaginated. Available from the Child Studies Unit, University of North London, Ladbroke House, 62–66 Highbury Grove, London NS 2AD.

19. Leon Jaroff, "Lies of the Mind," *Time,* November 29, 1993, 52.

20. Susan Chira, "Sex Abuse: The Coil of Truth and Memory," *New York Times,* December 5, 1993, 3.

21. Kim Ode, "A Couple on the Defensive," *Minnesota Star Tribune*, October 11, 1993, 2E.

22. Laura Davis, *The Courage to Heal Workbook*, 340.

23. Kim Ode, "A Couple on the Defensive," 1-E.

24. Jane Doe, "How Could This Happen? Coping with a False Accusation of Incest and Rape," in *Issues in Child Abuse Accusations* 3, no. 3 (Summer 1993): 154–165.

25. Jennifer Freyd, "Theoretical and Personal Perspectives on the Delayed Memory Debate," presented at the Center for Mental Health at Foot's Hospital's Continuing Education Conference: Controversies around Recovered Memories of Incest and Ritualistic Abuse (Ann Arbor, Michigan, August 7, 1993), 8.

26. Linda Myers-Williams, "Adult Memories of Childhood Abuse: Preliminary Findings from a Longitudinal Study," *The APSAC Advisor* (Summer 1992): 19–20.

27. Elizabeth F. Loftus, "The Reality of Repressed Memories," *American Psychologist* (May 1993): 518–537.

28. *Paidika, The Journal of Paedophilia*, 8.

29. Ibid., 9.

30. Quoted in "False Memory Syndrome Foundation," *Update*, National Center for the Prosecution of Child Abuse (July 1992).

11. *The Infantilization of Women III: The Demonic Dialogues*

1. Roland Summit, "Recognition of Cult Phenomena in MPD," *Fourth International Conference on Multiple Personality Disorder-Dissociative States*, 1987. Alexandria, Virginia, Audio Transcript VIb-383.

2. Roland Summit, "Symposia and Invited Papers, Adult Survivors of Ritualistic Abuse," *Fifth International Conference on Multiple Personality Disorder-Dissociative States*, 1988. Alexandria, Virginia, Audio Transcript IVd-436.

3. Jean La Fontaine, "The Extent and Nature of Organized and Ritual Abuse: Research Findings," 1994. HMSO (Her Majesty's Secretarial Office), P.O. Box 276, London SW8 5DT.

4. Rosie Waterhouse, "Government Inquiry Decides Satanic Abuse Does Not Exist," *Independent on Sunday*, April 24, 1994.

5. Valentine Low and Paul Lewis, "Whitewash Claim Over Satanic Abuse," *Evening Standard*, April 26, 1994.

6. Jean La Fontaine, "The Extent and Nature of Organized and Ritual Abuse," 30.

7. Ibid.

8. Ibid., 24.

9. Ibid., 31.

10. Ibid.

11. Ibid.

12. D. Sexton, "Gaining Insights into Complexity of Ritualistic Abuse," The Eighth National Conference on Child Abuse and Neglect (1989), tape no. 28. Cited in Sherrill Mulhern, "Satanism and Psychotherapy," in *The Satanic Scare*, edited by James T. Richardson, Joel Best, David Bromly (Hawthorn, N.Y.: Aldine deGruyter, 1991), 159.

13. Sherrill Mulhern, *Investigation of Ritualistic Abuse Allegations*, Proceedings of a Think Tank, Salt Lake City, Utah, October 22, 1989; in conjunction with the Eighth National Conference on Child Abuse and Neglect c. 1990, by the National Children's Advocacy Center, Huntsville, Ala., 83. Distributed by National Resource Center on Child Sexual Abuse, 106 Lincoln Street, Huntsville, AL 35801.

14. Ibid.

15. Ibid., 82.

16. See Louise Armstrong, "Storming the Castle," in *The Home Front*, 63–89.

17. Holly Hector, M.S., *Satanic Ritual Abuse and Multiple Personality Disorder: Understanding and Treating the Survivor* (available from the National Counseling Resource Center, Box 87, Rochester, Minn. [1991]), 1.

18. See Peter Steinfels, "Psychiatrists to Meet with the Pope," *New York Times*, January 3, 1993, 22.

19. Peter Steinfels, "Psychiatry Gets Religion," *New York Times*, February 13, 1994, Week in Review, p. 2.

20. Holly Hector, *Satanic Ritual Abuse and Multiple Personality Disorder*, 9, 10.

21. Edward Cone and Lisa Scheer, "Queen of the Right," *Mirabella*, February 1993, 86–94.

22. Ibid.

23. See Daniel Ryder, *Breaking the Circle of Satanic Ritual Abuse: Recognizing and Recovering from the Hidden Trauma* (Minneapolis, Minn.: CompCare Publishers, 1992), 17.

24. Ibid., 100.

25. Elizabeth S. Rose, "Surviving the Unbelievable," *Ms.*, January/February 1993, 42.

26. Ibid., 40.

27. Ibid., 42.

28. Kenneth V. Lanning, Think Tank Report, 27.

29. Elly Danica, *Don't: A Woman's Word* (Pittsburgh and San Francisco: Cleis Press, 1988).

12. One Hell of a Trip

1. See Richard A. Gardner, *Sex Abuse Hysteria*, 87.

2. The most thoughtful and thorough exploration of the results of rape, battering, and incest on women as similar to "combat neuroses" is Judith Lewis Herman, M.D., *Trauma and Recovery: The Aftermath of Violence—From Domestic Abuse to Political Terror* (New York: Basic Books, 1992).

3. Shulamith Firestone, *The Dialectics of Sex* (New York: William Morrow and Co., 1970), 117–118.

INDEX